T0209342

ELLEN STOTTS

RESET
YOUR
HEART

LIVE IN HARMONY
WITH GOD
AND YOURSELF

WESTBOW
PRESS®
A DIVISION OF THOMAS NELSON
& ZONDERVAN

WestBow Press books may be ordered through booksellers or by contacting:

WestBow Press
A Division of Thomas Nelson & Zondervan
1663 Liberty Drive
Bloomington, IN 47403
www.westbowpress.com
1 (866) 928-1240

ISBN: 978-1-9736-4170-4 (sc)
ISBN: 978-1-9736-4172-8 (hc)
ISBN: 978-1-9736-4171-1 (e)

Front Cover Photography by Carolyn Weinland
Back Cover Photography by Carol Steiner
Interior Illustrations by Carol Steiner

Library of Congress Control Number: 2018911839

Print information available on the last page.

WestBow Press rev. date: 10/25/2018

To my Lord and Savior, Jesus Christ
who defeated the enemy, so I
can live in VICTORY!
I dedicate this book to the wonderful man I call,
"my husband," who has taught me so much;
who has never tired of giving me his unconditional love
and pointing out the way to my Heavenly Father.
And to my children, who know me as their "Mom;"
they truly are a gift from above.

FOREWORD

In the Bible, David describes God's desire "to heal the brokenhearted and bind up their wounds." Psalm 147:3. He desires to restore broken hearts and lives and make them whole again. Jesus can heal one's damaged past and resolve the emotional pain that has been experienced as a result of circumstances which happened in the past. Jesus invites us to come to Him with our pain so that we can find healing and rest in Him. Matthew 11:28-30.

In her book, *Reset Your Heart*, Ellen shares her personal journey of coming to heart healing and freedom. She experienced healing through being led in prayer to Jesus. I have had the privilege of personally counseling Ellen and her husband and watching as they found their hearts healed and their emotional pain replaced with the peace of God. They learned how to lead each other in prayer to Jesus and how to care for each other's damaged hearts, creating a strong bond of emotional connection.

There is a need for believers to understand how they can take their pain to Jesus in prayer to find healing. I have observed Ellen and her husband as they reached out to care for others who were damaged by life's circumstances. In a practical way, this book shares how to take whatever one has experienced (that caused emotional damage) to Jesus and experience freedom from that pain. Ellen shares some examples of those she has been privileged to lead to Jesus in prayer and how they experienced healing, peace, and freedom in their hearts.

I trust you will enjoy reading Ellen's book and that your heart will be encouraged, as mine is, to know the freedom Jesus can bring to a damaged heart. I encourage you to share the Biblical principles with others, so they can "reset their heart" and experience God's design and purpose for their lives. Jeremiah 29:11.

John Regier, Director
Caring for the Heart Ministries

SPECIAL THANKS:

- To the Lover of my Soul, Jesus Christ, for loving me so much that He could not fathom being in Heaven without me. He gave His life for me!
- To my husband, the first person to love me this side of Heaven, who still loves me today.
- To my friend, Elke Lim, for spending countless hours editing, polishing, and improving the manuscript; for giving advice, and for her enduring spirit, always being very patient.
- To John Regier, for understanding the pain in my heart and gently leading me to the Healer, Jesus Christ.
- To my dear friend, Carolyn Weinland, for capturing, with her camera, the visual image of a RESET HEART that graces my book cover.
- To my fellow laborer in the ministry, Merry Hamrick, for introducing me to her *Meditation Talk* and allowing me to use it.
- To Carol Steiner for walking into my life when I needed her and creating the illustrations at the beginning of each of the four main chapters.
- To countless individuals for seeing potential in me and believing in me to write this book.
- Finally to you, dear reader, for picking up this book with the hope of having your personal life RESET. My prayer is that you too will find freedom, just as I have.

CONTENTS

CONTENTS

INTRODUCTION

How can we reset our hearts? And why would we need to reset our hearts in the first place? These questions take me back to a familiar Bible verse, where a Pharisee came to Jesus at night and received a strange reply to his question.

> Nicodemus said to Him, "How can a man be born when he is old? He cannot enter his mother's womb a second time and be born, can he?" (John 3:4 AMP)

Nicodemus wrestled with the idea of how in the world it would be possible for an old man to be physically born again. Jesus's answer indicated that Nicodemus not think in the realm of the physical, but rather in the spiritual. Jesus shared with his friend that it is necessary to be born from above in order to be included in the spiritual family. Becoming a part of the spiritual family is our free gift from God:

> ...so that whoever believes *and* trusts in Him [as Savior] shall not perish, but have eternal life. (John 3:16b AMP)

Resetting our heart in the spiritual area is only one aspect of being completely whole. We also need to reset our physical, emotional, and sexual lives. These concepts may sound impossible or far-fetched, like an unrealistic dream, but as this book explores these four main areas, you'll discover that it's not only possible, but every single person who desires to be whole can have this abundant life.

At one time or another, most of us have found ourselves reviewing our past, and in so doing, realized that our past had actually become our future. The benefit of a personal reset is to enable us to live the life God intended for us and not to continue as what we have become. Every person has the potential to reset their life. They need the right tools, and they need to give God permission to recreate them by making them whole again. After we reset the four areas of our life, we will regain our original identity and be at our best. Then we can truly live in harmony with God and ourselves.

I have discovered throughout my life that there are four areas we need to direct our attention to yield to what the Bible calls the "abundant" or "overflowing" life. It is difficult for some of us to imagine what God intends when He speaks of an abundant life because, all around us, we see people struggling, surviving, getting by, and hoping for the best. For many years, I was in that group, in a rut. I constantly tried to manage and juggle life with all of its demands. Something felt way off, and I knew I wasn't equipped to face certain challenges. I wondered if it was God's plan for me to experience life this way. I believe the answer to this question is no. Our God does not set us up to labor for forty, fifty, sixty, or seventy years, only to long for it all to end.

So what was I missing? Why did I continue, year after year, only to find myself at the same place I began? I could never find the answer or put my finger on what was wrong. The answer did not drop out of the sky or come as a sudden epiphany out of nowhere. It actually came as I embarked on a journey of finding freedom in my heart. Then as time went on, I had the privilege of coming alongside many hurting people, assisting and helping them with their journey through life.

You may ask how my personal journey began. One day, a married couple seemed to walk directly into my path. These two offered my husband and me an opportunity to attend a seminar in Colorado Springs. It would be taught by an individual who had helped them with their personal struggles and marital difficulties. After spending just three hours with this gentleman, this couple's marriage was set on a different course, and their personal lives were enriched. I was surprised, stunned, and definitely skeptical. Three hours? What can be accomplished in such a short time that would change someone's marriage? As their story unfolded, it became clear to me that this was indeed a true account of what happened to them.

The invitation to attend this week-long seminar came with a gift, which included payment of all our expenses. With grateful hearts, we walked through this door God had opened. I had no idea this decision would change my life forever.

The time came for us to travel to Colorado Springs. We expected to learn all we could and then apply what we heard to the congregation my husband pastored at the time. I was prepared, with pen and paper in hand, to soak up all I could. God, of course, had other plans, like He so often does. His plan was to work on my heart.

From Monday through Friday, I felt like a steam roller was running over my heart and soul. What was happening to me? Session after session revealed the damage and pain I stored deep within my heart. All of it seemed to want to come out. The bandages I had carefully placed over my wounds began to peel off; the cuts and bruises were exposed. I had no idea what condition my heart was really in until I came face to face with the ugliness of all the cover-ups I had carefully erected to keep my heart safe. That week in Colorado Springs changed my life, my heart, my marriage (eventually), and my ministry. In the following chapters, I will share with you how God transformed me. He performed a sort of surgery on my spiritually wounded heart and changed me from the inside out.

Because of my transformation, I had the privilege of sitting down with people years later to listen to their hurts and disappointments. What happened to me also happened to these folks. My heart learned an important truth I had never really seen before. The truth was simple, yet so profound. God sent His Son, Jesus, in order to reveal His heart to humankind. We, in turn, would discover the condition of our own hearts. In Colorado Springs, I was exposed for the first time to the way Jesus dealt with people: on a heart level. Jesus accepted people where they were. He cared for their hearts and understood what was going on inside of them. Not for one second does Jesus condone or overlook our sinful condition; no. But when a heart has become damaged and hurts so much, Jesus longs to gather us under His wings.

I turned to God's Word for confirmation. I discovered that God indeed demonstrated this same truth in many of the stories and parables in the Bible. God left us His Word, the Bible, as a perfect record for us to use and to study. With a fresh set of lenses, I saw the answer had been right there all along. I had never seen it clearly. Jesus ministered to me in a real way.

I also remembered some words spoken by a friend some time before: "Do you know what the word *Bible* stands for? B-I-B-L-E stands for 'Basic Instructions Before Leaving Earth.'"

I should have listened to my friend and taken these words to heart, as that may have spared me many wrong turns in life.

As already mentioned, for many years, there was a season in my life where I sat with hurting folks. I simply utilized the same principles and methods that were instrumental in changing my life. As I witnessed the transformation of their lives, my heart was blessed beyond measure. Their eyes seemed to have new light, as a direct result of Jesus touching their hearts. I realized their hearts were opened just as mine was.

I felt compelled to write this book as a direct result of what happened in my personal life. I'm not a licensed therapist, so I don't feel qualified. At the same time, I believe that a book such as this needed to be written, not by an expert but by a regular person who can relate, firsthand, how you can reset your life and heart. My intent for writing down my story and sharing the steps that led me to freedom is not to proclaim that I have all the answers. The material I will present, however, may be the solution that will help you transform your life too.

My prayer is that you will discover a life that demonstrates to a dying world that God is still on the throne. He did not leave His children to figure life out on their own. In these pages, you will see that Jesus is the Healer. He restored my heart, and I will be forever grateful that He stepped into my life and changed everything. It was Jesus who opened my eyes and heart to the four areas in my personal life, in which I needed to grow and mature. Only then was I really equipped to face whatever His plans were for my life. Thank you, Jesus, for gently leading the way.

CHAPTER 1

WHY ANOTHER BOOK?

> so that by two unchangeable things [His promise and His oath] in which it is impossible for God to lie, we who have fled [to Him] for refuge would have strong encouragement *and* indwelling strength to hold tightly to the hope set before us. This hope [this confident assurance] we have as an anchor of the soul [it cannot slip and it cannot break down under whatever pressure bears upon it]—a safe and steadfast hope that enters within the veil [of the heavenly temple, that most Holy Place in which the very presence of God dwells], where Jesus has entered [in advance] as a forerunner for us, having become a High Priest forever according to the order of Melchizedek. (Hebrews 6:18–20 AMP)

I felt compelled by God to write this book in order to share with people some principles I have learned from Him along the way. There was a moment in my life when my eyes were opened, my mind understood, and everything changed. I knew that one day, I would need to share what my heart captured. God began to teach me how to live this Christian life the moment I gave my heart to Jesus. Because He has a perfect plan for my life, He revealed Himself to me by answering my prayers and being near. He instructed me and molded my inner being for the purpose of attaining a whole and complete life in Him. God's plan is for humankind to be whole and to discover the essence of four areas of life in which He wants us to grow and mature. When each of these areas is given proper attention, everything changes.

> You may ask yourself at this point, will my circumstances change? No. Will my daily struggle end? No. Will life be easy, smooth, and enjoyable every single day? No. But there will be a benefit: so that you may live a life worthy of the Lord and please him in every way: bearing fruit in every good work, growing in the knowledge of God, (Colossians 1:10 NIV)

These principles we will cover are especially important for this time in history, when God's creation seems to be out of touch with God and itself. Much has changed through the centuries, yet our God is the same yesterday, today, and forever. His plan has not changed. For this reason, what He has revealed to me has the potential to revolutionize our personal lives, even now in the twenty-first century. The four generations of people presently living on this earth are included in God's plan—five generations, if you think of them this way: The Builder Generation, the Baby Boomers, Generation X, Generation Y (millennials, and now Generation Z or Post-Millennials (1997-present). My goal is to share with you a better way to live by drawing our attention to God's truth for our lives.

Together, as we read people's stories and follow specific teachings presented in His Word, we will unpack four principles. At the same time, I will share my discoveries with you by including you in my own journey, and I will lay out the plan for you so you, too, can be completely whole. In order to live this whole life, God needs us to grow and mature in the following four areas:

- our physical lives
- our emotional lives
- our spiritual lives
- our sexual lives

My intent is that this book will move people to examine themselves as to where they are in their personal journeys. This book offers a four-step approach to having a closer relationship with Jesus and living a whole and fulfilled life. I believe we are all familiar with the concept that God created us as body (physical), soul (emotional), and spirit (spiritual). This is true, but God also created us as sexual beings. If one of these four parts has been altered or damaged in some way, we no longer have the ability to be in harmony with God and ourselves.

The wounds of the physical body leave scars that are visible. These scars heal in time, but the memories of the events that caused them will remain, creating pain in the heart. Eventually, over time, victims of physical abuse can look at their scars and make friends with them. This can only occur if they continue to grow and mature in their physical lives.

The wounds of the soul, or the emotional pain that settles in the heart, are not seen or understood by anyone, including the person who experiences them. However, emotional pain can be healed, and people can once again enjoy freedom in their hearts. In order to regain this freedom, they must grow and mature emotionally.

The wounds of the spirit, such as those caused by spiritual abuse, are rarely addressed or even acknowledged. Growing and maturing in the spiritual area is vital to understanding God's heart.

The wounds of sexual abuse are stuffed under the rug, tucked away deep inside the heart, and not exposed or talked about. Any hurt in this area will cause people to see themselves in a different light from what God intended when He gave us the gift of sexuality. Everything changes. Growing and maturing in our sexuality will bring us back to God's plan for our sexuality.

We can learn from people in the Bible, and from individuals we share our earthly lives with, by gaining a deeper understanding of them. We can discover what God wants from us in order to be sent into the world as His ambassadors. Through careful study, we will uncover the truths God wants us to know so we can grow and mature in these four areas.

Only after I attended a particular seminar did I grasp these simple truths, which had been there all along. They transformed me from the inside out, and my personal life was never the same. The teacher presented these truths as if they were common knowledge, but for me, they were secrets I had never uncovered. I knew others needed to discover these vital truths, as well. A new reality came into focus, and I realized I was far from being whole in any of the four areas of my life. No wonder I was just drifting, struggling, and believing life should be easier. But there was a simple answer: I was not whole, which is God's ultimate plan for us all.

Full maturity is essential for dealing with the challenges that come as we journey through this life. In order to maneuver through the ups and downs in our daily lives, we need to be stable so we can manage the sudden lows we are bound to experience. The valleys will be less frightening, lonely, and dark, and we can quickly move toward the upside and climb out of the valley. When we are in the valley, we are not naturally drawn to God. People who have walked with God for decades may forsake Him if their lives take them into a valley all of a sudden. The ideal circumstance for establishing a relationship with Jesus is on the mountaintop, when life is good and blessings are abundant. In many cases, this will sustain us as we travel through the valleys, until we find our way again.

The question to ask ourselves while we are in the valley is not why God has allowed this or why God has brought this into our lives. God always wants to teach us, and for this reason, He wants us to seek the answer to the question "What?" instead of "Why?" God wants us to ask, "What do You want me to do with this event or circumstance? God, what are You up to? What are You trying to do in me? What do You want to teach me?" The why may have to wait for another day.

In the Old Testament book of Job, we read that God tested Job by allowing Satan to attack him. Job loses his children, his wealth, and his health. Even his wife tells him to curse God and die, but he remains strong and faithful, and accepts his circumstances. Job did not blame God or say to Him, "Why me?" The Bible tells us, "Through all this Job did not sin nor did he blame God." (Job 1:22 AMP).

Job's friends responded to his trials very differently. They gave him lots of bad advice. They blamed his sufferings on his personal sins. In essence, Job's friends concentrated their efforts on trying to find the answer to the why. In their minds, there had to be a reason for everything that was happening. Finally, Job, influenced by his friends, wants to confront God and complain. In essence, Job wanted to bring his case before God, but he doesn't know how.

At the end of the book, God puts Job in his place and asks him, "Who are you to question the God of the universe?" God never answers Job's question as to why He allowed this suffering, perhaps for this reason: God in His sovereignty chooses not to tell us everything. God's ways are beyond our human comprehension, but clearly God does have a purpose in allowing suffering:

> Dear friends, *do not be surprised* at the fiery ordeal that has come on you *to test you*, as though something strange were happening to you. But *rejoice* inasmuch as you *participate in the sufferings of Christ*, so that you may be overjoyed when his glory is revealed. (1 Peter 4:12–13 NIV; my emphasis)

I believe one reason for Job's suffering was that God was testing him. He wanted Job to grow and mature in his knowledge of Him. At the end of the chapter, before God restores Job, God humbles him by asking Job a series of questions that can actually not be answered by anyone other than God Himself. At this point, Job understands. God rewards Job for his faithfulness and for his endurance through his suffering, and Job declares, "I had heard rumors about You, *but now my eyes have seen You*" (Job 42:5 HCSB; my emphasis).

God blesses Job because he endured. He did not endure as a suffering martyr, however. No, he displayed maturity, all the while placing his trust in God; all this, even though Job had no idea that in the end, he would receive an even greater blessing than he had before his trials even began.

Just like Job, we need to come to a place in our lives where we can fully experience what God intends for us. Then, no matter what is happening (or not happening) in our lives, we can continue to thrive and overcome. My prayer is that you will gain a deeper understanding and apply these principles in your own life.

Why Can't We Overcome the World?

Most of us cannot imagine living in this sinful world and, at the same time, live as overcomers. Jesus told us to overcome the world. That is all well and good, but how do we do that on a daily basis, especially knowing that we are still capable of being sinful? Most of us have never taken

5

inventory or engaged in any kind of self-examination to find out if we can be overcomers or if we are really mature in the four areas of our life.

If only one area out of the four categories we cover in this book is somehow out of sync or out of harmony with the others, it will affect the other three remaining areas. For instance, our physical life can be affected if our emotional life is out of control. If we never grow and mature emotionally, the pain we encounter in our lifetime will result in a damaged heart. We will live life with a heart that feels hurt, is lonely, feels rejected, and unloved. Our whole life is influenced by our emotions, but the heart cannot experience peace. If our spiritual life is not developed, or has not matured and does not function correctly, we really cannot understand the deeper things of God. Our intellect (mind) will absorb a little bit of what God wants to say to us as we read His Word, but the true message will remain hidden. In order to fully grasp God with our limited understanding on this side of heaven, we need to see His heart. Lastly, God wants us to grow and mature in our sexual area. He created us as sexual beings, and from birth to death, we need to be responsible for our sexual life. If this area was violated by someone, our sexual life will unfold far differently. We grow sexually as we celebrate one birthday after another, and it is up to us to mature in this area, as well, in order to delight in what God has given for our enjoyment.

Only full maturity will allow us to achieve the life of an overcomer and be victorious, feel close to God, and enjoy all that is available to us. If we have the opportunity to grow and mature in all four areas, we will be at our best. We will be able to give God our best. We will have the best relationships with others. We will be the wife or husband God wants us to be, and we will love our children and be able to tend to their needs. Just like an orchestra, we will make beautiful music in perfect harmony. In essence, everything would be different, life would be less of a struggle, and we really would influence our world.

The Christian community has not seen a real revival for some time. Why don't we long for it and seek it? I'm not sure if I can adequately answer this question, but I do know that the lives of all the people who have understood the principles I want to share with you in this book have changed, even as my own life has changed. A lot of talk centers around the cry for renewal, but true revival can only come after the heart of the individual has had the opportunity to be changed. It all begins with growing and maturing in these four areas. Only then can people's hearts be fully available to God and to what His plans are for their lives.

We Need to Know What God Knows

God knows not one person will travel through this life without ever experiencing pain or hurt of any kind. We fail to see that any one of us can be wounded at any time, in some way, by someone. When hurtful events happen, we act surprised. It is as if this is some kind of a new thing that has never been felt by anyone before. One reason we are so taken aback is because, when the hurtful event happens to us for the first time, it creates deep pain in our heart, and we have no idea how to get rid of it. Of course, we have witnessed or known of hurtful events that have happened to others. But when we feel the pain in our own heart, especially if it is the direct result of a hurtful event, everything changes in our personal life. These hurtful events can occur early on, in our childhood, or later during the growing-up years. Pain can be introduced by parents who carry unresolved issues in their own hearts. They have no other method of parenting other than that which emanates from their own wounded heart. Their parenting style reflects on the kids and influences their hearts, and the pain the parents carry will transfer to the kids. These children are not qualified to help the parent, nor are they equipped to shield themselves from the devastating effects these events can create in their own hearts.

Let me give you an example. If a child grows up in a home where one parent is an alcoholic and the other parent is depressed, neither parent is available to the child to meet their physical, emotional, spiritual, and sexual needs. The child will struggle to develop properly in these four areas. The parents are not available in the physical sense because alcoholic parents are usually not kind and gentle; they are often absent from the home. Their children are not cared for emotionally because alcoholic parents are consumed by the thought of when they can have the next drink. Alcoholic parents can only connect emotionally with their children on a 3 percent level.

Depressed parents separate themselves physically from their families by sinking away into a land of fog and funk. They also focus on themselves about 95 percent of the time and often sleep a lot. Depressed and alcoholic

7

parents have no desire to engage in spiritual things, and their children will not be given the opportunity to be exposed to God the Father in a way that will foster their seeking a relationship with Him. In the area of their sexuality, the deficit of having depressed or alcoholic parents leads to early onset of sexual experimentation. This is due to the child's loneliness. They will give in to the pressure of engaging in premarital sex. The sexual activity feels good and soothes the child, but in the long run, this can become a problem. Children in these homes feel rejected, not loved, not important; they have no value, and the list goes on. The hearts of these children feel this pain on a daily basis, and the little love and attention that comes their way is simply not enough to fill their hearts with what they need.

In many cases, these children grow up not knowing how to connect to anyone, not knowing what love is supposed to feel like. They find substitutes to become their new connections. These children will connect their hearts to an animal or a place to meet their emotional needs. In many cases, as they get older, they reach for alcohol, drugs, or something similar. These kids have no idea how to form relationships because they themselves have never had a relationship with anyone. Later on in life, when they choose a mate, the familiar is selected, and the cycle repeats itself. Nothing changes. The heart has hidden away all the pain and hurt, and will never again open up. Marriage becomes a déjà vu, where the only thing that has changed is the location of their house and the name of the person they share that home with.

The Questions We All Have Asked

These questions are asked almost universally by believers in Christ around the world: What is God's will? What is God's will for my life? What is His will for this or that? It seems we spend a great deal of time trying to figure out the answer. I must admit that reading several books on this topic and listening to others was not as helpful as I had hoped. Why is that? One reason is that these authors had their own ideas of how we can come to find out God's will for our life. But is it up to an author to point us in the right direction? Not really. Can we not find the answer in God's Word? I believe so. But how can we dig out the answer to this age-old question? Actually, the answer is quite simple, yet so profound. Once you realize the potential your life can have, it will direct you and set you on a different course, a course that God had set out for you all along. You will be in tune and less resistant. You will embrace God's will for your life because you will see it as God sees it. However, you will only come to totally understand or discern the will of God and His perspective if your physical, emotional, spiritual, and sexual lives have been cleaned up and placed under the foot of the cross. Only then will you be able to function and live as a whole person. Only then will you fully realize what it means to follow and obey God's plan. If you seek a whole life, everything will become clearer and more focused, and believe it or not, it all begins with you.

Speaking of beginnings, God's original plan was for us to be immortal beings. Because we yielded to sin, we lost our immortal state, but we are still God's creation. God also created us with an intellect that sets us apart from the animal world. But is our intellect enough to piece together God's will and purpose for our life? What is the Christian life supposed to look like in the real world, where you and I live?

I believe we can find the answer to this question in life itself when we put God's Word next to it. God is wise and reveals Himself in both the profound and the simple. We often chase after the deep things of God, and this is a noble task that gains a rich reward. At the same time, we overlook the simple things that are right in front of our eyes: the truth that has always been there, but was never really uncovered. This truth is that to which God wants to draw our attention. God is God, and you and I will certainly fall short of getting to know Him completely on this side of heaven. Yet God is often direct, straight to the point, easy, and user friendly. You might say the people who lived in the Old Testament era were fortunate because God gave them the Urim and Thummim to determine His will, to know what He wanted them to be doing in a particular situation.

> In the breastpiece of judgment you shall put the Urim (Lights) and the Thummim (Perfections) [to be used for determining God's will in a matter]. They shall be over Aaron's heart whenever he goes before the LORD, and Aaron shall always carry the judgment (verdict, judicial

decisions) of the sons of Israel over his heart before the LORD." (Exodus 28:30 AMP)

But God also spoke to individuals in dreams and through prophets. God still speaks to us this way, or through His Word, church members, other followers of Christ, our family, and our circumstances. Old Testament believers in God, the Father, needed to believe and be obedient to whatever God's plan was for them. The same is true for New Testament believers. In order to live a complete, obedient life, we need to be fully mature in all four categories: the physical, emotional, spiritual, and sexual. The following is a small sample of where His will for our life is revealed to us in His Word:

God wants us

- to be faithful (1 John 2:17),
- to endure suffering (Psalm 112:7–8),
- to be sanctified (set apart for Him) (1 Corinthians 6:11),
- to be thankful in all situations (1 Thessalonians 5:18),
- to do good and share with others (Hebrews 13:15–16),
- to be holy in our physical life (Romans 12:1),
- to be transformed in our mind (heart/emotional) (Romans 12:2),
- to build up our faith (spiritual) (Colossians 2:7),
- to be pure from sexual sins (sexual) (Ephesians 5:3), and
- to live the will of God (whole) (1 Peter 4:2–6).

We can know how to live life as God intended. Every person should live in such a way as to reflect His will. This, my friend, is what it means to know the will of God for your life.

God's will is all over the pages of the Bible; the obvious often seems to get the least attention, even if we believe we know it well. We expect no real revelations but miss life-transforming principles. Yet our God gives us messages through seemingly insignificant areas of life circumstances that can have a great impact and outcome for us as individuals. I don't know about you, but I prefer the simple rather than the complex things in life. God made it possible for us to reach, discover, and embrace the simple. With this discovery, we can more clearly understand God's will for our life and rest in our ability to grow and mature in the four areas.

Let me say it again: Only then will we be whole and live in harmony with God and ourselves. I totally understand we all want God to give us a simple yes-or-no answer, preferably accompanied by some kind of external sign. In essence, however, it would relieve us of the responsibility of making the decision on our own. Each of us must choose to either voluntarily bow to the will of God or live life according to our own will.

Don't let Satan and his suggestions define you. Don't let circumstances and the storms in your life define you. Let your standing in the Lord, Jesus, define you. One of the biggest reasons we falter and do not know God's will for our life is we do not know who we are in Christ. One resource that has been especially helpful to me is *Victory over the Darkness*, by Neil Anderson.[1] If you choose to fellowship with worry, you have taken your eyes off Jesus. When you keep fellowship with fear, you will panic in the midst of the storm, and you will reduce the power that lives within you: Jesus Christ, the Conqueror.

As already mentioned, the answer to what God's will is for my life came out of my life experiences. Real-life events helped me grow and mature steadily in my physical, emotional, spiritual, and sexual life. As I met with countless individuals and heard their stories, my eyes finally opened for the first time to the obvious. God's will for our life is, foremost, to be whole beings in each area of our life. I should have known, as it had begun this way with me once my heart understood what was missing. Knowing God's will personally changed everything concerning His other assignments for my life. I had never considered that perhaps I was not whole.

The answer to how to live according to God's will was there all along. First, His will was revealed to me in His Word. Second, His will was revealed to me the moment I changed my prayer life and began asking God specific questions and then listening to the messages He sent to my heart. It was at this point I experienced freedom, peace, and the assurance of being His beloved, no matter what I had done, where I had been, or what others had done to me.

After taking these two steps, it was suddenly so clear and straightforward that I never challenged the personal words God had for me again. I had believed that everybody already knew about this and lived by these same principles. I uncovered the mystery of listening to the heart of God when I brought Him into every area of my life. For the first time, I listened to what

11

God had to say to me. The messages were soothing words that fell on my hurting heart. This activity of listening to God's heart was so new to me.

A new desire immediately entered my heart: to lead others to Jesus and show them how to listen to God's heart and receive the personal messages He had for them. When I took the time to listen to God, He shed His light on all my shortcomings, failures, hurts, and pain. I felt understood, cared for, and accepted. It was as simple as asking the right questions and then listening to and receiving God's message. Throughout this book, I will show how you too can enter into this kind of relationship with God.

As I look back over my life, I believe God provided me with many opportunities to develop the art of listening, as He placed me in several different vocations. He prepared me to sit with hurting people later on, to listen to them.

Learning Listening Skills

For me, listening to people had its beginning when I worked as a nurse. In this line of work, you have countless opportunities to listen to others.

Then, working as a cosmetologist opened up a whole new area of listening opportunities, as people came to get their hair and nails done. The phrase "only your hairdresser knows" is really true. During this time, listening took on a new dimension. I wanted to hear what people had to say. I understood how important it was for them to dump on someone and let things out. In some unspoken contract, I became the secret keeper for each client. This was unlike my work in the hospital setting, where people's focus was entirely on themselves, on their own needs and circumstances. In each of my professions, it was always about what people wanted to tell me, not about what I might want to say to them. I learned that most relationships are built this way.

Several years later, I had a new role: to prepare myself and my family for the mission field. A new set of individuals, missionaries, entered my life. Listening to these folks added another dimension to my experience. Sitting across from seasoned missionaries as well as new missionary candidates, and everyone in between, made me realize that even this group struggles. This came as a surprise to me, and the more I became involved, the more I realized that missionaries hurt and carry a lot of pain. Are missionaries not already in tune with God and themselves? What is wrong with this picture?

As my journey continued, the unexpected happened: I became a pastor's wife. The title alone was frightening. This new role brought to me a congregation, a community that would share, tell, complain, criticize, and vent to me. There were times I wished I could turn my ears off. I became overwhelmed with the hurt, pain, and neediness of people. I wondered, "Has the church missed the boat? Has the church turned a blind eye to what God wants to communicate to His people? Why doesn't the church have a clue about how to function as a whole body, about how to live together in harmony with God and each other?"

The next chapter in my life was the most difficult and sobering. I sat face to face with the hurting, listening intently as the stories of their lives unfolded. Most people would call this profession "counseling," but for me, it was "soul care." A counselor is in reality a people's helper, so in that sense, I was counseling. This term, however, comes with a lot of baggage. I believe it would profit me more to stick with the title of "caring for the soul," or to be more specific, "caring for the heart of the individual."

Caring for a person's heart is the very essence of God and was demonstrated by our Lord and Savior, Jesus Christ, throughout His life. Do we get this? Not really. Do we pay attention to what Jesus modeled for us? No, not exactly. I had to admit that it took me half a century to finally catch on to what Jesus was trying to share with us. Jesus was the master of listening to and hearing people. He did not focus on the spoken words, per se. His focus was on what people's hearts wanted to say. Our hearts speak louder and more clearly than any words we can formulate with our tongue. But the art of listening to the heart is relatively unknown, not desired, not sought after, and not practiced. This is the real listening we all need to be doing, and unless we engage in listening to the heart, especially the heart of God, we will miss out on becoming a whole person, and God's will shall remain a mystery to us.

Over the years, I recorded the things I learned from all of these different groups of people, to make some sense out of it all, especially from God's perspective. All of these people I had encountered in my life taught me much, but on the other hand, we all had one thing in common: None of us could have testified to being completely whole. I was not whole. You may ask what was missing. This question deserves an answer, not my answer, but God's answer. The Bible does not spell these things out in a way we would recognize as God's blueprint for our lives, but they are there for all of us to see. We simply cannot function fully if we are not whole.

Exploring the "Whole Person" Concept

What makes a person whole? There is the physical part of us, the emotional, the spiritual, and the sexual. Each of these four areas has a vital function of its own, and together, they make us a complete, whole person. If these parts are not perfectly orchestrated like a symphony, the sound is anything but beautiful. Harmony between these parts is essential. Does God's Word have something to say about these four parts? Yes, actually, more than you realize. Together, we will embark on this journey of discovery, which can transform your life, as it has transformed mine.

Each of these four areas needs to be developed, not only by human measurement, but more importantly, by God's measurement. I discovered that people lack what God desires for them, and as a result, they cannot be fully available to Him and to humankind. God knows what can make us optimal, functioning, excelling, thriving, and flourishing individuals.

In the following chapters, we will unpack the truth of what this all looks like, so we can fully embrace what God wants us to experience, so we can be whole and find God's will for our life. God knows none of us can journey through this life without experiencing some kind of pain brought on by circumstances or events. Somehow, we must maneuver through these difficulties, and if we grow and mature the way God has intended, we will be able to accept and understand Him on a deeper level.

"We will be considering four areas. God desires that we mature

- physically,
- emotionally,
- spiritually and
- sexually."

The Four Main Chapters

Each of us has the capability of coming alongside others and demonstrating to them what God considers a whole person. In our world, we have countless opportunities to see the hurt and pain others carry. Some give the message very clearly. As we are confronted by the reality of others' pain, we often find ourselves turning away.

You and I may lack the professional skill to write a poem or take a picture that exposes the hunger of a child, but like Jesus, we must in some way make God's message visible to the world. Painters use paints, brushes, and a canvas to show us what is in their heart. What is put on that canvas, and what you and I can see, is in essence the heart of the painter. We have the privilege of discovering the heart of the painter, and only then will we see the painting as it was intended to be seen. Until this happens, what's on the canvas will be a picture that only pleases our eyes. Writers use words that are in their hearts to tell the world what they need to hear. The late J. R. R. Tolkien, linguist and author of the bestselling classic, *The Lord of the Rings*,[2] believed he was simply the typist of the words God gave to him. Did people who read his books, or later on watched the movies, get the message? I believe many missed what Tolkien wanted to share with them: the essence of his heart and the heart of God.

My desire is to assist you in your journey by keeping things simple. I also want to keep the personal discoveries I have made, and my personal story, very simple so everyone can take a hold of the principals presented, and apply them to their own lives. My intent is to write this book in such a way that even a child can understand it. Jesus wanted children to understand what He had to say about the kingdom of God because the kingdom of God belongs to those who are like a little child:

> But Jesus called the children to him and said, "Let the little children come to me, and do not hinder them, for the kingdom of God belongs to such as these. Truly I tell you, anyone who will not receive the kingdom of God like a little child will never enter it." (Luke 18:16–17 NIV)

Chapter 2 will stay focused on our physical part. Each of us is very familiar with the physical, which we can see and feel. But just because we have the physical right in front of our eyes, this doesn't mean we really understand it the way God intended it to be understood. This physical body was given to us by God to serve us while we live on this earth. For the greater part, what we have on earth is physical; therefore, our body is physical and something we can see and touch.

In 2 Corinthians 5:1, Paul refers to the physical as an earthly tent. In 2 Peter 1:13, Peter agrees; he gives the same message referring to the tent of his body:

For we know that if the earthly tent we live in is destroyed, we have a building from God, an eternal house in heaven, not built by human hands. (2 Corinthians 5:1 NIV)

I think it is right to refresh your memory as long as I live in the tent of this body, because I know that I will soon put it aside, as our Lord Jesus Christ has made clear to me. (2 Peter 1:13–14 NIV)

This physical body will one day be left behind and replaced with our heavenly body, fit for living in heaven. In the meantime, we have this one body, but "growing in stature" is not all we need to accomplish if we want to be mature in our physical life.

In chapter 3, we will focus our attention on the emotional part of us. Our emotional side has often been treated like the unwelcome stepchild of our being. Why? It is always in the background of our development, the forgotten member of our inner being. This part of us is overlooked; we have no idea how God wants us to grow and mature in this area. Not till recently have we been made aware of our emotional side. Many people are now identified as having a mental illness, but God puts the spotlight on our emotional side in a much different way. Our modern world looks at the emotional side of our being as a diseased or malfunctioning part. Mental illness awareness is at an all-time high. Don't get me wrong; I applaud our progress in this area. Countless people have had to suffer in silence, only to find themselves trapped in a world that is filled with unexplained pain. On the other hand, I see a new phenomenon happening. A professional will give the diagnosis of a mental illness much too quickly, and then the treatment often involves medication that alters the emotional state. Or instructions for cognitive behavior are given, and the prescribed exercises cannot be accomplished because the emotions are all out of sorts. In many cases, the sufferer is not given any kind of exit strategy. These forms of treatment will become a new and permanent way of life for the patient. This is not what God intends. God has more to offer, and for that reason, we need to know what He has prepared for us and find out how we can grow and mature emotionally and make peace with our past emotional pain issues.

The focus of chapter 4 is on the spiritual part of us. Yes, we all have a spiritual part given to us by God. We must realize that the physical came first, and after that, the spiritual:

> The spiritual did not come first, but the natural, and after that the spiritual. The first man was of the dust of the earth; the second man is of heaven. As was the earthly man, so are those who are of the earth; and as is the heavenly man, so also are those who are of heaven. And just as we have borne the image of the earthly man, so shall we bear the image of the heavenly man. (1 Corinthians 15:46–49 NIV)

If I were to invite you to come with me to visit a mall, and our purpose for doing so would be to survey people and ask them one question concerning the spiritual, it might go something like this: "Are you interested in the spiritual?" The answer would, in many cases, be yes. "Wow, that is fantastic," you say, but the reality is that interest in the spiritual is not what you might think. The spiritual encompasses the evil side *and* the heavenly side. Satan and his forces dwell in the spiritual realm and offer great power to humankind. From the beginning of time, humans have chased after power, and the evil one is always ready to give us what we desire. God is spirit, and so are the angels, His heavenly messengers. Of course, God is more powerful than Satan will ever be:

Little children (believers, dear ones), you are of God *and* you belong to Him and have [already] overcome them [the agents of the antichrist]; because He who is in you is greater than he (Satan) who is in the world [of sinful mankind]. (1 John 4:4 AMP)

So the survey outcome would be inconclusive due to the fact that there is great confusion as to what is spiritual. We are also confused about how God wants us to grow and mature spiritually.

Chapter 5 will focus our attention on our sexual being. God wants us to grow and mature in our sexuality. Most of us never think about this subject or consider what God has to say about it. Sex is as old as the hills, but it has lost the original function and excitement that God intended. Why does God want us to grow and mature sexually? Doesn't this area in our life just happen, and what can we do about it, anyway? This may be a new subject for all of us, but believe me, if we do not cover this subject and learn to see our sexuality the way God sees it, we will miss out big time.

So there they are, in a nutshell: each area in which God wants us to grow and mature. Growing to full maturity in each of these areas will help us become whole and thereby ready to discover God's will for our life more clearly. If you have a car, you want it to run on all cylinders. If it doesn't, the whole car will suffer because of it. We too must run on all four cylinders, like a well-oiled machine. God has given us a blueprint that each of us can follow; so simple, but profound at the same time. Are you ready to unpack and unravel the mysteries for the purpose of being whole people, fully functioning, as God intended?

The path we choose in life will be influenced by how well we have grown and matured in the *physical* area, the *emotional* area, the *spiritual* area, and finally, the *sexual* area. If we have deficits in one of these areas, that means we did not grow and mature as God designed. We will make decisions that are based on limited resources, because actually, we are not whole. For this reason, we continue to experience difficulties with ourselves and others.

CHAPTER 2

GOD WANTS US TO GROW
AND MATURE PHYSICALLY

"Therefore I tell you, do not worry about your life, what you will eat or drink; or about your body, what you will wear. Is not life more than food, and the body more than clothes? Therefore do not worry about tomorrow, for tomorrow will worry about itself. Each day has enough trouble of its own. (Matthew 6:25; 34 NIV)

Our physical life is like a journey that takes us from birth to death. In the classic book, *Pilgrim's Progress*,[1] we travel with Christian as he is urged by Evangelist to leave the city of Destruction and travel to the Celestial City known as Mount Zion. He had to get up and go with his physical body, to begin his journey. Along the way, he encountered many mysteries and also some physical challenges. The road he travelled was not always smooth or easy. On the contrary; it took him uphill many times and often proved very tiresome.

You and I were given one physical life, and we too were asked to travel the road that God ordained for us. Along the way, we will endure hardships, and our physical bodies will experience fatigue, become weary, and eventually wear out and deteriorate.

It is for this purpose we need to prepare our physical bodies as best as we can: to face the many challenges it will encounter. We need to intentionally choose how we will grow in our physical stature, but growing, alone, is not enough. Our physical body needs to mature as well, so we can reach the end of our journey and look back, having finished strong. Only with a mature body can we fully enjoy what God has given us, no matter what comes along the way. In essence, maturity is growth and development, or improvement, toward a goal. The Bible often uses the word *perfection*. We realize none of us will ever achieve perfection in any area of our lives, but God sure wants us to try to be more and more like His son, Jesus Christ, who was a perfect picture of our heavenly Father. We read this short account in Luke: Jesus's parents went looking for Him in Jerusalem, after discovering He was not with his relatives, traveling home after the feast of Passover. Jesus was twelve years old at the time:

> And Jesus grew in wisdom and stature, and in favor with
> God and man. (Luke 2:52 NIV)

What does this mean as it concerns our physical body? To begin with, we need to come to the understanding we only have this one body, and we are given stewardship over our body. It is up to us to care for it, provide for its needs, and satisfy its constant demands of wanting to be cared for, and so much more. Our parents are the first who have the responsibility to fulfill our physical body's needs, but the baton is soon passed on to us.

God's Idea, Not My Idea

I was born the fifth daughter in a well-known, respected family. My beginning was not at all what my parents envisioned. The older I got, the more obvious this became. You see, the hope was that I would be a boy. A boy was needed to follow in my father's footsteps, to inherit the business. Then all would be well. After four tries and four girls, the anticipation of having a boy was great. That was the extent of the excitement, however. Aside from the fact that I would be the long-expected boy, having one more child was not anticipated at all.

Later on, my mom often said to me, "I wish you were never born! I wish you were dead."

"Why would she say that?" I wondered. "Was it because I was born a girl? Or was it because I was here at all?"

My heart refused to accept this message, and I told myself Mom was having a bad day; that she really did not mean what she was saying. "Of course, she wants me and loves me," I tried to convince myself. Yet what I was really doing was denying the fact I was, indeed, not wanted. This eased my pain somewhat, and to escape the harsh words, I chose to never allow myself to go down that path. I could not imagine or wrap my mind around the possibility: "What if Mom really meant what she said?"

My father was often physically absent. He was a man who had lost his dreams a long time ago. While he fought in World War II, his father, my grandfather, started the business. This was later passed on to my dad and was to be the inheritance for the boy he was to have. Starting a business during difficult war times was a daring and courageous endeavor; however, there was one aspect of this my grandfather did not count on. The business he was building to pass on to his son was not the life my father wished for.

My father had always dreamed of becoming an electrician. There is nothing wrong with that profession, except this was not what happened. After the war ended, my dad came home, and by this time, his future was set in stone. The only option for him was to roll up his sleeves and take over his father's business. There was no joy. There was only the constant pressure to grow bigger and better. My dad and one of his brothers became partners, and this eased the burden somewhat, but it was still not the future Dad had planned for himself.

Under these circumstances, I came into the world. My arrival in my parents' bedroom was attended by my grandfather, who was also rooting that I would be that much-anticipated boy. Also present were my mom's physician and my dad. Later on, I was told by one of my sisters that the moment I was born, the atmosphere in the room changed. My grandfather left, obviously very disappointed, and my dad followed suit. There was nothing to celebrate. I was left with my mom, who most likely felt rejected and blamed herself for having produced another girl.

Well, I was here, and I was determined to stay. God blessed me, not with looks or outstanding physical qualities, but He gave me a quick mind and an outspoken personality. Early on, I realized I was cared for very well, physically. I did not lack any physical comfort; those needs were met. Money was available, and we enjoyed a life of near luxury.

I soon realized, however, that status, money, and friends really don't mean much unless you can enjoy them from the heart. My father was an influential man. Even his stature pointed out to others that he was a man of authority. All kinds of people looked up to him, admired him, and maybe even secretly wanted to be in his shoes. My mom lived the life that was expected of her and portrayed that all was well. But what people outside of our home did not know was that in some ways, my parents were one couple in public and quite the opposite in private.

When the door closed behind my parents, it was open season for hypocrisy. All seven of us learned to become pretenders. What is a pretender? Movie stars become pretenders in every role they play. The better they can pretend, the more they are liked by their followers. We all remember John Wayne, the Cowboy. Did he play his roles well? Yes, and of course, we all wanted more of it. But in a home, pretending is neither needed nor wanted.

In my next chapter, we will discuss the hurt and pain that is created if the heart is never really cared for, if it never has the opportunity to grow and mature as God designed it. For now, let me say that my physical needs were cared for while I was little. However, the constant rejection of my gender and my actual presence made me eventually realize that I never really had the opportunity to grow and mature in my physical life, as I had believed. My existence was a daily effort to prove my worth. This left a huge vacuum that followed me for years.

As I grew older, however, the physical care seemed to slack off. I was expected to know it all and somehow figure things out by myself. I grew physically like any other girl, but nobody in my household took the time to share with me that some major physical changes would occur in my teen years. There was a day I would much rather not remember, but I believe the telling of it will help the reader fully understand the impact of how important it is that we grow, and eventually also mature, physically. During the years I lived at home, it was my parents' responsibility to teach and instruct me concerning my physical body, its care and possible changes that would occur, so that one day I could live on my own and care for my own personal needs.

The fateful day came. It was a sunny afternoon. I was fourteen years old, living life by staying out of everyone's way. Each day blended into the next; I had accepted the fact that my mom was happier if we kids would go outside for hours and just stay out of her way. So my sister and I would roam the countryside. We were the youngest and clung to each other. We were very close and shared some very precious memories together. In the winter, we spent hours outdoors, mostly sledding. We were so cold by the time we returned home, we thought we would never thaw. In the summertime, we spent most days at the public pool. Because my town is a very popular travel destination, we had fun with unsuspecting tourists who were surprised by adventurous children who came up with various antics to make their life more interesting. My, we had fun.

We knew every day must come to an end and that we would eventually have to go home. At home, we were expected to behave, be polite, do our chores, not speak, and to put it simply, mind our own business. The only talking that was done was for the purpose of passing on information we needed to know. When my parents were together, the atmosphere was drastically different. The verbal fights were intense. I just hid in my room. Following these violent outbursts, a lengthening silence fell between them. That was enough to let me know this was how it would always be.

Now, back to that day in my past where I realized that I had to take charge of my physical being. I was in the restroom when I noticed something was dreadfully wrong with me. The only conclusion I could come to was that I was dying. My body was bleeding. What was wrong with me? I was so afraid, and not knowing what to do next, I just yelled for my mom. Finally, the door opened. By that time, I was crying and carrying on. I cannot recollect what I actually said to her, but I do remember what she did. She opened the door, shut the door, then opened the door again, and threw something at me.

She said, "Put that in your panties and change it every now and then."

"Okay, and then what?" I had no clue what was happening, but I knew it could not be good.

In my panic, I finally confided in my sister and shared my problem with her. Can you imagine how she reacted? She laughed at me. My emotional state was anything but calm. Why did everybody think that nothing was wrong and everything was fine?

My sister then told me in a few words what was happening to me. What a relief; I was not dying. But why didn't Mom let me know, ahead of time, about these physical changes I would eventually experience? Wouldn't it have been wise for her to pass on to me the instructions I'd need to care for what would happen to my physical body? In many ways, I grew up living in the Dark Ages. Nothing was shared or passed on to assist me with issues concerning my physical body.

I share this part of my life with you to point out that we are constantly changing, and for that reason, we need to grow and mature physically. God's plan for my life was to be a girl, which is very different, physically, from a boy. Right from the start, my physical appearance became a constant reminder that I was not what was expected. My physical body knew how I would develop. I needed to learn to care for this body God had given me.

Having four sisters was a blessing because every time I had questions concerning my physical body, they gave me the information I needed. My girl body was never considered something of beauty, and so it simply became a way to exist on this earth, something that wanted to be fed, washed, and clothed.

My mind-set adapted over time to the constant message I heard, especially from my mom: "I wish you had died at birth!" To make my presence more tolerable, I had the idea to dress like a boy, have my hair cut short, and behave like a boy, but I realized that didn't help my cause or gain affection from my parents. At the end of the day, I was still a girl. I was here to stay, and I needed to be cared for. Nothing could change that.

As an adult, I somehow became aware that if you never learn to grow up to be healthy in your physical life, you also struggle to mature in your emotional, spiritual, and sexual life. One cannot happen without the other; they are tied together in an unspoken bond. You cannot truly live life to the fullest and consider yourself a whole person if even one area is not in harmony with the others.

Physical Neglect

We live in the twenty-first century, and you would think that physical neglect would have been eradicated by now, especially in the Western world. But to our surprise, that is simply not the case. So what is wrong with our society? We live in a world of abundance, modern conveniences, and excess. Why do children and adults still have to suffer the effects of physical neglect?

These questions are not easy to answer. Why? Because where there is physical neglect, we are often faced with more than this one isolated issue. It is a symptom of lack of growth and maturity in the other areas, which we will be discussing in this book. Physical neglect can be a direct result of other areas not having the opportunity to develop together, namely, the emotional, spiritual, and sexual areas. If one area is lacking, individuals have no chance to properly grow and mature the way God had in mind when He created us.

Let me explain: Right now, our generation enjoys an era of electronics, and in some way, we have become hungry for electronics. Human relationships are becoming a thing of the past, and electronic relationships are preferred. With an ever-increasing appetite, we pay a great price, the price of what we have lost and will most likely never regain: the beauty of personal relationships.

I'm not sure about you, my dear reader, but it hurts my heart to see many disconnected, absent-minded individuals engaged in totally deprived activity. If you are of the more seasoned generation, the wish for the olden days is a real longing for the past, when we treasured each other and invested our time in personal interaction. Why do we settle for less, for a machine?

As I gave this some thought, God reminded me that, in some ways, what is happening with our electronics is a reflection of times past. People carved idols out of wood or hammered a piece of metal into the shape of some imaginary person or animal, for the purpose of erecting them in prominent places to be worshiped:

> But their idols are silver and gold, made by human hands. They have mouths, but cannot speak, eyes, but cannot see. They have ears, but cannot hear, noses, but cannot smell. They have hands, but cannot feel, feet, but cannot walk, nor can they utter a sound with their throats. (Psalm 115:4–7 NIV)

Does that sound like an electronic device to you?

Yes, I realize that our electronics are not shaped in the form of a man, woman, animal, or some other thing, but their function is almost the same. I see individuals from all stations of life, both rich and poor, who cannot imagine being without their electronic devices. They panic if they are unable to find their phone, or if their tablet does not function anymore, or if their computer no longer worked. I have heard that people will go to the store at midnight and wait in a long line to buy the newest model hitting the market. We don't even get excited like that when a baby is born, or a student graduates from high school, or someone finds that personal relationship with God.

Can we turn this ship around and go back to how it was? Do we want to make that u-turn? Do we long for what was and no longer is? To tell you the truth, I'm not sure. Time will tell if our hunger for electronics will become an addiction, a tidal wave that cannot be stopped.

Don't get me wrong. I love my electronics and am glad God placed me in this time of history, able to enjoy the luxury of having the world and all it has to offer at my fingertips. At the same time, I never want my life to be about electronics and sacrifice the precious relationships God has allowed me to have. To tell you the truth, I would gladly exchange my electronics for the family and friends who are in my life. My life would be empty, though I could access the world with one stroke of my finger. No, I don't want to trade the living for the lifeless.

Due to the electronic tidal wave, we sacrifice face-to-face relationships. We choose to deal with personal problems via Facebook. We interact casually on Instagram, never able to add the human element of emotional connection. In essence, we have settled for less personal contact and exchanged it for a computer that does not require accountability, show sensitivity, or display humility. Our interactions with each other are superficial, nonfeeling, and disconnected from each other. Yes, everything we do is accomplished faster, but how far will we take this? Texting our children rather talking to them in person, texting our spouse in short sentences about what needs to be taken care of? We might as well invest in a robot because that is exactly the relationship we will have. We have separated ourselves from each other in such a way that it borders on physical neglect. Several of us live in one household, yet we exist apart from one another, engaged with the cyber world.

Physical neglect is a visible, in-your-face reality that cannot be denied or explained away. I came face to face with physically neglected children when Mike and I were foster parents for seven years early on in our marriage. Never in my wildest dreams had I considered that we would be confronted with physically neglected children and meet countless other foster parents who would have similar experiences.

Of course, these foster parents never knew their child's condition before receiving him or her, or how long one would live in their home. Fresh beds and loving arms awaited each one. In addition, many of these parents looked forward to the opportunity of introducing these children to their heavenly Father. Every foster home had a desire to love and care for these kids and to show them a picture of what a real family looks like. The hope was that when the children would leave their homes, the images and experiences would never be lost, but rather desired for their own future.

In many cases, as the door opened to a foster child for the first time, the initial glimpse revealed a child dressed only in their underwear and a dirty T-shirt. Social Services often brought the children directly from the pickup location and delivered them to their respective homes. Seeing the sad, unresponsive, scared, and bewildered looks on their faces felt like someone had punched us right in the stomach. When a family finds itself alone with a new foster child for the first time, in some way, everyone is at a loss as to what to do next. The first thing that needs to be taken care of is to offer these kids a fresh pair of pants and a clean shirt. All of the foster parents we knew had a stash of extra clothes handy just in case a child was brought from a physically neglected situation.

For these children, almost everything their new family does seems out of the ordinary and kind of strange, for instance, sitting down for supper. This is at times the first indication that what the social worker might have shared with them about the child was indeed true. Some of the kids we had in our home had to live in unimaginable circumstances. And who knows how long they had endured this kind of upbringing.

When food is passed around at the dinner table, a family simply digs in and enjoys the offerings. Not so with foster children. They say, "No," every time food is offered or simply shake their heads. The foster family has to realize all of their surroundings have changed, and the children are very afraid of what is happening. So a lot of patience has to be demonstrated by encouraging the simple foods, such as a slice of bread with peanut butter and jam. This offering is, after all, universally accepted by all children and carries the least threat to them. Just watching some of these kids can tear one's heart out. Ever so slowly, they work on accepting the food offered, almost as if it were a new food group to which they were just introduced. These kids never look anyone in the eyes. With downcast heads, they simply endure what is going on.

During the seven years we were foster parents, our adopted daughter also lived with us. She was several years older than the kids we fostered and always reached out to them in her own way. She most likely remembered her first day in our household. When she was dropped off by the social worker at only six years old, her world changed and would never be the same again. Her foster family, Mike and I, became her forever family. So with every child who came into our home, old memories of past pain were resurrected. She understood the needs of these precious kids better than we did. When she encouraged them to play with her, they followed her, trusting her in some way.

Before a day ends, there remains the hurdle of encouraging these children to enjoy a warm bath or shower. Just putting fresh clothes on the kids does not erase the dirt accumulated due to their situation. In our home, taking a bath was a fun occasion. Our kids always enjoyed the bubbles, toys, and warm water. Not so with children who never were given the opportunity to care for their bodies on a daily basis. A child's first bath or shower, in the host home, needs to be supervised to ensure their safety. Of course, we never knew if this routine was familiar to them. So we offered our services for a while, till we were sure the children were not afraid, and we'd offer instructions on how to take care of their physical body. Mike and I were extremely careful to guard the privacy of the children and never mixed the genders. If we had a boy, he would take over the supervision of bathing, showering, dressing, and so on. If the child was a girl, I took over these duties.

All foster children have a background, a story, a history of events that happened in their lives. The adult who now takes care of their needs must learn from the child the dos and don'ts of their personal care. Social workers don't always have helpful information in this area, and we often discovered, via trial and error, what was needed and what we had to be aware of. These moments became teachable windows through which we had the privilege of demonstrating love to these precious children.

Many times, as Mike supervised the boys, instead of having fun playing in the tub, horrible screaming would come from the bathroom. I knew the water was not too hot, and he never filled the tub to overflowing. What had happened? The children were so afraid of the whole experience that baths were often abandoned. When they would emerge from the bathroom, they would be dressed in their fresh pajamas, still dirty, hanging on to Mike for dear life. We never said very much and figured when the time was right, they would enjoy their baths. At this point, we simply offered some warm milk and led them into their new bedroom to read a bedtime story together.

Caring for physically neglected children taught me to never take for granted the daily activities we do without much thought. These daily routines, such as brushing teeth, taking a bath, or sitting together at the dinner table, had never been a part of these kids' lives. They often were physically not provided for; these normal functions were as foreign to them as speaking a language they had never heard before. Eventually, the day would come when they adjusted and would feel secure enough to venture into the welcoming comfort of a warm bath and want to become a part of a family who loved them.

Cycle of the Physical Life

The perception is often that caring for our physical bodies begins after we are born. In actuality, this begins in the womb of the expectant mom. Her physician advises her to care for herself by eating the right kinds of food, to take extra vitamins, and to continue with safe exercises during her pregnancy. All this, to assure that the life within her will receive from her the best nutrients for building bones and organs and all that the baby needs to grow healthy inside. At the same time, God does His work in the womb:

> My frame was not hidden from You, When I was being formed in secret, And intricately *and* skillfully formed [as if embroidered with many colors] in the depths of the earth. Your eyes have seen my unformed substance; And in Your book were all written The days that were

31

appointed *for me*, When as yet there was not one of them [even taking shape]. (Psalm 139:15–16 AMP)

Entire volumes of books have been written, and continue to be written, about our physical bodies. The more we discover, the clearer the picture becomes; we are indeed wonderfully made by God. Our physical body was also designed to naturally heal itself. For instance, when we injure our skin, the body will respond by repairing itself. I remember when our twins were about five years old, my husband and I decided it was time for them to have their first bicycle. Riding bikes had been part of our own growing-up years. Christmas came, and two shiny bikes were ready to be united with their new owners. The delight on the faces of our kids filled our hearts. We set all else aside and headed outside for them to show off their skills. My kids didn't realize this new adventure wouldn't be easy. It seemed like hours passed that day as we assisted, cheered, and encouraged our children, as they fell again and again. Thank God for good helmets and quick responses on our part. We ended up with only some scraped knees. Did they give up? No, they got up and tried again, just like an athlete or musician. We taught them that by repeating and practicing a new skill over and over again, they would eventually master whatever we wanted them to learn. Our children also knew that the damaged knees would heal themselves and they were a small price to pay for their adventure. As parents, we constantly instruct, correct, and at times discipline for the purpose of helping our children to grow up physically.

We can see with our own eyes the condition of our physical body. The years from infant to elder are short and few, yet in all cases, the changes are dramatic. From crib to death, we change constantly; the physical body continues to grow on the outside and on the inside. Over a lifetime, the physical body can be drastically affected by cancer, the loss of hearing or sight, the unpleasant effects of an autoimmune disorder, or the debilitating disease we call Alzheimer's.

When I worked in the geriatric unit of a nursing home in Germany, I came face to face with Alzheimer's. Previously, it was something I had heard about and understood somewhat, but I had never had the opportunity to care for people who had changed, in this manner, from who God had originally created them to be.

Each day was a challenge, as I took care of folks who could no longer care for their own physical needs. Insignificant tasks had been forgotten, and were it not for the caretakers in their life, the physical part of them would have been completely neglected. The physical body needs attention from morning till night, and these needs do not go away. When a person with Alzheimer's can no longer verbally communicate their physical needs, they employ other means to draw attention to themselves.

I can still clearly see a woman sitting in her chair, when all of a sudden, there was a terrible noise. It sounded like the scream of a wounded animal. I was the nurse responsible for meeting her needs and providing for her comfort. It was my job to decipher what this sudden outburst meant. Something was needed, and requested, but could no longer be given a voice. A blanket often soothed the person, or a kind touch let them know they were not forgotten. When their need was met, they calmed down.

In many ways, taking care of an infant requires that same skill. An infant cannot communicate with words what is needed or wanted. Only a cry will draw attention, and if the caretaker is in tune with the infant, the right need will be met, and the infant will go back to being itself.

Because of the nature of Alzheimer's, it is up to the caretaker to become the person's surrogate. What I mean by surrogate is simply this: The Alzheimer's patient can no longer distinguish what is happening, but I can. They may no longer know who they are, what they are doing, and so on, but I do. I considered it an honor to be their eyes, ears, and whatever else, in order to preserve their dignity and help them finish strong until the end of their life.

Sometimes, when family members came to the unit to visit their mother or father, I would meet them before they entered their loved one's room. I would share with them that this morning Mom was talking to them, believing I was the daughter. I would enter the conversation as if I was the daughter, and we enjoyed a lovely exchange of words with each other. This simple thing, me being the surrogate, or stand-in, was enough to keep the family members connected with a parent. I became a bridge that connected a mother to a daughter in such a way that it almost felt the person was still very much with them, in their mind, interacting with them.

My own mother suffered from Alzheimer's and eventually died from complications of the disease. Since I was living in the States by then, I did not have the opportunity to be involved in her care. In some way, however, having assisted other individuals throughout my nursing career gave me some closure, and I hope there was a nurse in my mother's life who came alongside to help her finish strong.

Physical growth happens when we give our body the fuel it needs, that is, the food we eat. The cycle of eating and growing repeats continually as we pass through the various stages of life. We call this "getting older." Each year brings evidence that we are growing physically. To stop the process of physical growth, we would need to quit eating and drinking; our physical body would die. All people have been given stewardship over their body. At the beginning of our physical life, we need instruction and training on how to care for it so it will last. As already mentioned, the responsibility of caring for our bodies is eventually passed on to us, and we may not necessarily continue what we were taught. We can choose to care for this one body we were given, or we can neglect it. The choice is truly ours and ours alone. Our physical body is very resilient, but years of neglect will eventually be acknowledged, when something does not work right or hurts. It is at these times we pay attention to our physical body, and out of desperation, we seek a quick fix to get back to normal.

Nourishment is essential to keep our body going. We make choices through the filters of how we were raised and what was modeled for us. Providing for our physical body, however, can be a daily battle, waging war with our desires. When the time comes for us to live on our own, we can choose for ourselves what to eat and what not to eat. Food takes on new meaning. We are free to do as we please, but the choices we make will affect our physical bodies, for better or worse.

A long time ago, I heard the saying, "You are what you eat." If the body gets the wrong fuel, the cycle of our physical life will be affected, and this has the potential of contributing to what we become. We were created for a higher purpose. In *The Purpose-Driven Life*,[2] Rick Warren encourages us to discover God's purpose and to be fully available to fulfill His plan for our lives. In order to fulfill what God desires from us, we must do our part and keep our physical body in the best shape we can. This brings us to the question, what does God want from us?

What Does God Want from Us?

As the years went by, my mind-set, and especially my heart attitude about myself and who I am, changed. Over time, I fully accepted (and actually celebrated and rejoiced over) the fact that I was a girl. I no longer cut my hair to look like a boy. I enjoyed putting on pretty things and having my hair styled. I realized my heavenly Father had plans for me, and years later, I found the scripture in Isaiah that says:

> "For My thoughts are not your thoughts, Nor are your ways My ways," declares the LORD. "For as the heavens are higher than the earth, So are My ways higher than your ways And My thoughts *higher* than your thoughts." (Isaiah 55:8–9 AMP)

God knows what is best for us, and it doesn't matter if the rest of the world agrees or not. While I was growing up, I didn't realize how much I was missing. I was not wanted. I was not honored as a girl, especially as it pertained to my physical appearance.

I strongly believe God wants us to grow and mature physically. Why? Because He knows that our physical bodies change all the time, and if we don't grow and mature, we can have real challenges with that part of our being. As already mentioned, and it is worth repeating it again, to grow physically means "to have a fully grown or developed body, a body that has grown to full size" (according to the Merriam-Webster Dictionary).[3] On the other hand, God also wants us to have a mature body. "A mature physical body is one that has completed natural growth and development" (Merriam-Webster Dictionary). The key word is "development."

Developing or maturing adds a new dimension to everything we have discussed so far about our physical growing-up years. Maturity happens over time and often comes as a result of enduring hardship or difficult circumstances in life. God does not need trials to teach us to mature in our physical bodies. He assists us in many different ways. He knows the importance of having a mature physical body, because only then can we truly accept all other changes that will occur in our physical growth.

How do we actually develop mature physical bodies? As already mentioned, we need to take responsibility for our physical body, no matter its shape or size. If the physical body has challenges, or deficits, or other problems evident since birth, the task of caring for it takes on a new direction, and extra care is needed to ensure the best quality of life is achieved.

Over the years, I have met sick, healthy, wealthy, poor, and average people. Each one was different, yet they had one thing in common: They bore the mark of physically maturity. No matter the condition of their body, these people had accepted what was happening in their physical bodies and had in some way made friends with their bodies. They had found a new normal and continued to praise God.

I also encountered people with physically healthy bodies, in excellent condition, strong, beautiful, and functioning very well. If you would ask me, however, if these physical bodies were mature, I would have to say no. Why? Because, over time, these bodies were used to serve their own selfish purposes, viewed as indestructible, and neglected in many areas. Some were punished and inflicted with unnecessary pain. These onetime healthy, perfect, physical bodies were eventually torn apart by choices made. Let me explain:

Athletes will push their physical body to the limit in order to be faster and better than the next person, and they may not give their body the rest it needs. We may enter challenging races without adequate preparation; this grueling activity takes its toll on the body. We know of entire cultures where people seek to find favor with their gods and have their prayers answered by appeasing them by punishing their physical bodies and inflicting pain and suffering upon themselves. You might remember the Old Testament account of Elijah when he met with the prophets of Baal on Mount Carmel:

> At noon Elijah began to taunt them. "Shout louder!" he said. "Surely he is a god! Perhaps he is deep in thought, or busy, or traveling. Maybe he is sleeping and must be awakened." So they shouted louder and slashed themselves with swords and spears, as was their custom, until their blood flowed. (1 Kings 18:27–28 NIV)

Were these prophets mature in their physical bodies? No, not really. They were willing to do whatever it took, mutilating their physical bodies to gain favor from their god. Our heavenly Father can use a person with any kind of physical body, anytime, and anywhere, but the more mature the body, the more likely that it will remain steadfast and endure great challenges and difficulties. Our heavenly Father needs us, when He calls us, to go to a dying world on His behalf.

> And He said to them, "Go into all the world and preach
> the gospel to all creation. (Mark 16:15 AMP)

If the physical body, however, does not have the opportunity to fully mature, then Satan will, in times of difficult challenges, step in with his plans to hinder our life and ministry. The physical body will succumb and give up. You may be familiar with the book by John Foxe, *The Voice of the Martyrs*.[4] I was never able to complete reading this book because each story reveals how Christians were willing to suffer for their faith, in their physical bodies. These faithful servants did not give a thought to their physical bodies and what was happening to them. Actually, the opposite was the case. The greater the physical suffering, the more deeply they felt connected to Jesus, who had suffered for them.

Now, to go and make disciples does not always mean to get up with that physical body and go. It can also look something like this. When Mike and I lived in California, I had the privilege of hosting a Good News Club[5] in my garage each Monday afternoon. I would set up several benches that would fill up with children when the school bus dropped them off near our house. I had a snack and a story prepared, and eager eyes and ears were ready to receive what I had for them. The kids had a favorite story and begged me to tell it over and over again. Eventually, I would give in.

I had heard this story about a boy who lived around the late 1800s. The kids could identify with this boy because he was about their age. The story inspired me personally as well and made me evaluate my own commitment to witness to the unsaved.

The tale begins with the boy's many health issues, severe enough that he had become bedridden. On top of it all, he was born into a poor family who could not afford the mounting medical bills to take care of his needs. He no longer had a mom or dad to take care of him, so the authorities placed him into the care of a relative to live out his days. This relative was a very bitter person who did not really want to care for a child in his condition. He was of no use to anyone and only lay in bed and ate her food. She had little choice in the matter but, since he was considered to be an orphan, reluctantly agreed to give him a room. She put him way up in the attic, where a small bedroom served as his new physical prison.

So here was this little boy, lying in his bed, day in and day out. Food would be brought to him twice a day, and this was his only interaction with the person who was supposed to care for him. During these brief visits, he kept begging for a Bible and a pencil, or something he could write with. Again and again, he was denied his request. The caretaker had no use for the Bible herself and wondered why a boy would want one. Eventually, she gave in to his repeated requests. He was elated. He could now read his Bible each day and also write notes in the margins. His lonely days were filled with God's Word and God's love for him.

This young boy had a personal relationship with Jesus. This means there was a time in his life when he recognized that Jesus came to this earth to take on the sins of the world and willingly die for humankind. This included him. He knew he was born with sin, like all of us, and that there was nothing he could do to change this. He also knew, from the Bible, that sin can never live in heaven, and this is where he wanted to live with Jesus someday. This boy understood that Jesus, being sinless, was the only Substitute for his sin condition. Jesus died for him and all of humankind on Calvary.

His heart believed Jesus was his Savior, and with a sincere heart, he had invited Jesus to come into his life and forgive him for all the wrongs he had done. This was the day the boy became a child of God. The same can happen to each one of us, if we believe in our heart that Jesus came, died, and was resurrected. Because of his relationship with God, the boy wanted to learn all that he could about Jesus, who had given His life to save his.

He had found a relationship with God, but there were others who had never had the opportunity to accept Jesus into their hearts. As a result, they would not be with God after their life on earth ended. He told God he wanted to be a witness, to lead others to a saving knowledge of Him. But what could he do?

One day, he had a thought. Over the boy's bed was a small window. He was not sure which direction this window faced; nevertheless, he knew exactly what he needed to do. Each day, he carefully selected a scripture passage from the Bible, painstakingly tore the section out, and rolled the small piece of paper into a tight roll. Next, he would use all the strength he had left to pull himself up to the window. He was able to open the window only slightly, but enough for him to drop the roll of paper outside. He would collapse back into his bed, praying that this Bible verse would find the right person and lead them to Jesus.

One day, an older gentleman was walking past the building where this little boy lived. He saw something flying down from the upper window, and it landed right on top of his hat. He took off his hat, and to his surprise, he found a small roll of what he recognized as a page from the Bible. He carefully unfolded the little scroll. The verse on that piece of paper moved his heart in such a way that he determined to find out who had thrown it out of the window.

He entered the building to inquire about what had just happened in the street. He met the caretaker, and after a time of discussion, she led him up the stairs into the boy's room. The gentleman entered the room where the boy lay, and his heart melted. The room was cold; the only furnishing it held was a bed. He approached the little boy, touched his hand, and cried. The man sat down next to him and retold what had happened to him on the street. The boy was so excited; his heart felt good.

Right then and there, the gentleman promised he would do whatever was necessary to take care of the boy. After several weeks, he brought the boy into his home and cared for him until he died a few years later.

This is not the end of the story. You see, the Bible that the boy used was sent to a relative of this man, who served as a missionary in a foreign country. The missionary used this Bible and the notes the boy had written in the margins for all of the time he served there. One day in heaven, it will be revealed just how many lives were touched, how many found Jesus Christ as their Savior, all because a physically sick little boy cared about others and not himself.

This boy could not physically go, but in some way, he used his physical body to do what he could. His physical body was mature because he had accepted his fate and had come to peace in his heart. God needs all of us.

The people who have a healthy body surely can go. The sick can seek God as to where He needs them. Some of you may have seen the movie, *The War Room,* directed by Alex Hendrick, released in 2015.[6] "Going" can mean to retreat into a prayer closet and pray. We all can do that. If we ever find ourselves lying flat on our backs, our ministry of being a witness to others does not stop. The plans God has for our lives are still directed by Him.

If we have grown and matured physically, we can do so much for our Savior. We can go to places that need to hear the message. We can be the hands and feet of Jesus, showing a world that He still saves today.

In essence, God wants us to trust Him, completely. *Trust* means "to have full confidence in God." When Job experienced his struggle, God was testing him. We all want a testimony but don't want to go through the test. God was looking for an answer: Would Job choose to love and serve Him?

> The LORD said to Satan, "Where have you come from?" Satan answered the LORD, "From roaming throughout the earth, going back and forth on it." Then the LORD said to Satan, "Have you considered my servant Job? There is no one on earth like him; he is blameless and upright, a man who fears God and shuns evil." (Job 1:7–8 NIV)

God allowed Satan to attack the physical things belonging to Job, first his kids, then his goods, and eventually his body. Satan wasted no time and got to work right away. In one day, Job's life was changed completely from the way he knew it, but his response to God was:

> At this, Job got up and tore his robe and shaved his head. Then he fell to the ground in worship and said: "Naked I came from my mother's womb, and naked I will depart. The LORD gave and the LORD has taken away; may the name of the LORD be praised." (Job 1:20–21 NIV)

We are all eager to share with the world our blessings, exclaiming, "God is love," and "He loves you very much," and this is true. Yet in the midst of physical suffering, our voices remain silent. Suddenly, we believe God is not so great or loving toward His creation.

What Does God Desire for Our Physically Mature Bodies?

If God wants us to grow and mature physically, what does that mean? As already covered, a mature physical body has nothing to do with age or one's outward adornment and appearance. Physical maturity is achieved when we are ready to accept and adapt to the constant changes that come our way. This physical body, our earthly tent, needs to continue to grow and mature to be fully functional and available to God and His purposes for us.

In scripture, Paul gives us a picture of the physical body as a "tent" that allows us to be part of the human race. God breathed into this physical body His breath of life and enabled us to become a living being. The breath of life is also in every living creation.

There was a time in my life where I was consumed with the welfare of my physical body. In October of 1988, my husband and I, and two of our kids, found ourselves living in North Carolina. To be specific, we lived at the JAARS Center, that is, the support branch of Wycliffe Bible Translators'[7] Jungle Aviation and Radio Service. Our purpose was to prepare ourselves to serve God in missions overseas. One day, it hit me. I had discovered an area in my life in which I was not willing to trust God.

My mind was preoccupied with the thought, *What if I catch a sickness from these people I will be ministering to?* My thoughts were self-focused and only went down a one-way street. My selfish thoughts about my own physical being did not even extend to my family members. In order to still my fears for the well-being of my physical body, I had to talk to God about it. In my reading of the scriptures, some verses from the Psalms stood out. God wanted me to pay attention too:

> The angel of the LORD encamps around those who fear him, and he delivers them. Taste and see that the LORD is good; blessed is the one who takes refuge in him. Fear the LORD, you his holy people, for those who fear him lack nothing. (Psalm 34:7–9 NIV)

Right away, my thoughts shifted to angels, and I tried to envision lots of angels surrounding me, along with the promise of God that I will have no wants. I made a resolution right then and there, in my living room, to trust God with my physical body, and the physical bodies of my family.

In order for this promise to become a reality, I needed to give my physical body to God and trust Him every step of the way.

If I had not made that conscious decision to follow God, my concern on the mission field and beyond would always have been for my own physical welfare and comfort. I made a promise to myself to continue the process of maturing in my physical body, waiting with expectation on how God would use me in the lives of the people.

Health Challenges That Affect the Physical Body

I have journeyed this world for over half a century. I am not quite in my twilight years, but on the other side of sixty. During my nursing career, I saw my share of physical bodies, both healthy and sick. In many cases, the sick bodies seemed to have no life in them, appearing like a shell, yet somewhere in that shell was the real person. I saw also the physical bodies of visiting relatives who also showed signs of being sick. Their bodies were hunched over, burdened by some unseen force that pulled them down as well.

Prolonged or short-term illness can be accompanied by loneliness. Life seems to come to a standstill, and in some sense, the patient reverts back to being a little boy or girl. Family members go on with life, but everything has changed for people suffering in their physical body. Their new normal is filled with constant pain, physical discomfort, and despair about the lack of improvement. In addition to the physical challenges, mental and emotional issues can threaten to overwhelm a person completely, the longer the sickness continues.

The caretaker may begin to mirror the sick person, especially if a prognosis of "no hope" has been given. The focus is on the task of caring for the sick individual, never on the caretaker's personal needs. In the same way, aging parents or children with physical disabilities can be solely dependent on the caretaker. At times, it seems the living and the dying are alike. Like the dying individual, the living person can quit wanting to live, in some way.

God still listens, hears, knows, and understands all of our concerns and fears. I realize the prayers we offer often seem to go unanswered; things do not move in the direction we hope for. Yet I would encourage you to continue to boldly bring your requests to God, then quietly trust Him for what is best, just like Jesus prayed boldly in the garden of Gethsemane and then acknowledged whatever God wanted is what He wanted as well:

> And after going a little farther, He fell face down and prayed, saying, "My Father, if it is possible [that is, consistent with Your will], let this cup pass from Me; yet not as I will, but as You will." (Matthew 26:39 AMP)

I have also met precious folks who were born with physical limitations or horrendous physical challenges, right out of the gate. Some of these people became harsh, bitter, and angry with what happened. Others, with time, made friends with their physical bodies, with the way things were, and continued to enjoy the best things in life. Their physical bodies matured in the process, accepting what was. Such was the case with Craig, my brother-in-law.

My husband's brother was born with a physical defect that was not discovered till he was about seven years old. When Craig was born, he seemed the same as his other siblings, in the physical sense. As he got older, he struggled to walk, and an x-ray revealed that his ankles had not developed properly. Craig was fitted with a cast that extended from below his knees to his toes. He learned to walk in this cast and needed a new one every two weeks. There were no other signs of anything one would refer to as slightly abnormal; nothing that would point to the real issue. Later, during one of his routine visits to the pediatrician, the doctor noticed that his chest was a bit more pronounced and coming to a point, rather than flat and spread out.

Craig's siblings describe him as having a funny nature. He smiled a lot and joked around in such a fashion that nobody suspected he was different or sick. To his family, he was just like any other kid. As mentioned, his physical defect was not discovered till, at the age of seven, he was admitted to the hospital for some tests. Nobody really realized how sick this boy really was. The family doctor suspected that Craig had a kidney disease. His belly had swollen up, though he was losing weight. His urine had changed to a brown color. An appointment was made, and without even examining the boy, the doctor announced that Craig had an enlarged heart. His heart was pushing his ribs outward. While in the hospital, he had to undergo a battery of tests.

The tests revealed that he had a malfunctioning heart valve. Open-heart surgery was suggested, but at that time, it was still a new procedure, and survival was put at 50 percent. During his hospital stay, Craig had a stroke. God's timing was perfect, in that he had his stroke in the hospital; his roommate called for the nurse. An entire team was available to meet his new needs right away. The stroke he experienced that day was, in many ways, the beginning of the real problem. Why would a seven-year-old boy have a stroke? In the hospital, the truth became evident, and after several more tests and x-rays, it was confirmed that Craig had been born with Marfan syndrome.

Marfan syndrome can be mild, or it can be severe; the disease tends to worsen with age. The doctors pointed out Craig's features. They included a tall and slender build; disproportionately long arms, legs, and fingers; and a protruding breastbone. The disease is caused by a defect in the gene passed on by the parents; sometimes, it just develops on its own.

When I first met Craig, he was twenty-three years old. In his gangly way, he was a kind, caring, funny person. I discovered he was also a physically mature individual. With all of his setbacks and challenges, he grew and matured with what he was given. Even with the condition his body was in, he always enjoyed having lots of friends; in a visible way, he became a living gospel. Yes, Craig freely shared words from the Bible and talked about his Savior, and he never complained. He was truly a mature man who lived till he was twenty-six years old. We all can learn from my brother-in-law. Now in heaven, Craig is whole, rejoicing that even in his mortal physical body, he was able to become the visible Jesus to countless others.

At his funeral, several of Craig's friends realized he was now with His Savior in heaven. This was the deciding factor for these men to give their lives to Jesus, as well. Craig was a witness, not in the sense we often would describe. His physical setbacks did not hold him back from sharing Christ and His love with others.

In 1977, Philip Yancey wrote a book titled *Where Is God When It Hurts?*[8] He wrote that book especially with suffering in mind. "Many people want to love God but cannot see past their tears," Yancey wrote.

Thinking again of my brother-in-law, Craig, it would have been easy for him to come to the conclusion that God had in some way betrayed or abandoned him.

Jesus did not come to this world to alleviate physical suffering, and He did not always heal, rescue, or make things better for humankind. When Jesus came to the pool of Bethesda, we read the following:

> Here a great number of disabled people used to lie—the blind, the lame, the paralyzed. One who was there had been an invalid for thirty-eight years. When Jesus saw him lying there and learned that he had been in this condition for a long time, he asked him, "Do you want to get well?" "Sir," the invalid replied, "I have no one to help me into the pool when the water is stirred. While I am trying to get in, someone else goes down ahead of me." Then Jesus said to him, "Get up! Pick up your mat and walk." At once the man was cured; he picked up his mat and walked. (John 5:3–9a NIV)

A little later in that same chapter, we read the man's reply. After the Jewish leaders asked him who had healed him on the Sabbath, his reply was as follows:

> He answered them, "The Man who healed me *and* gave me back my strength was the One who said to me, 'Pick up your pallet and walk.'" They asked him, "Who is the Man who told you, 'Pick up your pallet and walk'?" Now the man who had been healed did not know who it was, for Jesus had slipped away [unnoticed] since there was a crowd in that place. (John 5:11–13 AMP)

Did Jesus heal only this man, or did he heal all the others who were around that pool, seeking to get well that day? The Bible is not clear. In the verse, we read that Jesus slipped away in the crowd. But we know one thing for certain: why Jesus came to this earth. The words Jesus spoke to Zaccheus while He was at his house reveal this:

Zaccheus stopped and said to the Lord, "See, Lord, I am [now] giving half of my possessions to the poor, and if I have cheated anyone out of anything, I will give back four times as much." Jesus said to him, "Today salvation has come to this household, because he, too, is a [spiritual] son of Abraham; for the Son of Man has come to seek and to save that which was lost." (Luke 19:8–10 AMP)

How Can You Reset Your Physical Life?

1. Identify if you can completely love your physical appearance.
2. If you are presently experiencing physical challenges, bring Jesus into the situation. (Follow the examples I applied in my own life, as described throughout this book.) Pray without ceasing till you are able to accept your physical setbacks. God does not expect you to love your physical circumstances, but He does want you to make friends with your physical challenges, to demonstrate you still trust Him. Also, go to the Word and read till God gives you a verse that speaks directly to you.
3. Strengthen and prepare yourself for future unexpected physical changes in your body. Include God in this process. We should not be surprised when these things happen to us.
4. Be realistic, as different seasons are part of our physical life cycle.
5. Find a new normal, with God's help, to accept temporary or permanent changes in your physical body.
6. Go to your physical safe place often (see chapter 6).
7. Record your losses, not for the purpose of having a permanent reminder of what was lost, but to allow yourself to begin the grieving process. Grieving eventually brings closure to what is happening in your physical life.
8. Invite Jesus by bringing your questions to Him, and give Him the opportunity to speak to your heart till His peace fills you up. (see chapter 3).
9. When you are ready, speak to God about forgiveness. If others have sinned against your physical body, grant forgiveness.
10. Finally, I would highly encourage you to clean up all of your personal sin issues. Unconfessed sin can lead to physical issues. You

can secure a copy of the *Biblical Concepts in Counseling Workbook*[9] to assist you with this process.

I'd like to cover another area that not many of us are aware of. The first time we gave in to Satan's temptation and engaged in sinful behavior was the point in our life when we invited Satan to set up a base of operation in our life to influence us. In other words, he now has a stronghold in our life. The Bible warns us in Ephesians, "And do not give the devil a foothold" (Ephesians 4:27 NIV).

When Jesus died on the cross for the sins of this world, He died for our past, present, and future sins. What we do not realize is, the influence, or the place, or the foothold we gave to the enemy needs to be dealt with, as well. We do this in prayer by first renouncing our involvement and second by asking Him to give back to us the ground we gave to the enemy through our sinful involvement. The *Biblical Concepts in Counseling Workbook*[9] can assist you with this process.

How Does My Physical Life Story End?

My physical life story has not ended yet because I'm still very much alive in my physical body, as of this writing. My journey to grow and mature continues and is on the course that was ordained by God. My entrance into this world was anything but good news, but now, looking back, it was what shaped me into who I have become.

The rejection I felt from my parents, and eventually from everybody who criticized my physical appearance, was a constant thorn in my side. The words my mother hurled at me haunted me for years. Even though I was a social butterfly, I never felt quite safe enough in the physical world. Most of my friends were male, and I felt they accepted me and wanted me. Unlike my female friends, who were more concerned about how they looked, I just wanted to be accepted for who I was. People would have described me as outgoing, fun, and always on the move. But the reality was much different.

When I was alone, my heart ached. My physical body became a reflection, in the mirror, that I despised. Not only did I feel rejected as a person; I felt like the ugly duckling who tries to fit in. The day I brought Jesus into my hurting heart changed everything.

In prayer, I asked Him, "Jesus, the day I was born, I was a disappointment to my parents. I was not the boy they longed for. What did this rejection do to my heart? Jesus, if you could show me a picture of my heart, the way you see it, what would you show me?"

To my surprise, I saw a heart with a big, jagged break all the way through.

"What happened to my heart?" I asked. "It's broken." I prayed some more, wanting to know. There was no answer. So I continued on, "Jesus, when did my heart break?"

I offered Jesus several options as to how old I was at the time my heart broke, but there was only silence from His end. There was only the picture of the large heart changing, becoming smaller and smaller. By now I had arrived at my birth, and I saw a very small heart that was broken in half.

Finally, I asked Jesus, "Lord, can you take me back into my mother's womb and show me my heart there?"

The moment the words were out of my mouth, I saw the tiniest heart I've ever seen, and yes, even this heart was broken.

What happened next has changed my life forever. Again I asked Jesus what had happened to me; my heart was wounded before I was even born. The answer to my question came again in the form of a picture. It was as if I was looking out of the womb, and Jesus gave me a picture of my future. I saw my parents fighting, shouting, and saying hateful words to each other. The more I heard, the more I pulled back, farther and farther, to escape the hateful words and violent tempers of my parents.

All of a sudden, my heart understood, and a deep sorrow washed over me. I also wanted to know if Jesus was excited the day I was born. He confirmed the message to my heart: He was ecstatic that the world would finally see His special, little girl, created for His pleasure. His love poured all the way through my weary soul. I continued asking Jesus if He was there and had heard my mom's words when she told me she wished I would die. Jesus was there; He had heard everything, and He cried for me.

At this point, I asked Jesus to hold me and comfort me because I had no idea what would happen next. My tears flowed, and in some way, I allowed myself to grieve the many losses I had experienced from the moment I was conceived. The love I felt that day was so real.

As Jesus held me, my wish was that this moment would never end. Like a movie unfolding in front of my eyes, my heart realized that what Jesus showed me, what had happened to me in the womb, was true. My heart now fully grasped the reality that as God was forming me in my mother's womb, my heart broke and became wounded, because I was not wanted by my mom. Jesus also showed me I had placed my physical body, in an imaginary way, back into a dark attic. Way back in this lonely, dark attic sat a little girl, shivering, rejected, not wanted by anyone. I had no idea if I had any worth in the eyes of Jesus, but I asked Him if He would come to this frightened little girl and sit with her. He did. He continued to hold me and comfort my heart. Jesus wiped away my tears and whispered that I was beautiful, and He created me exactly the way He wanted me to be. Jesus gave me a special image of how He saw my physical body. The picture I saw was of Jesus holding in His hands a very large multicolored jewel, shaped in the form of a heart. As I looked at this enormous jewel resting there in the hands of Jesus, my physical body seemed to change right in front of me. I was still the same person, but I felt different. I felt free, accepted, lovely, beautiful, cherished, and honored. The next time I looked in the mirror, I saw what Jesus saw, and from that day on, I have always seen myself as this priceless jewel, the woman God specially designed and gave life to. No, it was not a mistake I was born a little girl. God knew all along what His plans were for me, and I was finally able to celebrate and embrace my physical life.

The healing I received from Jesus on this day was overwhelming, wonderful, and amazing. For the first time, I felt completely accepted in my physical body. I accepted my body as a perfect gift from the Father. At the time I was praying and seeking healing from God for my physical pain issues, I was not ready to forgive my parents for the emotional pain they caused me or the spiritual pain I had to endure by being taught that God was harsh. I was also not ready to talk to God about my sexual abuse. What I took away from that day was that God would give me all the time I needed to allow Him to step into my other areas of pain, when I was ready.

Outwardly, my physical body went through countless changes, but one thing remained throughout all these years: The way I see myself is still the same as the day Jesus spoke His message of love to my heart. As different physical changes have happened in my body, I have been willing to accept and adapt. I realize this earthly tent is beginning to fold up and one day will be laid aside for a body that is fit to live forever in heaven with my Savior.

I learned to view my physical body, created as a girl, as a gift from God. I am able to come alongside my Savior and make a difference in the world. Once I was a little girl who was completely out of her comfort zone. Then, like a caterpillar, I developed into a beautiful butterfly. As I now enter the latter half of my earthly life, I know that physical challenges will come my way. It is my prayer that I hold fast to God and His promises:

> For I am convinced that neither death nor life, neither angels nor demons, neither the present nor the future, nor any powers, neither height nor depth, nor anything else in all creation, will be able to separate us from the love of God that is in Christ Jesus our Lord. (Romans 8:38–39 NIV)

Only we have the power to separate ourselves from God, and it is for that reason we must grow and mature physically in order to be prepared for what God has ordained for each one of us. Then, we can begin to live that life that God has given to us, the way He designed it to be on this side of heaven.

The next chapters will discuss how God wants us to grow and mature emotionally, spiritually, and sexually, in order to reach our full potential.

CHAPTER 3

GOD WANTS US TO GROW AND MATURE EMOTIONALLY

Do not be anxious about anything, but in every situation, by prayer and petition, with thanksgiving, present your requests to God. And the peace of God, which transcends all understanding, will guard your hearts and your minds in Christ Jesus. (Philippians 4:6 NIV)

The concept of God wanting us to grow and mature emotionally may seem kind of strange to some. It was for me. In the Western world, we place the seat of our emotions in our heart. The Bible has a lot to say about the heart; hundreds of verses talk about it. I've often asked myself, "Why did God place so much emphasis on the heart?" One day, I had a light bulb moment, and it dawned on me. Jesus understands, and He also knew our heart would be damaged by others. When individuals speak painful words or inflict traumatic deeds, to others their actions result in an emotionally damaged heart, filled with pain. As Jesus asks us to give our emotional heart to Him, we need to pay attention to His leading. If the heart is this important to Him, it should be important to us and draw our thoughts to what God wants to do in our hearts. He wants to set us free from emotional pain and restore our emotional heart. Few of us have given this much thought. Jesus not only died for our spiritual sins; He also gave His life for our emotional, broken heart at the same time. Once this concept became crystal clear to me, my whole world began to change.

We never consider the fact that Jesus wants to come into the places in our heart we locked up at some point. We lock our pain in an imaginary room, deep inside of our being, and often forget it is still there. We want no one to see these secret places. We will not surrender or open up these places of pain to others or even ourselves. This includes Jesus, because we have come to believe that not even He understands or can help us in any way. Jesus simply cannot feel how hurtful and painful these events were. So these secret rooms, down into which we stuff all of our pain, remain under lock and key. The key is not surrendered to anybody. We know very well that if we were to open up these rooms, we would make ourselves vulnerable and disclose information about ourselves that others could use against us. The risk of doing this is far greater than keeping it all hidden and locked up.

It took me years, not days or weeks, but years, to open up my own locked doors and let others see and hear what was hidden from the world. In the pages that follow, I am writing from my heart, and in doing so, I am exposing my inner self to the world. I want to give you a clear picture of what created pain in my heart, how I identified my pain, and the steps I followed to find freedom. My desire is that you will see yourself in these pages and that you, too, would be willing to take a good look inside of your emotional heart.

As covered in chapter 2, we grow up physically, knowing we also need to mature, but we never realize emotionally, we are stuck. How can this be? We laugh and smile, deceiving ourselves, believing we are fine, yet the true picture is that we live in an emotionally vacant pit. We are so physically oriented that our inner being is often neglected, perhaps not even considered. Yet God created us as emotional beings, to exist in relationships. For this reason, we need to know ourselves on the inside. In order to reach wholeness in our life, our emotional side plays a major role. Our body and soul live so close together, they catch each other's diseases. If we have grown and matured physically, spiritually, and sexually, but our emotions are out of sync, then all of the decisions we make will be affected. How we perceive life will be influenced by this imbalance. We find ourselves asking, "Why did I do that?" or "I'm at the same place I was before; why does nothing change?"

It seems that no matter how hard you try, the outcome is pretty much the same. You may choose the same type of boyfriend, over and over. The names change, but each time, your emotional needs are not met. It could be you find yourself at a loss, again and again, as to what to do next, feeling helpless and all alone. You cannot seem to manage your choices, and it always ends up in a disaster of some kind. Over and over again, you give love and attention to others, all the while not realizing you need to be loved and paid attention to, as well. At first, this realization may surprise you and seem rather selfish, but on the other hand, you resonate with the thought of being on the receiving end of being loved and cared for.

In this chapter, I want to offer you a path of how God can step into your life and heal your emotional wounds and scars. Once this process has taken place, you will be able to continue to grow and mature emotionally, and the decisions you make in life will be in harmony with everything else. I found this to be true in my life, and I cannot wait to share this information with you.

Emotional Scars from My Past

In chapter 2, I described many moments in my life where I identified struggles that related directly to my physical person. I shared with you the fact I was supposed to be a boy, and to top it all off, any physical changes that took place in my body were dealt with in the quickest way possible. As a need arose, attention was given. The greatest hurdle I had to overcome in my physical life was to accept the fact that I was an ugly girl, not wanted and good for only one thing. To accept God's decision for my life, and who He created me to be, was a process, and without Him, it would have been impossible to achieve. Yet not only in my physical life did I need to come to Jesus and ask Him to step into my pain in order to grow and mature. I also needed to do this in my emotional life; the inner part of me had become severely damaged by all that had happened. This damage occurred early in my childhood and was like an unseen thread that wove itself all through my life. I had become a survivor of some sort and finally I found freedom and rest in my heart.

A total of seven people made up our household, so one would think we were showered with love and affection. This was not the case. One question remains unanswered: Would I have received all that I needed emotionally, if I had been born a boy? To tell you the truth, I really don't know, since all my siblings were girls. Looking back, it seemed that each of us received the same treatment, but I was so focused on my own needs that I did not once consider my sisters' needs for love and attention.

While I was still very young, I realized my heart was not in a good place. It felt lonely, not wanted, not valued, and rejected. In some ways, I felt invisible to everyone. Being invisible in a family can happen more often than you think. I was surrounded by four sisters and two adults, and except for the sister who was just a few years older than me, I was invisible to the rest of the family. When my mom wanted me to do something, she would often call me by one of my sisters' names. Finally, she would just say, "Hey you." My given name was seldom used, and I never really liked my name till I was much older.

Later on, after I had developed the art of listening to other people's hearts, it became quite obvious what they wanted to say to me. My ears no longer focused on their spoken words, but rather on what their heart was trying to say to me. What they wanted me to understand was that their home was like a dormitory, or felt like a tomb, and in the end, it was a place where people just existed. How well I could identify with them. While I was still living with my parents, if you asked me how my home life was, I could not have told you what I was feeling. All I knew was that I was not noticed and felt really unhappy, deep down. I figured this was how all families were.

My extended family was very much a part of my growing-up years. I only knew my Grandpa on my father's side for a few years. He was a very strict, opinionated man, commanding everybody around to fulfill his needs, and I stayed away from him as much as I could. The way he treated my mom and dad made me cringe inside. I still remember the day he died. I wondered if my parents were relieved to have him pass. There were uncles and aunts who offered me the same cold shoulder I received from my parents. Our get-togethers were formal affairs, rather than getting to know each other. Drinking and partying was always on the agenda, and of course, we kids just tagged along for the ride. Needless to say, we did whatever we wanted till it was time to go home again.

In spite of all that my father represented, I noticed there were moments when he was gentle and kind. He had a generous heart. He also gave things to homeless people and helped cared for them. Destitute individuals could come to my dad, and he met them with grace and a helping hand. His workers spoke of him as being a fair, giving man. My dad was respected by his employees, and I often heard them say he was a great boss. I saw this side of my dad every once in a while; my heart longed to be the recipient of this kind of outpouring of kindness.

When I was about ten years old, something special happened. My father announced that an older couple he knew were moving into town. He arranged all the moving details, and some men from his company assisted in the relocation of this couple. My mom was asked to make an effort to get to know them and offer her time to them as needed. A few days later, Mom told us to get ready to visit this couple. Only my sister and I were still living at home. I sort of did not want to go; I wondered what I had in common with two old people. Nevertheless, I had to go.

When we arrived at these strangers' home, we were met by a jolly old man. He was round and somewhat short, but what caught my attention were his twinkling eyes. A petite lady then came to the door as well, and she reached for my mom and gave her a big hug. Well, that was new; I wondered how Mom would respond to that?

Mom explained who she was and why we were there, and we were ushered into their small living quarters. The way the apartment was laid out was kind of funny. It all seemed like one long hallway. The three of us sat down on the couch, and more formal introductions began. Of course, we were encouraged to take tea with this couple, and to my surprise, my mom accepted. We spent the afternoon getting to know these two people, and my heart was strangely drawn to them. I never met my paternal grandmother, and not knowing anything of my maternal grandparents, I never knew what having grandparents was like. This was new, and it felt good.

All too soon, we said our goodbyes. Before we left, the lady looked at me and my sister and made us promise to come over as often as we wanted. The lady's husband added his approval to this invitation, and my heart grew excited for my next visit. My mom said that it would be fine and she would give it some thought.

A few days later, both my sister and I tested the waters and asked Mom if we could go over and spend more time with the two elderly people. To our surprise, our wish was granted. We were given a time to return, and that was that. The two of us ran over to the next street to start our great adventure. You should have seen the look on the lady's face when she opened the door. She was truly delighted that we came and hugged us to her chest. Before we knew what was happening, we were sitting together at the kitchen table, playing a board game and enjoying lemonade and chatting away. This couple let us talk. They listened to us and enjoyed our company. My heart felt good. I felt wanted and, in some way, accepted.

From that day on, we ran over to this couples' house as often as we were allowed. Our times with them were awesome. My father even invited them to our family affairs, and knowing that my adopted grandma and grandpa would be there changed everything. Not till I was an adult did I realize the gift my heavenly Father gave me by sending these two lovely people into my life.

A few years after our original meeting with this older couple, the husband died. My heart was shattered. I still remember his funeral. My heart was so sad, and my loss was deep. Now it was only Grandma, my sister, and I. Our times continued much as they had before, but we all knew they would never be as rich as they had been.

Then, the unthinkable happened: A year later, Grandma died as well.

My first thought was, *Who would love me now?* I missed these two precious people very much, but my parents had no idea that their little girl had connected her heart in some small way to these folks. My parents had no idea how this brief moment gave me a glimpse of what love might feel like and what a heart connection looked like.

My father was an alcoholic. He never connected his heart to mine in any way I can remember. I actually feared him. He never physically abused me or harmed me in any way, but because of his drinking and immoral behavior, which I will cover in a later chapter, I did not respect him. I often saw him when he was drunk with soiled pants. I was embarrassed for him, and shame filled my heart. My father's friends seemed to just take this in stride, but for me, it was humiliating. My dad sat on the city council and ran a successful business that was the largest in town, but I had no idea who this man really was.

I longed for him to sit me on his lap, hug me, and tell me how much he loved me. It never happened. In all of my growing-up years, I never heard my dad say these words: "I love you." My father only touched me to punish me, severely. His eyes showed me that I wasn't accepted. His mouth spoke words that devastated my world. Words were hurled at me that made me recoil on the inside and changed everything my heart believed. Actually, my father's favorite comparison was that my back side was as big as a horse. Remarks like this were a constant reminder that something was definitely wrong with me. Eventually, these words became my new identity, and my heart believed this was exactly who I was.

My mother had her own favorite sayings about me. In the rare moments she looked at me, she would point her finger in my face and declare my awaited future. Her outlook for my life was that the only thing I was good for was to be a prostitute, and because I was so ugly, I would have to pay a man to take me. Her face was so stern and sincere that I believed her. Why couldn't my parents just accept and love me? Neither of them was emotionally available to me. What I didn't realize was that my heart was drained, and without me even knowing what was happening to my little heart, which was already in a far corner of the attic, it retreated even more into the dark space.

How I longed to have someone love me and say kind words to me. I never saw love from anyone. It seemed that all the people who were a part of my growing-up years did not love each other or care for each other. I despised the idea of marriage because all the couples I saw were miserable. My entire extended family was immoral, and the effects of their lifestyle robbed them of being able to connect with each other. Why be miserable in a marriage where you are not wanted, loved, and cherished? Early on in my life, I had a thought that I would check myself into an abbey, live like a nun, and all would be well.

I voiced this idea to my mom, and her only response was a sarcastic, "That is just what they need ... you."

I lived in my parents' home till I was fifteen years old. In the country where I was born and raised, we attended school till the ninth grade and then went on to higher education. We could choose high school, trade school, or college. My dream was to be a nurse; I was ready to move on to the next chapter of my life. To get to this new level and to get accepted into the nursing program, I had to get everything done by myself. My goal was also driven out of the need to get away from my parents, out of their house, and on to bigger and better things. At least, that's what I thought.

Once in college, things were better in many ways. I made friends quickly and truly enjoyed my studies and my exposure to hospital life. Yet somehow, something was missing. What was missing? One day, it dawned on me, and I actually admitted to myself the truth of what I had become. I was a domineering, angry, self-sufficient young lady who could not connect to anyone at a heart level.

Now my heart knew the truth, and it actually did not really ruffle my feathers one bit. I loved what I had become. My goal was to advance in my career as fast as I could, and if that meant using people, or stepping over some bodies, that would be just fine with me. I was very goal oriented. Relationships were a waste of time. By now, the lie that nobody wanted or needed me was deeply planted in my heart, and my life reflected what I had become.

However, my beloved heavenly Father, whom I did not know at the time, had other plans for me. Just as He sent my surrogate Grandpa and Grandma, He sent another angel to my aid. A young lady started her second year of nurse's training at the same time I began nursing school. She and I became best friends and were inseparable. In many ways, we were the odd couple because we had totally different backgrounds. She was brought up in a close-knit family, which was foreign to me. But that was not what made our friendship unique.

My friend was born with no chin, had glasses that looked like bottoms from a coke bottle, and wore a hearing aid that was fitted to her glasses. When she took her glasses off, she was deaf and blind. Her physical appearance was not what the world would call "flattering," but to me, she looked perfect. The two of us bonded right away, not so much on a heart level, but on having the same interest in boys.

When my graduation day arrived, it was this friend who was there for me. My parents never came to any of my graduations. Even when I came home for weekends that first year of my studies, my mom didn't care about my presence. It was my friend who cheered me on and gave me approval. The two of us got into a lot of mischief but always managed to stay on top of our grades. She saw me at my worst, especially when I'd accept any man who wanted to go out with me and let him have his way with me. She never bucked me but accepted me for who I was. I began to reveal bits and pieces of my childhood. She really had no idea how to help me; she just let me talk. I could never cry or feel any kind of emotion when I talked about my growing-up years; it was like telling someone else's story.

My quest for looking for someone to love me became a desperate search. My thought was, if I give people what they want, of course they will love and accept me. I was wrong. Over and over again, my heart was rejected, not wanted, not valued. As time went on, a cycle repeated itself, over and over again. I would meet someone, be friendly, spend time with them, give them what they wanted, and off they would go to meet someone else. Or I would push others away, believing they wanted something too. My heart finally got the message that I need to behave in a certain way, give everybody what they want, and life will be fine. In the end, I got so tired of it all.

I passed from childhood through my teens into adulthood, and not much changed. Finally, I decided that being loved and given attention was not what I needed, after all. Me, myself, and I, we did just fine. Eventually, I returned to my so-called friends the same treatment they were giving me. I took from them what I thought I needed and then left them in the dust. I went from one boyfriend to another, only to be pushed aside for the new thing. Once alone in my little apartment, I would feel the loneliness, but just as quickly as these emotions came, I put them out of my mind for the purpose of seeking success, instead.

The Visible Signs of a Heart That Is Empty

Some of you reading this book have now discovered you may have never had a real heart connection with anyone. You might even feel the pain of unresolved issues deep within your heart. Perhaps you are becoming aware that what you are experiencing is connected to the emotional damage you are still carrying. Your heart may be telling you that your loneliness has its roots in your past. Whatever is bubbling to the surface is a reminder from God, to draw your attention to what is still unresolved inside of your heart. If you are willing to take an honest look at these past unresolved issues, you are ready to bring them to Jesus.

God is wise and placed within us a deep need to both give and receive love. Love is a broad term because love looks different for each of us. To some, love looks like another person understanding them, to some, fully accepting them, or to another, giving them attention, and so on. But in order to give love to others, we must first know what love is, and if others give love to us, we must be able to fully receive it. A heart that has received what it needed knows how to minister to others. To receive love or other things that we need from others is to be able to take into our heart everything that someone wants to pour in. These are good things that make us feel loved, wanted, important, significant, and cherished. If a person can give love, but not receive love, the heart is locked. I call this a single locked heart. If a person can neither give love nor receive love, then they have a double-locked heart. At the beginning of our lives, we first look to our families and close friends to meet our deepest needs; later, we look to those we work with. Somebody needs to satisfy that need, but if it is never met, then the heart does not have the opportunity to grow and mature emotionally as God intended.

A heart that has a single lock cannot receive love from another person. This individual will miss out when anyone wants to care for them on a heart level. No matter what is given or how hard the other person tries, it falls on a hardened heart. If the emotional heart is starved for love, it will wait for a long time for someone to fill it, but there comes a point when the heart will give up waiting. At this point, the lie from the enemy settles in their heart: Nobody will ever meet their emotional needs. The lie from Satan, that they are unlovable, now becomes their new reality and new identity. Satan attacks our identity. He wants to steal it away from us, and if we don't know who we are or who we are in Christ, we succumb to his scheming. We believe the lies he places in our hearts, and they become our new truth. As stated earlier, the need of being emotionally cared for is so strong that people will wait years, hoping and longing for someone to recognize what they need. It's really up to the person closest in their life to discover what the other is craving. All we know is that something is missing, and damaged hearts cannot share with others what's missing or what their needs are. Damaged hearts cannot give a voice to what is needed and cannot clearly say what would fill their hearts. The years go by, and nothing changes, and the heart eventually goes into hiding and dies.

The double-locked heart is even more desperate because it cannot give or receive love. At some point, it will built protective barriers to keep itself from becoming more damaged. The heart will actually go far away, or be put in some kind of secret place only the person knows about, or perhaps it's been so long the person can no longer identify the place. At times, the heart can be lost. All the pain experienced is locked away in the recesses of the heart, not to be resurrected until the painful event is triggered. When a heart has been severely damaged over a long period of time, only Jesus knows where the heart was hidden. In prayer, we can ask Him to look for that heart, so it can be restored to the person.

One teenage girl described it like this: "I see myself sitting inside a deep hole, and far above me, I hear faint voices. There are moments I see people passing right over me. They never look down to see me or acknowledge me in any way. Each day becomes lonelier and more isolated. Occasionally, I can see the fun others are having, and their laughter drifts down to me, only to bounce off the walls, never reaching my empty heart."

As I listened to this young lady, I could see the sadness in her face. I could feel the emptiness in her heart.

I gently extended my arms, inviting her into my embrace. Would she come? Could she come? I was not sure, but I gave her all the time her heart needed to decide. You see, it was not her head or her intellect that ultimately made that decision to allow me to hold her. It was her heart that rushed into my arms and was finally able to cry. As I held her, I asked her if I could take her to Jesus. She just nodded her head, crying and holding on to me as if I would vanish into thin air.

As I led her to the lover of her soul, she followed my soothing voice, shaky at first. Then, with a new determination, she repeated my words in her own voice and asked what her heart wanted to know: "Jesus, do you see me sitting all alone in that deep dark hole?"

Yes, He saw. He knew. Just the fact that Jesus knew, and saw, and understood her heart brought on a fresh flood of tears.

"Jesus what happened to me? Why can't I get myself out of that lonely place?"

In her heart, she received the message Jesus wanted to share with her, and little by little, she understood the truth in her heart. Jesus literally opened her heart, just like the song, "Open the Eyes of My Heart."

Jesus prompted her heart by letting her know what He wanted to say to her. Jesus can speak in an audible voice if He chooses, but in my experience, He speaks by letting the heart know what He wants to say. Jesus not only gave her a knowing in her heart, He gave her a picture. He showed her those moments in her life when her heart became wounded and received pain. Over time, the pain in her heart became so great that she put it away into that dark hole so nobody would hurt it again.

She asked, "Jesus, can you help me out of that hole? Can you heal my heart from all the damage it has received? Would you help me to forgive the people who hurt me so deeply?"

Together, we prayed though all of the pain we had identified. She forgave, from her heart, all the people who had hurt and damaged her emotionally. Step by step, her heart came to the surface. Was she scared? No, she actually felt free. Now that the heart was free, it needed to be cared for by someone so it could stay in freedom.

Where Does Emotional Pain Come From?

Most of us look at our immediate circumstances and attribute our emotional state to what's happening right now. We never put the dots together as to where our emotional pain really came from or began. There is a beginning for everything, and if we do not go back to the cause, we will never find the solution. As just stated, the reason we are unable to seek a solution is, we no longer know the cause from when our heart first felt pain. The moment we experience a new painful event, our heart is in such a place, we cannot even get a handle on all the feelings that are going on inside; eventually, we just adapt and live with it. We stack one painful event on top of the other, without realizing how damaged our heart has become. We make a feeble attempt to manage life in the middle of it, yet our emotionally wounded heart has stopped developing over many years. Each hurtful event, word, or action that we ever experienced damaged us in some way. These things will not go away on their own, and until we deal with all the damage our hearts received, we just stuff it inside. Over time, the more hurt our heart has experienced, the greater the pain it will feel. If we have pain in our hearts, then life is lived in the shadows.

There are several ways we compensate for the pain that has settled in our heart. One way is to give pain a voice. We become angry, dominant, and controlling; pressure others with high expectations; and develop a critical, judgmental spirit that becomes our new norm. We believe that venting to others actually makes us feel better, but we never calculate the risks involved because in doing this, we alienate people. Instead of getting our needs met, the opposite happens. Also, over time, the anger will sit deep in the heart and become a way of life.

One other way we compensate for pain is that we try to fix our broken heart, by placing a bandage over it. It does seem to feel better for the moment, but the reality is that this is just a temporary fix and not what the heart needs in order to be healthy and whole. Some of our self-made bandages are things that soothe us for the moment. Alcohol and other drugs dull our senses and make us feel okay, but after the high wears off, we have to face our desperate, lonely heart again. The danger with all self-medication is that we become unaware that each and every substitute has the potential to thrust us into full addiction. All of a sudden, we need the substance, the distraction, that outlet, and we're no longer in control. It has control over us.

When we are under the influence of our self-medicating, the world is fine, temporarily. The alcohol never tells you that you're not important and have no value. The drugs never suggest that it's always your fault and you're stupid. The women from the magazines and the internet accept you, seem to love you, and give you what you want. They will never shout in your face that you're a loser. But all of this is a direct lie from Satan himself. He always offers us a cheap substitute, anything to keep us away from God, the Healer.

Even the expression on our face reveals the condition of our heart. The eyes are called the window to the soul. When the heart is in pain, the eyes reflect this very fact because they no longer light up or dance with delight. Darkness has engulfed them. We never realize that what we have received in life from others can potentially hurt or damage us. What we did not receive that we should have gotten can hurt us, as well.

Most of us hold on to the belief or impression that we are emotionally damaged by what our heart received emotionally at times in our life. This is, in many cases, the obvious reason why our heart is now damaged and in such a desperate state. If children were raised by parents who physically and verbally abused them, they assume that all their damage came from these experiences, and in part, that is true. The heart is damaged by receiving this kind of treatment. What we miss is this: The heart is also damaged by never, ever being given what it needs. A child's heart needs to know their house is a safe place, that someone will protect them if danger is present, that people care about their hearts and want to know how they feel, what their opinions are, and what their dreams are. In other words, the heart is not only damaged from what it received, but also from what it needed and never got. As a result, all throughout their lives, people will long for what was needed.

Once our heart has become empty, out of desperation, we take away emotionally from others. One example would be an expectant mother. While she is carrying her unborn baby inside, she can take away emotionally from her unborn child for the purpose of meeting her own needs for emotional fulfillment, especially if she is depressed. The little one inside of her becomes emotionally drained and begins to emotionally detach from Mom. After the child is born, it does not long to be held often, because the infant no longer seeks an emotional connection. Most likely, the mother will continue to emotionally drain the infant by taking from the child what she herself needs. The mother gives nothing back emotionally, and after her emotional needs are met, the child is neglected. Mom may hold her baby, meet his or her physical needs, but the child will know if Mom is truly emotionally connected or is detached. The child will feel empty and lonely.

I'm not an expert, but one can read secular studies on this very phenomenon. In our office, we have encountered many men and women who may have emotionally connected with their child in the beginning. Then when the child reached a certain age, all of a sudden, the nurturing quit because painful memories of events during their own lives surfaced. The parents do not realize the disconnect is related to their own experiences when they were exactly the same age. On the other hand, when parents are emotionally mature and healthy, then the parent-child relationship will be as God designed it. Each of them will be able to freely give and receive emotionally from one another.

In the Old Testament, we have these beautiful words describing how Naomi cared for her grandbaby's emotional needs:

Naomi took the baby and held him in her arms, cuddling him, cooing over him, waiting on him hand and foot. (Ruth 4:16 MSG)

How We Reach inside Each Other's Hearts

Wives, husbands, singles, teens, and kids all have a cry in their heart: to be emotionally loved, accepted, understood, and cared for by someone. A close friend of ours invited us to attend one of his workshops, and during his presentation, he said, "Emotional 'intimacy' equals 'In-To-Me-You-See.'" When I heard these words, my heart leaped for joy. It all made sense. That which I had tried to communicate and had wanted to say to others all along; this concept of someone understanding me on the inside, knowing me on a heart level, really taking the time to get to know what my heart needs, and on top of all that, being willing to give it to me. This revolutionized my world. Secretly, I went down a list of names of people I knew, trying to identify individuals who would sacrificially take up the quest to seek my heart. Devastated, I came up empty.

Then I turned to my husband Would he be willing to accept and care for me on a heart level, even with all the pain that he was still caring around himself? Yes, I believe he would, and he also would be the perfect person to get to know me deep inside. During our attendance at this workshop, he had shared with me that it was time for him to be free from the painful memories of his childhood, the lingering horrors of Vietnam, and the man he had become.

I know in some ways this sounds like a very selfish request, to look to a person and expect that they will now meet all of your emotional needs. But the circle of soul mates, individuals who truly long to get to know you on the inside, does not have to be only one person. However, in my experience, this group is rather small. But ask yourself this question: Is it selfish? Doesn't God call on us to love one another, meaning, give to each other what is needed? Yes, we can give emotionally what is needed to another person, but we should never forget that God always accepts, cares, and understands. Ultimately, He is the one who knows precisely how to care for our hearts. We are, however, physical people, and if a person is willing to duplicate the Father's love for us, our heart will feel emotionally cared for.

"A new command I give you: Love one another. As I have
loved you, so you must love one another. (John 13:34 NIV)

My heart longed for me and my husband to know each other on a heart
level, to quit pretending we had it all together and that everything was fine.
I had a new mission: to explore the word, intimacy, from an emotional
point of view. When we take the word *intimacy*, we come up with two
definitions. The first is the physical intimacy that we enjoy within the
bonds of marriage. Being sexually involved with your spouse is the closest
you can be physically. We will never have that kind of intimacy with our
Lord and Savior, Jesus Christ. The second form of intimacy we can have
with each other is emotional intimacy, or the heart connection, the getting
to know one another on the inside. The person who wants to emotionally
connect needs to know who we truly are, or find out what brings us joy,
knowing what our dreams are, and so on. This emotional intimacy is
exactly what God the Father, Jesus, His Son, and the Holy Spirit long for
us to have with Them. God is asking us to get to know Him on a heart
level. He gives me, a simple mortal being, the opportunity to know His
heart, and this is where He and I need to tabernacle together. I want to
receive all God has for me in my heart, offer Him my heart, and worship
Him from my heart. At the same time, God wants me to discover and
understand His written Word with my heart. It blows me away that the
Creator of the universe wants to have this intimate relationship with me.

There was a time in my life when I was not willing to let God see inside
my heart. I was scared, ashamed, and so much more. Now I love to be with
God in my special place, my heart, where He knows me, and I want to
know Him. There is no longer any fear because my heart is whole and free.

I want to point out that helping a heart come to freedom from past
hurtful issues is one thing. It begins with identifying and owning our
emotional damage and admitting our sin. We need to fully understand
what happened in the past and how this made us feel. Though we cannot
change our past, we need to move forward, or the past will become our
future. Staying in freedom for a lifetime is another thing. In order to stay
free, we must have someone in our life that cares for us. This person of trust
must care for what had happened to us in the past and never repeat the

pain we suffered. They have to be willing to take their eyes off themselves and focus on the person they want to emotionally care for.

Sadly, I must report that this is where the fabric unravels. You see, by the time people identify their damage, whether they were damaged by something they received, or they were damaged by something they needed but did not receive, their need is now so great that they become very needy. I cannot emphasize this enough. If a person will now care for their needs, the caregiver will feel like they are being run over by a train. My husband felt this way. When he began to care for my heart, I could not get enough. I wanted more and more. It will take a great deal of patience to meet the unmet emotional needs of a person. Jesus will always care for our emotional needs, but He also calls on us to be His hands and feet.

The earlier in life the heart was damaged, the greater the pain. Adults who were damaged while still in the womb, or as a baby, or as a young child up to the age of eight, felt severe pain. Young children will not know their heart was damaged by an experience, but they will know that something happened that was painful. For instance, a woman shared with me that her daddy left home one day, when she was five years old. Every day, for six weeks, she would run out of the house, sit on the curb, and wait for her daddy to come home, but he never came.

After six weeks of this, her mom sat down by her side, and all she said was, "He's never coming home again."

That little girl had no idea why her daddy would not come home, why he would leave her. From that day on, her heart felt unprotected and no longer safe. Now she was an adult, and she still felt unprotected, not safe, and feared that her husband would one day just leave her, without saying one word.

If emotional damage was experienced by children between the ages of nine and nineteen, the pain in their heart is still very great, though not as severe as if they had been younger. They will still have a lot of pain in their heart. For example, imagine if Mom posted a note on the refrigerator that said, "I wish I could have stayed, but I need to go, and I am not coming back." If her twelve-year-old daughter were to find that note, her heart would be confused; she would feel angry, abandoned, and hurt. She was left behind with a father who was more interested in drinking than raising his daughter.

"Why didn't my mom take me with her?" will be a constant cry of her heart. When this child becomes an adult, she will struggle to trust anyone because she was so deeply betrayed by her mom.

Any damage that occurs after the age of twenty will still result in substantial emotional pain and is considered adult pain. We cannot lessen the effect of any kind of pain that came from damage that occurred in a person's life, no matter what the age. In some ways, adults can handle the blow from an event better than children. A lot depends on what created the pain. From that moment on, life as they know it has changed, and a new normal has to be established. Damage that creates pain, at any age, changes their heart, and they won't know how to get rid of the pain on their own.

Some time ago, I was visiting a foreign country where horses were used as a means of transportation. For the most part, the horses I saw in the corrals and in the countryside seemed healthy, well fed, and happy. But there was one horse in particular that caught my eye; still, to this day, I cannot get the image of this horse out of my mind. The horse was pale in color and just stood in a fenced-off area. I saw the eyes of this horse, and the look was horrifying. The sadness that came from that horse was overwhelming. Never before in all of my life have I seen one of God's creatures in such deep sadness. If that horse could talk, I wondered what pain I would hear lodged deep within his heart. Believe it or not, I have seen similar eyes in people I've met, people who were like shells, walking around with no sense of belonging anywhere, hopeless, hurt, wounded, and emotionally drained.

Only Twelve and Wanting to Die

A twelve-year-old girl lived with her family in the same town as us. She was involved in our youth group. This girl was a bundle of life and joy. One day, however, I received a phone call that painted a totally different picture. I was told that this same girl wanted to take her life; she wanted to die. "No, that cannot be true," I said. "I would have seen some signs, wouldn't I?"

Before too long, the adults in her life sat around my table, and I had to admit that what they shared sounded like the truth. My heart was devastated for the deep pain this young girl must be carrying inside her heart. I had no idea what my role in this young lady's life would be or how

I could help her. A few days later, the girl's family asked me if I could spend time with her, to help her in some way.

At the time, my husband was a pastor in a midsize town. My role was to function as his wife. I loved my role, as it truly satisfied my soul. It was also a time in our personal life when we had just discovered Caring for the Heart Ministries. This ministry showed us clearly how Jesus modeled, in the scriptures, the way we need to help ourselves and others He brings our way. After we discovered this simple, yet unique, style Jesus demonstrated in reaching into the hearts of people, we were eager to apply these principles in our own life. We wanted to deal with our many unresolved issues so that we could truly come alongside people in our congregation.

Based on my newfound freedom and the training I received from Caring for the Heart Ministries, I felt led by God to see this young lady two times a week. Our first meeting came like a freight train. Was I ready? Was I prepared? No to both questions. If that young lady could have seen my knees, she would have known that I was a wreck inside. Praise God that my heart immediately settled as I focused on the words of Jesus and His promise: "And lo, I am with you always [remaining with you perpetually-regardless of circumstance, and on every occasion], even to the end of the age" (Matthew 28:20b AMP).

We started talking about several things. All along, I was trusting God to show me clearly the heart of this girl because He would know its condition. If I could not understand her heart, I would miss what she needed to say to me and not know how to lead her to Jesus for a solution. I listened carefully to every word she had to say. Would she expose her heart to me? This young lady guarded her heart so well, and by no means would she give me access to that place. "Well, God," I said, "it's up to You to show me what I need to do next. I continue to place myself completely in your hands." That was my prayer at the time and for all the meetings that would follow.

These questions needed to be answered: Why would a twelve-year-old want to die? What had happened to her that she saw no way out other than to quit? Several weeks later, I had my answer. She wanted to die in order to put an end to what was going on in her life, something that had been going on for years. The only way she could figure out to stop what was happening in her home was to take her life by her own hands.

During one of our sessions, I had a thought. God revealed to me what I needed to do. When she arrived, our session started the same way all the others had, but now I had a plan, a direction. In one of our earlier times together, I discovered that she loved to draw pictures. She had a sketchbook full of drawings she had put together over the years. What God revealed to me was to have her draw me a picture with a specific purpose in mind. My prayer was that we both would see the root problems in her life.

I placed paper, various pens, pencils, and markers in front of her so she could choose how to draw her picture. My instructions were simple: "Would you please draw me one room in your house?" I watched her as she selected her choice of colors, and with determination showing on her face, she set out to please me by honoring my request. We continued to have a light conversation to break up the silence that would have overshadowed the moment. Before too long, she passed the finished picture over to me.

I immediately noticed that something was missing. You see, part of my instruction to her was to draw one room in her house and to include herself in the picture. Where would she be in the room? If she had drawn her bedroom, she could have included herself lying on the bed or reading a book. If she had drawn a picture of the kitchen, she could have included herself washing the dishes or eating at the table.

I chose to bypass, for the moment, that she had not included herself in her picture. Instead, I remarked that this looked like her living room. There was a TV in the corner, a sofa, and some chairs. She smiled at me and confirmed that my guess was correct. At this time, I looked at her and mentioned that she had forgotten something in her picture. You would never guess what her response was.

She said, "How do you know what I have in my living room?"

She was right. I had no idea what was in her living room, since I had never set foot in her house. I gently reminded her that she missed putting herself in the picture.

At this moment, everything in the room seemed to change. Her voice turned into a whisper. She moved closer to me, pointed with her finger to the upper corner of her drawing, and said, "You cannot see me because I am invisible."

My heart resonated with hers because the very moment she said these words, I knew exactly how she felt. Gently, and in an equally quiet voice, I asked her if I could come and visit that girl who is invisible.

"No," she said immediately. "No one can come for a visit."

Our session had to end, but from that day on, I knew that the only person who could come to this invisible girl and minister to her hurting heart was Jesus.

> "Come to me, all you who are weary and burdened, and I will give you rest ... for I am gentle and humble in heart, and you will find rest for your souls. (Matthew 11:28a, 29b NIV)

At our next appointment, after talking awhile, I asked my friend if she would allow me to lead her to Jesus in prayer. When I lead a person in prayer, I ask them to give me permission and to trust me to lead with words that the Holy Spirit lays on my heart. The person, if they are in agreement, repeats the words to Jesus after me with their own voice. My husband and I had learned this method of praying by applying it in our own life. When a person's pain is great, they don't really know what to pray for. With this prayer method, a person can relax and follow you. Jesus can be asked questions the person may never have thought of before.

In our request to have them follow our lead, we include the direction that they only repeat the words that are true to their circumstance, correct as to their story and what their heart wants to say. It is not our intent to produce a parrot-like atmosphere, where the person repeats our words to the exact letter. No, the person has the right to use the same words as I have given them, but they are free to add their own thoughts to the prayer. We also instruct the person to not say anything they are not ready to say. This prayer is always done with an audible voice.

In the case of my young friend, she agreed and was eager to talk to Jesus. She felt completely comfortable praying and letting me lead her. She sat in front of me, and I touched her arm so she would not get lonely. I also had her close her eyes so she could concentrate on Jesus. I asked her if she could go in her mind's eyes into that living room and just sit in the corner she had described to me. Almost immediately, she nodded her head to confirm she was there.

I asked again if I could come visit with her, and the answer was still no.

Then I asked her if Jesus could come for a visit, and she also said no.

I never pressured her to do something she wasn't ready to do. You see, anyone she would allow to come for a visit would be given access to her heart. Since she had hidden her heart far away, she wanted to keep it safe, and the only way she knew how to keep that heart safe was to be by herself in that corner.

At our next appointment, I asked the same question, if Jesus could come and visit her. In a small voice, she said Jesus could just come to the door. At this moment, something wonderful happened. I had my eyes open so I could discern from her facial features where I needed to lead her next in prayer. I saw in her countenance that something significant was happening.

She grabbed my arm, squeezed it tight, and whispered, "Jesus is standing at the door, looking at me."

"Are you afraid?" I asked.

No, she was not afraid, but at the same time, she did not want to talk to Jesus, nor did she want Him to talk to her. So I just left both of them enjoying one another, looking at each other.

In the following appointments, she asked Jesus to come closer and closer, and Jesus did exactly as the girl asked. You see, Jesus will never pressure your heart; He will wait for you to invite Him to come to you. The day when Jesus was finally with her in that corner, the dam broke. By this time, she also had asked Him if she could sit on His lap. She opened the floodgates of her heart to Jesus. This girl felt safe with Jesus and me. Out of her heart came the cry of a lonely girl who was afraid to go home. She told Jesus everything, as tears streamed down her face.

All these events in her life had created so much pain that her damaged heart was no longer able to cope and function, and the only way out, she thought, was to end it all.

There was a moment during our prayer time when I asked the question, "Jesus, do you want me to live or do you want me to die?"

The girl did not hesitate, but she repeated this question right away to Jesus, and He gave an answer in return: "I want you to live!"

What joy there was in her eyes as she looked at me.

This young lady who had just accepted Jesus Christ into her life over a year ago displayed such maturity that I was taken back. In the following sessions, I was a witness as she forgave all the people who had hurt her in some way. We asked Jesus to remove all the pain from her heart and replace all that she missed out on. Jesus began pouring into her heart the things she asked for, and little by little, something changed deep inside of her heart. Jesus gave her a picture of a healthy heart that was glowing, pure white. When I looked at her eyes, they sparkled.

After learning what was happening in her home, we notified the authorities and encouraged them to do a home visit. To our disappointment, the social worker's visit did not have the results we had hoped for. These wellness checkups are usually done by appointment. This means the family is called by the social worker, and an appointment is set for the visit. By the time the social worker actually arrives, the home is in perfect shape, and all involved parties have had time to get their act together. In addition, the child is interviewed in front of all the people who live in the home. Children are scared to reveal the truth or talk in front of the adults about what is really going on in the home. The social worker sees and witnesses a good family. In the case of my friend, she was never asked any questions.

A few weeks later, she knocked at my door and informed me that she and her mother were moving away. With a firm voice, holding my hands in hers as if I needed comfort, she told me not to worry because her mom really wanted to try to be a good mother, and most importantly, Jesus would go with her wherever she went, and whenever she needed to, she could crawl into Jesus's lap and tell Him everything.

> In him and through faith in him we may approach God
> with freedom and confidence. (Ephesians 3:12 NIV)

My heart knew that this girl would be just fine and that she would continue to grow and mature in her faith, because she had met Jesus in a real way. He was the only one who could have given her freedom. Did all the things she had endured in her short lifetime really happen to her? Yes. So what was different now? Together we identified her pain, gave it to Jesus, and asked Him to remove it, and finally, she asked Him to give her what she had missed out on.

Can We Know the Age of Our Heart?

How old are you emotionally? Have you ever asked yourself that question? My guess is, probably not. I hadn't either. It sounds kind of strange, unnatural, and totally out of context to even entertain a possible answer to that question, but we can know and should know how old our heart is, emotionally.

The age of our heart will determine our emotional state. The younger the heart, the more the heart will struggle. A six-year-old emotional heart will respond to the pressures others repeat. Choices in life are influenced by an unstable heart. For this reason, God needs us to grow and mature emotionally so we can function out of a mature heart: make decisions, raise our children, be responsible with our finances, and know how to treat each other, and so on.

Overall, people do not know how old their heart is. They cannot point to a specific event in their life where the heart was damaged, after which they were possibly no longer able to grow and mature. But Jesus knows exactly what has happened to us and what we missed out on. He will reveal to us not only the condition of our heart but its age, as well. Often, it is by asking the right questions in prayer that a picture emerges, that shows us either a little girl or a little boy. We have become wounded children living in an adult body. One reason Jesus gives us a picture of a child is to give us a visual to help us understand the age of our heart.

All too often, I hear from people who cannot remember their childhood. It's like that part of their life never existed or was somehow erased. Memories of parents are vague, but if you ask questions long enough, a hero emerges. A hero is simply a person, object, or place that we had a close connection to at one time. We may not be able to recollect our younger years and how our parents or others related to us, or we to them, but we will have a vivid picture of who did connect to our hearts.

At times, kids grow up in homes where they are emotionally neglected and never have the opportunity to intimately bond with someone, so they bond to an object, to an animal, or even to a place. The bonds that are established are very real. These kids grab on to a substitute, such as a stuffed animal, a pet, a place, an activity, an imaginary friend, or a fantasy. These substitutes fulfill the need of feeling loved, wanted, valued, and everything children crave emotionally. For example If a girl gives her heart to a stuffed animal, it is because this is the only safe thing she can connect to with her heart. This stuffed animal becomes her secret keeper; it never neglects her, always listens to her, loves her unconditionally, and is always there for her when she needs it no questions asked. The girl will sleep with that trusted friend, knowing at all times where it is. The girl will protect that stuffed animal with all her might. Even after she has grown physically and is an adult, this precious item is often kept in a secret place.

What is really happening? The girl transfers the love she has to give to that stuffed animal, and in return, the stuffed animal gives to her what she needs. Now she will no longer look to the people in her surroundings to provide for her emotional needs because she has found a substitute. Along the way, if people repeat, over and over, the same pain that drove that child to seek out a substitute in the first place, her heart will stay connected to that substitute. The heart will pull away from others and will feel safe behind a wall, or a hedge, or some other secret place. The same connection that was established while she was young is still in place, and the heart is still with that established substitute.

When we recognize and understand this mystery, a light bulb moment takes place. Our heart deceives us by letting us believe we have given all of our heart to another, but we know that is simply not the case. Many women have shared with me that they were unable to connect their hearts to their children or their husband; they had no idea how to love because nobody ever loved them. Emotional trauma experienced by parents gets passed down through the father's or mother's line, as well. Countless men have opened up their hearts and declared that they feel so confused as to who they are. They lost their identity, and out of that deep pain, they disconnected their hearts from their spouse and kids.

Each of us has learned in some unspoken way to just live with it. Deep down, inside, we realize that something is definitely wrong, but we cannot put a finger on the problem. So we do the best we can, operating out of an emotionally deficient heart. Is this God's plan for us? No.

I already mentioned this before, but it is worth repeating again. What is wrong is simply this: When our emotional heart was wounded, in some sense, it stopped connecting emotionally with others, and later on, after we had children of our own and they reached the physical age of our emotional damage, we emotionally disconnect from them. I have sat with individuals who confessed they needed to have one baby after another in order to connect with them emotionally. When their babies reached the age at which their own emotional heart was damaged, then Mom or Dad would physically and emotionally detach from them. In prayer, Jesus needs to do the healing or switching in these hearts. He heals from the inside out, not as others try to heal from the outside in.

I would like to encourage you to take the following steps so you can know if you have truly given all of your heart to your spouse, to your children, or to a trusted person you are close to. Here are the steps I would strongly recommend:

Sit across from each other with cell phones off and no distractions of any kind. Look into each other's eyes and have some kind of bodily contact, like holding each other's hand. Then ask these simple questions, one at a time, to one another:

One person asks the other, "How much of your heart have you ever given to me?" The answer will often be, "100 percent." At times, our heart knows we have never given 100 percent, nor can we give that much. But we say it anyway, deceiving even ourselves. At times, a person chooses to be totally honest and does admit the number is a lot lower than 100 percent.

The next questions to ask are, "How much are you able to receive from me? Do you receive the 100 percent I'm giving to you?" Believe it or not, a spouse never, or rarely, answers, "I am receiving 100 percent from you." Why not? There can be many reasons why a full 100 percent is not received. One possible reason is that the recipient's heart has, from its beginning, never been given what it needed emotionally. Or the tone, body language, and manner in which spouses who believe they are giving 100 percent care for the other's heart seems like pressure or rejection to them. This small exercise will be a great indicator as to what is happening inside one's heart. All that is left to do is to explore the reasons why the heart cannot receive completely what is given.

If both hearts are free, this means all the issues that damaged these hearts have been identified, all the pain that was created by others is fully realized, and Jesus was given the opportunity to restore each heart. Then the results of asking each other these questions will be positive, because both hearts can give 100 percent and also feel and receive 100 percent.

The key again is to know, first of all, what did the person receive that should never be repeated again, especially by the person who now wants to care for them. Secondly, what did they not receive and still long for, that you are willing to give to them, as long as you both shall live. In essence, we take our eyes off ourselves and place them on the other person, being other-person minded. It is a beautiful thing to have two hearts open and not hiding away somewhere, crying, waiting, hoping for someone to find them.

The Formula That Will Change Your Life

Have you ever wondered if there is some kind of formula that would undo the emotional pain we have experienced? I never thought this existed, but I was wrong. As already stated several times, when emotional pain is introduced into someone's life, it changes everything. The formula to which I am referring is not my plan. It is God's plan, His idea. God knew that not one of us would journey through this life without ever getting emotionally hurt. For this reason, He urges us to grow and mature in our emotional life so we can flow through the ups and downs in life, always finding our way out of the valley.

People who do not constantly grow and mature in their emotional life will be hijacked by their emotions. Their heart can become locked up so that it is no longer emotionally available to anyone. But how do we begin to describe something we have personally experienced to someone who has never experienced it? What do you say when you wish to explain to another individual how you feel? Pain can be described in various degrees, from 1 to 10, similar to how it is done in a doctor's office. Patients describe their level of physical pain or discomfort to the doctor as best as they can, because they are the only ones who can assist the doctor in assessing the problem. The doctor needs a starting point in order to recommend a certain protocol. The emotional pain felt by people needs to be defined, as well. Only people who have experienced the painful event will be able to tell how they feel. They can use the same scale, from 1–10, to express their level of pain. It is, therefore, essential to use the best words to communicate and explain how you feel.

C. S. Lewis wrote, "Pain insists upon being attended to. God whispers to us in our pleasures, speaks in our conscious, but shouts in our pain. It is his megaphone to rouse a deaf world."[1] In other words, pain should wake up the world and serve as a reminder that we are under the curse because of sin. This is not how God intended it to be. God created a beautiful world that was perfect, with two healthy people. All that changed after sin came into the world. Lewis also said, "Mental [emotional] pain is less dramatic than physical pain, but it is more common and also harder to bear. The frequent attempts to conceal mental [emotional] pain increases the burden: it is easier to say, 'My tooth is aching' than to say, 'My heart is broken.'"[2]

He is right. The world barely understands what to do with physical pain or how to empathize with someone's physical suffering. But when we speak about the pain in the heart, nobody seems to know what we are talking about. The longer we carry emotional pain in our heart, the greater the possibility of developing physical health problems, as well. This finding has been well established and documented.

One lady recalls when she was a young girl, her mom suddenly died of cancer, and her whole world shattered into a thousand pieces. Her mom was her best friend, always knew what she needed, and loved her unconditionally. Now she did not know what to do. She suddenly felt lost. After the funeral, she ran up the stairs into her mom's bedroom, hid under the covers, and breathed in the familiar scent of her mom that still lingered on her pillow. After what seemed like a long time, she left the room. Years later, she was married, had several children, and could not understand why she was unable to connect her heart to her husband and kids. What was wrong with her? It was during her prayer time that what was hidden came to light.

After she asked Jesus where her heart was, she saw herself sitting next to her mother's grave. She was the same age as when her mother died.

"What am I doing sitting next to my mother's grave?" was the next question she wanted Jesus to answer.

Little by little, the message Jesus wanted to share with her became clear. This lady could not have known that the day her mother died, she left her heart with her mother. How did she do that? While she was lying in her mom's bed, the only way she knew to go on with life was without ever giving her heart to anyone. Under those bedcovers, she made a vow in her heart. Without really understanding what she was doing, she left her heart under the bedcovers. Jesus brought this memory back to her as she, in her mind's eye, sat by that grave.

Would Jesus be able to restore her heart to her so she could give it to her husband and to her children? She poured out her heart to Jesus, leaving nothing out. In return, Jesus restored her heart completely. It seemed like the whole atmosphere in the room changed, and the lady's countenance lit up like a Christmas tree. I asked her to open her eyes and continue following my words. Looking deeply into her husband's eyes, she held his hands and waited expectantly for me to lead her.

Our dialogue went something like this:

"Can you forgive me for not giving you my heart?"

"Do you want my heart now?"

"Would you care for my heart like my mom used to?"

"Are you interested?"

The dialogue seemed to go on forever, and in many ways, it felt like a new courtship or dating relationship was beginning between the two.

We should not be amazed that our hearts can go away, or that there are moments in life where we must put our heart in a safe place for the purpose of protecting it from more hurt. Over time, we cannot remember anymore when we put our heart away, or what the circumstances were that resulted in a heart no longer reachable by others and even ourselves. And we have no idea how to get our heart back, make it whole, be available to others to give and receive love. Jesus always knows why the heart had to hide, where it hides, and what condition it's in. He also knows how to return the heart back to the person, heal it, and make it whole. What is needed is for someone to come alongside Jesus in our physical world and continue the same care they received from Him.

Before you pray, it is important to have your issues identified. The more specifically you can pray, the more freedom you will experience. When Jesus touches the heart, a switching of some sort takes place inside of us. For so long, we have tried to change our emotional pain from the outside, but from the reports I hear, this results in debilitating and life-altering outcomes and does not give the desired results. God created us as emotional beings to feel love and to experience Him fully. If that part of us was damaged, He is the only one that can bring healing to our emotions. When Christ died on the cross, He said, "It is finished," or in other words, "All is paid in full." This includes our spiritual sins and our emotional pain.

I'm not a scientist, but I have read enough literature and reviewed enough studies to know that every time we experience a traumatic event and feel pain in our heart, the pain and the memories are stored in a particular section of our brain. I know that our brain has a small area called the amygdala, which stores all of the feelings we have ever felt. We store good feelings and bad feelings. Since events and how we feel are stored in this part of our brain, they become part of our history. It is for this reason we can occupy ourselves for hours rehashing past painful events, only adding to the fact our heart is not in a good place.

At times, out of the blue and totally unexpectedly, a word or scene can trigger a hurtful memory from years ago. The pain associated with my memory was still deep in my heart, and it seemed, from that first day, others would constantly trigger it. I had no idea how to rid myself of this pain, which was constantly triggered by others. I've spoken to several women who told me when their boyfriend hit them for the first time, the emotional pain he created was overwhelming. They felt afraid, devalued, humiliated, and violated. From that day, their world was not the same. Every time someone raised their hands, they would recoil. These women no longer felt safe or protected.

Jesus created our brain and knows exactly how each part of our brain functions. When we invite Him into our painful memories and ask Him to take the pain out of our heart, in essence, we entrust the pain to Him. Jesus will disconnect the pain that was created in the heart and carried around for years. We can ask Jesus to take it away for us. The women who had to endure domestic violence from their husband or boyfriend can ask Jesus if He understands their pain. Did He see everything these men did to them? What did that do to Jesus's heart? Jesus lets them know that He saw everything, including their tears, and He was crying for them.

"Can you take the pain out of my heart?" they could ask Jesus. "It is destroying my life."

In many cases, a picture of big black trash bags is seen, and Jesus throws the trash bags, one by one, over a waterfall. The more bags fall over the waterfall, the lighter the hearts became. All that is left is to ask Jesus to begin pouring into their hearts all that was stolen from them. At times, we need to ask Jesus to give us back what was taken from us, or even what we gave away, or what we missed out on and still need. Most often, being robbed has roots in the sexual area when we have experienced the traumatic events of sexually abuse. I will cover this issue in chapter 5.

This formula I just talked about sounds so simple, and it really is. I have witnessed countless individuals, including myself, entrust their pain and memories to Jesus. Everything changed. I sat with my husband when Jesus met the soldier on the battlefield, when he had no idea how to end the war within. With time, something beautiful will happen. The more pain from your experiences you give to Jesus, the more freedom you will have in your heart. There will come a day when you can look back down the corridor of your memories and be amazed that no pain is connected to the events. Only sadness will remain, and you will notice that others will be unable to trigger the bad feelings you once harbored in your heart.

How to Reset Your Emotional Heart

1. Begin by writing down your personal story and identifying the areas where you feel you were emotionally damaged. Go back as far as you can into your past memory. The memory will trigger pain, and you may cry. For example, emotionally neglected as a child, never noticed, never spoken to, or as a child, you were constantly bossed around by a domineering parent, and their controlling ways damaged your heart.

2. Go to the appendix and mark all the pain words you have ever experienced. Give each word a value ranging from 0 to 10. The number 0 means no pain is connected to this word. The number 10 indicates a lot of pain is connected to this word. For example, neglect, 10; abandonment, 8; rejected, 9; insensitive to my needs, 10; and so on.

3. After you have numbered all the pain words, take some colored pencils and select one color for each person who has surfaced in your memory who emotionally hurt you. At the top of the page, write the name of each person in the color you select for them. Now, in the color that corresponds with their name, place a dot next to the words you have identified as pain they have created. Do this with each pain word you have given a number greater than 4. For example, If you wrote "Mom" in red at the top of your page, then all the pain words associated with your mom that are rated

81

higher than 4 get one red dot. For example, Neglect (10) gets a red dot. Insensitive to my needs (6) gets a red dot. (It's not my intent to openly bash all parents as being totally dysfunctional. On the contrary, most likely you were parented by two people who experienced pain themselves and created pain in your heart out of their own pain and unresolved issues. Many times, the damage did not start with a parent. It could have begun with another relative or someone at school.

4. When you have identified your emotional issues by writing your story and marked your pain words, you can begin praying. It is best to bring only one issue at a time to Jesus in prayer. The enemy must be defeated at the point of deception. Apply the following steps for each unresolved emotional issue:

   a. Step 1: Identify one emotional issue; for example, emotionally neglected in my parents' home.

   b. Step 2: Bring Jesus into the area you just have identified. For example, "Jesus, did you know how lonely my heart was when I was a little girl [or boy]? What did that do to my heart?" Let the Holy Spirit give you an answer as you keep asking Jesus specific questions about the issue.

   c. Step 3: Ask Jesus to disconnect and take away the pain. For example, "Jesus, can you remove all the pain from my heart; the pain I felt when my parents never noticed me or included me? Jesus, can you throw all this pain away?"

   d. Step 4: Ask Jesus to begin filling your heart by pouring into it all the good things you need, that you never got. For example, "Jesus, can you begin pouring into my heart your love, peace, and whatever else my heart needs? Would you give me what I still long for or never received? Would you do that for me, Jesus? Would you show me a picture of a filled, healed heart? What would my heart look like?"

   e. Step 5: Before you close your prayer time, ask Jesus for an emotional safe place (more on this in chapter 6). Jesus may give you a picture, a scripture verse, portions of a Bible story, or even a song. You can go to your emotional safe place anytime others trigger your past pain. If Jesus gives you a picture, then every time someone reminds you of your past pain, you can lay this new picture over the pain, and your heart will enjoy peace again.

5. To stay in freedom, identify one person you can freely share your personal story with (if you are married, this should be your spouse). Include this person in your healing process by allowing them to care for your heart. The person caring for your heart needs to begin reversing all your pain words. It is vital to have this person help you live in complete freedom in your heart.

6. Locate the list of emotional healing words in the appendix. To begin with, mark no more than six new words or statements in order to not overwhelm the person who is caring for your heart. The person who wants to care for and connect to your heart will now use the new healing words to fill your heart. This needs to be done on a daily basis. New words can be added when the first selection of words have been planted firmly in your heart.

Any emotional pain you have experienced will always be a weakness. This means if you were emotionally neglected as a child, every time someone emotionally neglects you, you will feel the same pain as when the damage occurred the first time. For this reason, you need your emotional safe place and a person you trust to help you center yourself again.

God is wise and gentle, and He will only reveal one layer at a time. This means, in your personal story, you will identify the obvious pain issues you experienced, but God will continue to peel back the layers of your heart, over time, till all pain has been exposed, and Jesus is brought into it.

As already stated, live for the day when you can go down memory lane and see clearly the past issues that created pain at one time, that are now only laced with sadness. This is a great indicator you are healed. If, however, you choose to stare at your past pain, you can spin yourself into a new pain cycle again.

To stay in freedom, review your life experiences from time to time and check how your heart feels. It should feel free and light all the time. Your heart should be healthy and whole, and if the right people are in your life, you can and will stay in emotional freedom.

Jesus Restored My Heart

My personal journey to emotional freedom started when I began to identify events in my life, from my earliest memories, that could have possibly damaged my heart. This was a difficult task due to the fact that I had blocked out most of my childhood. The isolated memories I could piece together were enough to make me scared of what else I would uncover and need to deal with. I came to the conclusion that my heart would simply have to trust that Jesus would fill in the blanks of my life.

The moment this thought flashed through my brain, the answer came: "What the Holy Spirit will uncover, the blood of Jesus has already covered."

From here on, I knew God was with me all the way. What a comfort this message was to my heart. Having never trusted anyone, this was exactly what my heart needed to hear.

Right from the start, the moment I made the decision to deal with all my unresolved issues, a real battle began to rage in my heart. It felt as if I was being tossed around by all kinds of emotions. I knew very well who I had become: a self-sufficient, hardened, angry, domineering, and unloving person, completely the opposite of who I wanted to be. I longed to be gentle, kind, and accepting of others. I soothed these storms by quickly discovering that my heavenly Father would never ask more of me than I was able to handle, and He also would give me all the time I needed.

The question was this: Am I willing to take the first step, trusting Jesus to be there all the way, and can my heart follow the leading of Jesus? Instantly, my heart knew Jesus would only reveal one issue to me at a time. So I could bring any issue to Him, and when Jesus knew I was ready, He would reveal a new layer of my pain to me for the purpose of repeating these steps for my emotional healing again. Jesus would reveal more unresolved issues, and this would go on till all of the emotional damage and pain ever created in my life was gone. My heart would then be free and my burdens unloaded.

My journey was not a solo journey. I knew there was no way I could do this on my own. The man I referred to in the introduction of this book, the teacher at our first seminar, scheduled my husband and me into his office for a one-week intensive counseling session. I was so scared. All I wanted to do was run that first day. Jesus had already laid it on my heart to tell the truth and nothing but the truth. My days of hiding and living in secret needed to end.

By the time I sat in that hot-seat on the other side of the desk from this gentleman who was willing to help us, a new reality set in. You see, at the time we sought help, both Mike and I had been in full-time ministry for fifteen years. Our ministry had its beginning serving with Wycliffe Bible Translators[3] in a support role. A few years later, we had the privilege of going on a three-month mission trip to India. Then a few months after that, we found ourselves at a Bible school, where we served in various roles at first. My husband eventually graduated with his bachelor's in biblical studies. After his graduation, we had the privilege of leading a congregation. Why did we wait so long to deal with our issues? In some sense, we had become masters of disguise. We had no idea of the damage we had received along the way, of the pain we carried in our hearts. There had been moments we stared the truth right in the face, but our hearts were not willing to bare our souls to anyone, not even to each other. In the quiet times, I had to admit that things were not good on the home front.

The longer we live putting on one mask after another, the more the truth gets stuffed into the background, and the more comfortable we become with how things are. After all, we had what the world considered to be a good marriage. On the outside, we did look good, but to our heavenly Father, our unresolved issues were hindering us from being fully available to Him. It was out of our desire to assist our congregation that we finally realized, if restoration and healing does not begin with us, we have no business coming alongside others. For too long, we played the game of hypocrisy. It was time to take off all of our facades and masks and live like Jesus created us to be, not as what we had become.

Our first session started, and before I knew what was happening, my heart began to soften. For some reason, I wanted to tell it all. I felt no judgment, shame, embarrassment, or condemnation from this man. What I did feel was genuine acceptance. He demonstrated to me that he understood my heart, and I felt his caring personality. Was it easy to pour out my heart with all of its sinful issues that I had neglected and put away? Did I struggle to put into words the events that created so much pain that just talking about them brought the past back into full view? Yes, it was difficult, yet rewarding and freeing at the same time. The real healing and freedom in my heart came after I had put all my issues on the table and identified the damage that had been created and the pain that resulted. I anticipated bringing Jesus into all that I had uncovered. Still shaky and unsure, yet much more trusting, I approached the throne of God.

I still remember the first words I spoke to Jesus while my husband supported me, holding my hands. His warmth made me feel loved and cared for in a way that I had not felt before. I asked Jesus if He had some time to sit with me because I wanted to open up my heart to Him. I asked Him to walk with me through my childhood experiences, and if there was any pain or trauma in my past, to draw my attention to those events. All of my emotions seem to rush into my mind and heart, and it was difficult to sort them all out. The quiet voice of my counselor, as he was leading, encouraged me to forge ahead to seek with all of my heart what Jesus wanted to say to me.

My conversation with Jesus continued. I said, "Jesus, You have known me from the beginning, before You even spoke the world into existence. You alone saw me inside my mother's womb, and You were there at my birth. Did You see my heart? Do You know how I felt when …? Jesus, I was not allowed to be the girl You created me to be. Can You re-parent me and show me how a little girl is supposed to feel and who You say she is?

Finally, the dam broke. The tears began slowly, eventually breaking into sobs. My heart felt the touch of my Savior, Jesus Christ. He opened the eyes of my heart and revealed to me that from the moment of my conception, and when my mom fully realized she was pregnant with me, I was rejected by her, and my little heart was wounded. My mom did not want any kids, so her own heart was not in a good place. The more questions I asked, the more He revealed to me. Nine months later, my father rejected me because I was not born a boy. I was not wanted by my parents. Jesus let my heart understand that the angry words my parents spoke when I was a little older and the constant put-downs and sexual innuendos created more damage and pain in my heart.

While I was praying, Jesus revealed to me that I had never truly grieved the loss of never having had loving parents, never experiencing fun times with my dad, never hearing the words from him, "You are my beautiful little girl," never having a mom who wanted to hold me just because she loved me very much. No, my heart always knew I was a disappointment to my parents, and as a result, I became a rebellious, domineering, and angry woman.

Jesus showed me that day that my heart was very tiny. It was the smallest heart I had ever seen. He also let me know that this heart had a break right down the middle of it. By now, I was ready to ask Jesus anything, and I did. No more holding back. Pouring out both known and secret memories did not drain me one bit. On the contrary, the more stuff I let go, the lighter I felt. Eventually, I asked Jesus if He could touch that little heart and heal it, restore it, make it whole, the way He originally intended it to be, and as I shared with you in my physical chapter, the large jewel Jesus gave to me was a direct message from Him of how much He cared for me and loved me, and how He wanted me now to see my heart. Jesus was thrilled because now the entire world would see His creation, His little girl.

> With your very own hands you formed me; now breathe your wisdom over me so I can understand you. When they see me waiting, expecting your Word, those who fear you will take heart and be glad. I can see now, God, that your decisions are right; your testing has taught me what's true and right. Oh, love me—and right now!—hold me tight! (Psalm 119:73–76 MSG)

The day Jesus touched my heart and made all things new was the day a specific Bible verse became my favorite: "But Jesus called the children to him and said, "Let the little children come to me, and do not hinder them, for the kingdom of God belongs to such as these'" (Luke 18:16 NIV).

With each prayer, with every confession, with every release of emotional pain I had stored in my heart, and with each forgiveness granted, Jesus restored and renewed my heart. Something changed on the inside, and everything became lighter and joyful, especially when the moment came that I was ready to forgive my parents from my heart. My heart understood forgiveness was for me, and I gave up my right to hurt my parents or seek revenge or get even. At first, my voice seemed unsteady, yet the timing was right, and my heart was ready. In just a few simple words, but deep from my heart, I released my parents by forgiving them. My prayer to Jesus went something like this: "Jesus, have I ever forgiven my parents for rejecting me because I was not a boy? Was my heart damaged by my father and mother for not wanting me? Did you see my heart and feel my pain when I was never held, kissed, or cuddled in any way? My heart longed to hear the words, 'I love you,' but nobody ever spoke them. Jesus, I want to forgive my parents. Can you help me?"

Finally, I was ready to say these words: "Jesus, I choose to forgive my mom for not wanting me, for not knowing how to love me or care for my emotional needs. I forgive her for the pain and consequences she has caused me. Jesus, I also want to forgive my dad for never getting to know his little girl's heart and never giving me a chance to love him. I want to forgive him for the pain and consequences he caused me. Jesus, if I could sit on my daddy's lap, and he would listen to me and I could tell him anything I wanted, what would my heart say to him? 'Would you just hold me, protect me, and make me feel secure? Would you give me your full attention and tell me I'm pretty? Would you just love me always so my heart can feel secure? We both missed out, because now I know your own heart was wounded, and you could not love me.'"

Eventually, I took Jesus to my picture of a girl sitting in the dark attic all alone in a corner, shivering and scared. The moment Jesus stepped into the attic, the light shone down on me. The corner was now illuminated with the bright glory of God Himself. I cannot even describe to you what this moment felt like. My heart was finally able to begin to relax and just enjoy Jesus and me being together. This was not the occasion where I actually left this attic; my healing journey was not complete, but when Jesus showed me this picture, I was completely satisfied, as if nothing more would happen.

I had one final request. I asked Jesus if He could give me a safe place, a picture in my mind and heart that would be there for me every time someone rejected me, abandoned me, or did not accept me. Right away, a picture came into view, and to this day, the picture has never changed. Every time someone steps on my past pain issues, I go to that safe place. Jesus is always there, waiting for me. As I've said before, the picture is always the same. My back is leaning against a giant redwood tree. My legs are drawn up, surrounded by my arms, and my eyes are resting on the rays of the sun, streaming into the edge of the forest. Just beyond that scene, my eyes are greeted by a lush, soft green meadow. The peace I feel is real. When I'm in my emotional safe place, my heart knows that Jesus is right there beside me. If others in some way trigger my old memories, I don't allow them to take me down. I immediately go to my safe place. My heart now realizes the emotional pain I experienced. It will always be my weakness, and the enemy continues to parade people into my life who try to tell my heart that nothing has changed. Praise God for my emotional safe place.

After our prayer time ended, I felt so excited. Words cannot adequately describe what I felt. My heart was at peace. For the first time, I had truly forgiven my parents, who had rejected me and hurt me so deeply. For the first time, I was honest with all that I had done and what I had done to others (with the exception of my sexual abuse; it took a little longer to finally bring Jesus into this area of my life). And for the first time, I truly felt I was a new creation. I know the day I gave my heart to Jesus; His promise to me was:

> Therefore, if anyone is in Christ, the new creation has come: The old has gone, the new is here! (2 Corinthians 5:17 NIV)

I now understood. Because my emotional heart was so young and full of pain, I was not capable of functioning as would be expected. My emotional heart was not the age I was physically, and over and over again, I made wrong decisions in my life. I had no clue my heart had become so emotionally detached. This was the reason I could not love, couldn't connect to others, and always felt alone. Now my heart was filled with all the good things I needed, and I didn't want to lose what I had found.

I turned to my husband, who still held my hands, and saw the tears running down his cheeks. He was crying for me. I rushed into his arms; we held each other. Instantly, a new bond began to form. After twenty-four years of marriage, it seemed a second honeymoon was just beginning. Now, fifteen years later, I can testify that our honeymoon is still in progress.

I asked Mike if he would be willing to help my heart so it could begin to grow and mature, to assist me and help my emotional heart align with my physical age. I wasn't sure how he would do that, but he said he would try.

A few days later, he made good on his promise. He took me to the playground and let me be a kid. We horsed around and had so much fun together, I almost forgot I was a grown adult. A few days later, we raced to the ice cream truck to get a treat. My husband gave me a second opportunity to experience what it was like to be a happy child. He became my surrogate father, the one I never had. For the next week, he came up with different activities that a father might have enjoyed with his little girl. He helped me catch up emotionally and develop that part in my heart, standing in for my dad and my mother, who never emotionally connected her heart to mine.

He often asked me, "If you could give me three words or statements that I could say to you, that would make you the happiest girl on the face of this earth, what would you say?"

At first, I had no clue how to answer, but eventually the words came.

What I want to share with you now seems really out of the ordinary and kind of bizarre, but this is exactly what happened. After this first week ended, my heart was all of a sudden no longer satisfied with the childish activities or the question he would ask me: "What does the little girl need from me today?"

I went over to my husband held his hands in mine, looked deep into his eyes, and said, "I want to date you."

Wow, did you just read that? Yes, you did. My heart wanted to date his heart, and right away, I knew my heart, emotionally, was no longer that little helpless, wounded infant.

True to his word, my husband changed his tactics, and we began to date. My heart felt so good and was filled with so much joy. Now I was also able to reciprocate to my husband what he needed from me emotionally so that his heart was able to grow to match his physical age. We had a blast, and I imagine that, up in heaven, Jesus was elated.

Once again, after one week, a strange thought entered my mind. I was no longer satisfied hearing, "What does my girl need from me today?" My heart was emotionally a fully grown woman, ready to move forward with God's plan to mature in His knowledge and wisdom. These next words that I spoke were a total surprise, even to me, but I could no longer hold them back: "Will you marry me?"

I realized that my heart wanted to be married to his heart, and from that point on, our hearts were truly one. Our connection was now on a heart level, something we had never experienced before. In many ways, we felt this may be exactly how Jesus loves us.

One other very important step in our healing process was to share with each other the new healing words we had selected, things we needed to hear from each other. Staying in freedom for the next sixty years (or till Jesus returns) is an everyday commitment we make to each other. For this reason, your spouse or trusted friend needs to know what it is you need in order to stay in freedom. These positive healing words will never create pain and will never spin either one of us back into our old pain cycle. Actually, the opposite is true. Our hearts will constantly feel cared for.

A few weeks later, we stood on the beach. It was my husband's favorite spot and loved by me as well: two hearts beating as one, hands joined together, our eyes looking deep into the other's heart. Standing in the soft breeze with people all around, I spoke the familiar words: "I, Ellen, take you, Mike, to be my beloved husband, to have and to hold, from this day forward, for better, for worse, for richer, for poorer, in sickness and in health, to love and to cherish, till death do us part."

CHAPTER 4

GOD WANTS US TO GROW AND MATURE SPIRITUALLY

Anyone who lives on milk, being still an infant, is not acquainted with the teaching about righteousness. But solid food is for the mature, who by constant use have trained themselves to distinguish good from evil. (Hebrews 5:13–14 NIV)

Throughout the centuries, as far back as we can trace the history of humankind, God has been misrepresented by His creation. Simply put, the very essence of God has been distorted and become altogether false. Of course, God's enemy, Satan, has played a major role. He has been whispering constantly into our ears and fabricating lies about God. He knows who God is, but the truth he presents is always repackaged. God's creation buys into these lies and believes Satan's version of who God is.

False religions, make-believe institutions, and cults maintain a trace of the truth, yet millions have been betrayed by believing in gods who do not even come close to the true God of the scriptures. Humankind willingly embraces these gods because they fit into their lifestyle, expectations, and desires. Actually, this is not a twenty-first-century phenomenon. Groups and so-called churches have deceived entire cultures since the beginning of time. Solomon records the following for us in the book of Ecclesiastes:

What has been will be again, what has been done will be done again; there is nothing new under the sun. Is there anything of which one can say, "Look! This is something new"? It was here already, long ago; it was here before our time. (Ecclesiastes 1:9–10 NIV)

Entire generations and people groups have bought into the message from false, counterfeit gods who promise to transform the world into a better place. Why are we so easily deceived? What causes our belief system to change so drastically? Do even born-again believers find themselves stuck, unable to grow and mature in the truth the way God has laid it out for us in His Word? Have some of us been spiritually abused so that now our picture of God is completely distorted?

Growing and maturing in Christ is perhaps more needed in this century than ever before. There has never been a time in history when true believers in Christ were not persecuted for their faith, and persecution is still on the agenda of our enemy today.

One day, as I was listening to a program, the speaker made a profound statement. In essence, he said, "Prayer is the new pornography." Wow; what a statement. But if you give it some thought, it is a true reflection of our present culture. Right now in our time period, individuals are targeted by groups from within the church (and from without) to quit praying in public, to stop praying over meals, and to remove all religious symbols from their neck and their property. Seniors are being told they can no longer pray over their meals at senior centers.

With these things happening, we must all reach deep into our soul and answer this question: What would I do if I were persecuted for my faith in Jesus Christ? Only if we have learned to live and function as mature Christians can we live through perilous times and emerge victors.

With this chapter, it is my desire to attempt to lay bare God's design for His children, regardless of what they have experienced or were told about Him, things which may have interfered with their process of growing and maturing in God. I would also like to address spiritual abuse: what it is, and the impact it can have on our relationship with God.

"God": I Almost Missed Him

My parents met when World War II was in full swing; each of them served their county in different ways, on opposite sides of the continent. My mom fulfilled her duties as a surgical nurse in France. She never spoke of the horrors she must have seen or the physical and emotional impact this had on her future. My dad was in the infantry, and he, just like my mom, never talked about the war. As fate would have it, when my dad was wounded, he ended up in a French hospital. While in battle, a bullet entered his side, sliced through his pelvis, and exited from the other side of his body. My mom oversaw not only his operation but also his recovery.

During one of their conversations, they discovered that both of them were from the same town. What a small world, even then. As time went on, they took a liking to each other and reconnected after the war. My father proposed, and the marriage between two hurting hearts was sealed. My parents never told me any details of their courtship or romance. Over the years as I grew up, I received bits and pieces of information about my parents' earlier years from my relatives.

You may wonder why I am sharing this part of my story. You see, it was at this point in my parents' life that a decision was made that eventually affected me. My father aligned himself with one faith and my mom with another. When they married, my father's church had a set rule. If he chose to marry my mom, she would have to convert to his faith or sign a paper promising that his children would be brought up in his faith. My mom chose to stick to her faith but relinquished her right to bring us up in the way of her church. So all five of us, girls, were automatically absorbed into my father's church and had to embrace his faith.

This was the beginning of my spiritual life. It was chosen for me by my parents and was in essence all the exposure I had growing up. The memories I have from this time are anything but pleasant. Every Sunday was the same. A couple who lived upstairs from us was very active in their church, and as it happened, it was the same church my father was a member of. In all of my growing-up years, my parents never darkened the doors of a church. Both held on to their respective faiths, but neither of them was a practicing member. So we were picked up by this couple every Sunday (or whenever the call was given to attend).

Our Sundays started in silence and continued very much like this till the morning service ended. It seemed to me this couple just went to church and then walked home again. I learned to accept my fate and dragged along in silence. The church atmosphere was rather cold, even when it was not winter. The whole building on the inside fostered a coldness that made my heart afraid. The building was constructed entirely out of stone; even the flooring was made up of large, uneven stone slabs. The church was filled with incense and smells that always overwhelmed me, and on top of it all, large stone statues stared down at me, pointing their fingers in my direction. I felt out of place and very uncomfortable.

I had to sit in the front row, in full view of the elderly, who made it their mission to supervise and correct us from their pew right behind us. Whenever I had to cough or make the slightest noise, a hand would settle on my shoulder, reminding me that this was unacceptable. Of course, there were no bathroom facilities, and I always hoped my body would co-operate with me. Sitting for two hours, perfectly still, was not my way of doing church. Once the actual service began, the time really dragged on. The only things that were somewhat pleasant were the songs. At least I could read the words from the hymnal and follow the organist somewhat. The music was at times kind of majestic. The organ, way up on the balcony, urged us on to sing as loud as we could, and as the notes resonated in the building and vibrated in my heart, a quietness seemed to settle in. Yes, the singing was good. The message, on the other hand, was very difficult for me because it was given in Latin. I could not understand one word. Other than my sister, there was never anyone I could ask if they had the same trouble as I did, understanding what was said. Does God only speak Latin? This question was constantly on my mind.

So each Sunday, I followed a protocol, being told when to sit, stand, kneel, or do this or that. The faces of all the people in attendance were anything but happy. Maybe this was the reason my father never attended church with me, because he too had to endure the silence of the people in his childhood. During this time, without realizing what I was doing, I made a vow in my heart to never attend church again once I left my parents' home. Why would I want to be a part of something that does not want me to be a part of it? The congregation functioned in many ways like puppets on a string. We were expected to behave a certain way and do exactly as the church prescribed. Many questions swirled around in my heart, but no one ever gave me the opportunity to ask them. It seemed unlikely that anyone would ever give me answers.

The years went by, and I almost counted the Sundays remaining before I could leave this church and its rituals behind. If there really is a God, does He want to be worshipped this way? Does He expect us to follow strict orders and nothing less? Could I love a God who seemed so far away from everybody? Deep in my heart, I could not love such a God and also knew there was no way He would love me. After all, not even my parents loved me. Finally, I had to admit to myself, I really had no use for such a God, and He would be better off without me. I would be a constant disappointment to Him, anyways.

Based on that philosophy, I entered my adult life and laid aside the Bible I had never really opened. Life felt unrestricted, and I convinced myself that everything will work out in the end. I never attended any church, had no desire to, and did not want to hear about it from others. I had no use for it. My friends were of the same cloth as me; there was never any pressure from anyone to include church in my life. Of course, the lack of my spiritual understanding took me down the lane of self-destruction and bad choices. I did not withhold from indulging in many things and saw nothing wrong with doing those things my church would have shuddered over. I believed there would be no consequences, so I did as I pleased. I had no idea how destructive my life would become and how desperately my soul would need to be rescued by a Savior.

In 1978, when I was in my early twenties, I met Mike, my future husband, and he suited me just fine. His idea of going to church was exactly like mine. We were a perfect match. Even after we were married, we continued to live in sin, without any thought of our afterlife (or the present life, for that matter).

But then something began to change. One day, my husband asked me if I would attend a church service with him.

"If that's what you want," I replied, "okay, let's try it."

I had no clue why he wanted to attend a church, but I thought I would just do him that favor. Not knowing where to start, we got out the Yellow Pages and found a church that was in our area. What came next took me by complete surprise. The best way to put this into words is to describe what happened the first Sunday we attended. The service was unlike anything

I had ever experienced. The pastor shouted so loud, I was actually afraid he would attack me. Needless to say, we only attended a couple of times, not sure where to go from there.

In 1981, shortly after we moved to California, my husband repeated his request to attend church. This time, I was ready, and I welcomed the idea of finding a church where I hoped to get some answers (by this time, something had happened that impacted my entire world). Once more, we consulted the Yellow Pages to find the perfect church for us. Before too long, we found ourselves seated in a mortuary. Yes, this church was in its infancy, and its first church building was a mortuary. I reminded myself that we were, nevertheless, a live congregation.

You may wonder why I was now willing and actually eager to attend church. Here is why: In April 1979, Mike and I got married, and in September of the same year, we moved to the States from Germany. One month later, in October, I received a telegram notifying me that my father had died. This was unexpected, as death most often is. When I left Germany, he seemed to be himself, and there was no reason to expect his passing any time soon. I still remember the day I said goodbye to him. My father actually reached out his arms, and I walked into his embrace. This was the first time he ever hugged me, and I noticed a tear sliding down his cheek. What a precious gift. Now, holding this telegram in my hands, I had no idea what to do. My head told me to stay in America and just let it go, but my heart gave me a different message. For some reason, I had the urge to go to Germany to be at my father's funeral.

I finally decided to take my husband's advice and follow my inner prompting, and we made arrangements for our trip back to Germany. The day we arrived, we were informed that my father's funeral had taken place the day before. The telegram had given the wrong date. *Now what?* was my first thought. Panic filled my heart because I had no idea how to handle this sudden change. If I had been at his funeral, I could have blended in with the many people in attendance, pretended I was a grieving daughter, and be done with it. Now I was the only one who had not been at the funeral, and the prying eyes of my relatives would examine my reaction to my father's death.

I came up with a plan. I proposed to go to the cemetery and ask my family, my husband included, to stand off to the side. This way, I could approach the grave by myself. Then, after I had given it the appropriate time for my supposed grieving, I would return to my family, and all would be well. I applauded myself for having a good solution to this problem. That was my plan, but God had another plan for me.

> "For I know the plans I have for you," declares the LORD, "plans to prosper you and not to harm you, plans to give you hope and a future. Then you will call on me and come and pray to me, and I will listen to you. You will seek me and find me when you seek me with all your heart. I will be found by you," declares the LORD. (Jeremiah 29:11–14a NIV)

The time came to go to the cemetery. I stood before my father's enormous, decorated, freshly dug grave. Flowers and wreaths were piled so high, the grave looked like a giant monument, erected for the man who called himself my father. The thought crossed my mind, if I had a match, I would light it all up and have a bonfire. Deep inside my heart, I felt so angry. I had no idea what to say or where to begin. It might as well have been a stranger's grave I was visiting. Standing there, not knowing what to do next, sparked a sudden, rather unusual need to get the answer to a specific question. I knew I was alone, out of earshot of my family, so I went ahead and gave in to this nagging thought. Before I knew what was happening, the question was asked, out loud, in my own voice. Unknown to me, I actually directed my question to God, since He was the only one who could provide me with the answer.

I asked, "I would like to know where my father is right now."

Suddenly, I had the answer. It was as if an invisible hand wrote it on my heart. "In hell," was the answer. To my surprise, this revelation did not bother me one bit. Then an even stranger urge came over me, and without giving it a thought, I asked, "What if that was me down there? Where would I be right now?" "You would be in hell," this inner voice replied. "No way, hold on, that cannot be." At this point, I felt a panic rising up within me. Instantly, my heart understood. I would be with my father in hell, the two of us together, forever.

It is difficult for me to describe what happened next. It almost felt as if something was chasing me. I whirled around, approached my husband, and told him I had to find the next bookstore and purchase a Bible. That's all I said, and off we went. I bought a Bible written in German, because at the time, I could not speak English.

For the next year, I sat on my couch every single day, terrified of dying, reading the Bible. There had to be an explanation as to why the answer given to me pointed to hell. I needed to find the way to get to heaven. From the religious upbringing I had received as a child, I was familiar with a place called heaven and a place called hell. These two destinations really did exist. Eventually, with words that did not even resemble a prayer, I told God that if He was real, He had to show me how I could be with Him in heaven after my time on earth ended.

I was completely ignorant as to how to read the Bible and didn't know where to begin. I flipped to the first book in the Bible, Genesis, and started reading. Day after day, I sat and read. As already stated, it took me over a year to finally come to the passages that changed my life and my final eternal destiny:

> "For God so [greatly] loved and dearly prized the world, that He [even] gave His [One and] only begotten Son, so that whoever believes and trusts in Him [as Savior] shall not perish, but have eternal life. (John 3:16 AMP)

> And this is the testimony: God has given us eternal life, and this life is in his Son. Whoever has the Son has life; whoever does not have the Son of God does not have life. I write these things to you who believe in the name of the Son of God so that you may know that you have eternal life. (1 John 5:11–13 NIV)

During this stressful time in my life, we attended church in the mortuary, but for some reason, my heart could not fully absorb all the messages, and our attendance was not quite as consistent as it should have been. But during my daily Bible readings, God found a way into my heart. When I discovered the above scripture passages, it all suddenly became crystal clear.

I remember the day as if it were yesterday. The verses I read made sense, and I understood in my heart that Jesus gave His life for me. He became my substitute and extended to me an invitation to live with Him one day, in heaven, for all eternity. The tears began to fall, and slowly I slid off my couch.

The words I spoke were simple but from my heart: "Jesus, I understand the sacrifice You made for me, that if I would have been the only person on planet earth, You would have died for me. You could not fathom to be without me. Today, I want to ask You to come into my heart. Would You accept me, forgive me of my many sins, and give me the right to become a child of God?"

My heart knew the answer right away. God wanted me and loved me. I cannot recall how long I stayed on that floor, but it seemed like an eternity. The love I felt was so real, I did not want it to end. There on my knees, before my Savior, I began my journey of forgiving my parents. My heart already felt so light.

The day I accepted Jesus Christ as my personal Savior, I realized God gave us the right to choose, and that includes where we want to live life after death, our eternal destiny. God draws us to Himself, but He does not violate our freedom to choose.

God created us with a body He formed out of the dust. Then He breathed His life into this body, giving us His Spirit, and the result was a soul (who we are). We became a living being. When a person dies, the reverse takes place. The breath of life (spirit) departs from the body, the soul no longer exists, and the body returns to the ground from which it was taken. Each individual's spirit will live forever, somewhere; it truly is our choice. All of us were created in the image of God. He created us and gave us a part of Himself: the spirit, which is eternal:

> Then the LORD God formed a man from the dust of the ground and breathed into his nostrils the breath of life, and the man became a living being. (Genesis 2:7 NIV)

> And the dust returns to the ground it came from, and the spirit returns to God who gave it. (Ecclesiastes 12:7 NIV), or as the Message puts it, Life, lovely while it lasts,

is soon over. Life as we know it, precious and beautiful, ends. The body is put back in the same ground it came from. The spirit returns to God, who first breathed it (Ecclesiastes 12:6–7 MSG).

We had been attending church for several months now, and my desire was to learn all I could about my Savior. Church became my refueling station. In 1981, the same year I found Jesus as my Savior, I requested to be baptized. I wanted the whole world to know I was a born-again Christian, a follower of Christ. I was forgiven, loved, and accepted in the Beloved.

By this time, my husband had found a relationship with Jesus as well, and the day arrived that both of us were to be baptized. The setting was in the back yard of my friend's home, where a big sparkling pool served as our baptismal font. When it was my turn to enter the water, my heart was ecstatic. I cannot even describe it. In the arms of my pastor, I was gently put under the water, and when I emerged, I felt like a new person. I took my pastor in an embrace, and my heart was full of joy. I belonged to Jesus for all eternity. A deep sadness seemed to be present, as well. If it was true that my father was in the place God had revealed to my heart, I would never see him again.

My whole perspective changed. I had a hunger to learn God's Word. It seemed as if God had given me a new set of ears. Every Sunday was exciting and filled with teaching and instruction on how to live this Christian life. For the first time, the truth of who God really is found its way into my heart.

The Four Stages of Spiritual Growth

I would like to focus our attention on four spiritual stages we need to know in order to grow and develop to live the mature Christian life. We all begin at the Spiritual Infant Stage, but we only reach the Spiritual Mature Stage (or Father Stage) if we take a personal inventory of the various stages we will be discussing. I cannot take you to specific scriptures where these four stages are clearly spelled out, but I have included some scriptures to demonstrate the principles of this concept. Throughout the Bible the lives of the patriarchs and New Testament believers demonstrate that indeed a transition took place between the infant and the mature stage.

We begin to grow spiritually at the point of salvation. As the Holy Spirit comes to dwell in the born-again believer, He helps us move from the infant stage to the mature stage. This development can proceed rather quickly, depending on how much time we spend on spiritual things. We start fresh and our trust is small, but it eventually develops into complete trust in God and His Word. The more we occupy ourselves with God, the more our interest will be sparked, resulting in our knowing God at a heart level. God is wise. He knows if we reach the Spiritual Mature Stage, we will be able to handle every situation that comes our way. The biggest reason we struggle living this Christian life, or even life in general, is that we try to manage life's circumstances while still in the Spiritual Infant Stage. Because we live in a fallen world and not the world God created for us, the question is not, will difficult circumstances befall us but, rather, when will hardship enter our personal life or the lives of our loved ones?

We will move through the four spiritual stages at a faster pace if we make it our mission to chase after God's heart. The Bible refers to this process as knowing God intimately on a heart-to-heart level. Our heart can know His heart. Just this thought alone should boggle our minds and excite us at the same time, because it is actually possible. Can you imagine that God, the Creator of the universe, gives us the opportunity to know Him at a heart level? This is the relationship He wants to have with us. Reaching this level of intimacy requires each of us to do our part and maybe even let others assist us and spur us on.

One of the gifts I received at the beginning of my spiritual journey came immediately after I put my faith in Jesus Christ as my Savior. There was a lady in our church who felt led by God to take me under her wing. She was instrumental in my life, teaching me to seek the heart of God. Not only was my friend my teacher; she consistently modeled a true walk with the Lord. The longer I spent time with my friend, the more my heart desired to reach the same level of oneness with God. Was the road easy? No, not really. The books *The Pilgrim's Progress* and *The Dream Giver*[1] demonstrate metaphorically the journey from the day of salvation to the final destiny: heaven. The pilgrimage presented in these books is not always smooth sailing. I quickly realized my former lifestyle was not fitting into the new life I now desired to lead. There were moments where my friend held me accountable for my actions. She pointed out to me that certain things were no longer acceptable. Did I mind? Not, at all. In actuality, I eventually urged my friend to always steer me in the right direction. For the next nine years, I was in school, being discipled.

Because of this one-on-one discipleship opportunity, I was able to serve God, beginning with caring for infants in the nursery and then eventually teaching small children. After some time, I sensed the leading of God to teach the older kids, and finally to my long-awaited goal of opening the Bible with adults. The more I learned, the more I wanted to give; that goal has not changed. Later on, as I served alongside my husband as a pastor's wife, there were years of opportunities to teach, disciple, and open the Word of God. I slowly realized I was not only growing in knowledge, but more importantly, I was maturing in my faith. Each of us needs to be willing to take a personal inventory of how we are doing in our physical life, our emotional life, and in our spiritual life.

In the previous two chapters, I shared with you that God's will for our life is to grow and mature physically and emotionally. We discovered that we can know how old we are in these areas. The physical is the most obvious because each year we live on this earth, we count our physical years by the birthdays we celebrate. Even if we did not commemorate our physical birthdays, we would see the outward aging process by simply looking in the mirror.

Our emotional being, or the inner part of us, also referred to as the heart, reflects how old we are emotionally. It's often difficult to discern the condition of our emotional heart or the age we are emotionally. We may never consider the age of our emotional heart, but as you have previously read, we certainly can. This inner emotional part of us needs to have the right environment to grow till it finally reaches maturity. The physical age and the emotional age need to match. Only then will harmony exist between the two. In the final chapter of this book, I will flesh out this principle in more detail; it actually takes all four parts to live a whole, abundant life. Likewise, everyone should know, and can know, how old they are in their spiritual life. The following will take us through the four spiritual stages as revealed in God's Word.

The Bible points to the first spiritual stage in our growing and maturing process as the infant stage, where we are starting out like babies:

Brothers and sisters, I could not address you as people who
live by the Spirit but as people who are still worldly—mere
infants in Christ. I gave you milk, not solid food, for you
were not yet ready for it. Indeed, you are still not ready.
(1 Corinthians 3:1–2 NIV)

This should not surprise us one bit, since our physical life begins at
this same stage. Few people remember how they behaved as infants; we
rely on our parents, siblings, or other family members to fill in those gaps
for us. The stories we are told reveal that we had to be totally cared for
by someone who was older than us. Our very survival depended on our
caretakers. We were unable to communicate clearly or let our needs be
known. The best we had to offer was a cry or continued wailing to get
the attention of someone to take care of our needs. To sum it up, infants
only think of themselves and want to be served. Infants cry but never sing.

The Spiritual Infant Stage is in essence very much the same. Spiritually
speaking, we are at the beginning, needing others to serve and assist us.
We may have our first Bible and be ready to explore the words of God.
We may for the first time rub shoulders with church culture and feel like
an outsider, not sure what to do or what to say. Our spiritual eyes begin
to open to a new set of values on how to live this Christian life. Each day
is a learning experience.

It is at the infant stage where we fully realize that Satan is God's enemy
and ours. We can only recognize and learn to fight against our enemy if
we continue to grow and mature in Christ. Infants cannot engage in this
spiritual warfare or discern if a teaching is according to God's Word. They
will simply succumb, falter, give in, and be easily persuaded:

Then we will no longer be infants, tossed back and forth
by the waves, and blown here and there by every wind of
teaching and by the cunning and craftiness of people in
their deceitful scheming. (Ephesians 4:14 NIV)

I think back to my own spiritual infancy. I relied on others to locate
a certain book in the Bible, find the right chapter, and eventually get the
verse. Little by little, just like an infant, I learned and mastered new things.

My heart was satisfied, knowing that Jesus loves me very much. I found fulfillment in reading Bible stories I had heard from others. I discovered these stories did indeed happen the way others had told me. Each day when I read my Bible, something new jumped off its pages, and before I realized what was happening, I entered the second stage of my growing and maturing process.

The second spiritual stage we can identify is the Small Child Stage. Even the disciples of Jesus had to be gently rebuked by the Lord because their faith was like that of a small child. Their focus was very narrow. Jesus let His disciples know that their faith was very little, not big enough to trust Him for all of their needs.

> Then Jesus said to his disciples: "Therefore I tell you, do not worry about your life, what you will eat; or about your body, what you will wear. For life is more than food, and the body more than clothes. Consider the ravens: They do not sow or reap, they have no storeroom or barn; yet God feeds them. And how much more valuable you are than birds! Who of you by worrying can add a single hour to your life? Since you cannot do this very little thing, why do you worry about the rest? ... You of little faith! (Luke 12:22–26; 28b NIV)

I have some vague and sketchy memories of this period of growing up physically, but I can imagine I acted like any small child would. This season in a child's life can be characterized by learning the system. A small child can be untruthful and jealous of other children, especially younger siblings. Discipline is very difficult during this stage, since small children never believe they are in the wrong and often have temper tantrums. The art of copying grownups is a favorite pastime; children may repeat things in public that were meant only for adult ears. A small child is still very much focused on self yet on the other hand is capable of doing some things on their own. The more children try to master new things, the more successful they become. They begin to sing a new melody, unique to their personality. Moving ahead is just within their reach.

Spiritually speaking, the Small Child Stage is marked by venturing out, digging deeper into the Word of God, and getting a little more involved in the activities of the church. Individuals who find themselves in this stage are still learning, not leading. Just like people who try to convince themselves and adults that they are ready to lead others, this stage is still a time of preparation. Some ministry opportunities, however, can be recommended. Opportunities such as taking care of infants in the nursery or assisting others in their ministries can be good exposure to what ministry is all about. It's like being an apprentice. Learning is at the top of the list.

When I was spiritually at the Small Child Stage, I really did believe I could teach a Sunday school class or be the leader of an Awana Club.[2] When I volunteered in these classes, however, I found out rather quickly the kids knew more than I did. My spirit was dampened, and so I thought I would never be qualified to teach anyone. My mentors were kind and loving, and they gently gave me all the time I needed to catch up. Before too long, I reached for a higher goal, and this set me on a new path, the next stage in my maturing process.

The third spiritual stage we want to reach is the Young Man's (or Young Woman's) Stage. (The Bible is presented to us in the masculine form, but the teaching and its principles clearly include woman, as well). In the Bible, we find a brief dialogue where Jesus and a young man have a friendly exchange of words. The young man asks Jesus what good thing he has to do to get eternal life. You see, this young man believed that what he was doing would be enough. Jesus answered him by saying:

> "Why do you ask me about what is good?" Jesus replied. "There is only One who is good. If you want to enter life, keep the commandments."
>
> "Which ones?" he inquired.
>
> Jesus replied, "'You shall not murder, you shall not commit adultery, you shall not steal, you shall not give false testimony, honor your father and mother,' and 'love your neighbor as yourself.'"

"All these I have kept," the young man said. "What do I still lack?"

Jesus answered, "If you want to be perfect, go, sell your possessions and give to the poor, and you will have treasure in heaven. Then come, follow me."

When the young man heard this, he went away sad, because he had great wealth. (Matthew 19:17–22 NIV)

When I was physically between twenty and thirty, my life was anything but mature. I was involved in senseless activities and made unwise choices. I was, however, mature enough to pay my bills and care for my needs. It was like a yo-yo season in my life. There were stretches where I acted totally mature and fully grown up, and there were other times when I wondered what in the world I was doing. During these years, college plays a major part. As young men and women grow, they have to stand on their own faith and can no longer ride on their parents' shirttails. What does this mean? When we are small children, we see Jesus from our parents' perspective, but as we grow up, we have to decide who Jesus is to us personally.

Here are some trademarks of a young man or woman: Young people, unlike infants and small children, are vibrant, fully engaged in life, and very much in control of their circumstances. The days of basic training are finished, and the school of hard knocks has begun. No longer are we under our parents' care; we've accepted the role of being our own caretaker. Usually during this stage, people get married, and the whole world changes again. Depending on their maturity level, people can be successful wives or husbands, and even prove to be wonderful parents. Life is filled with visions for the future and marked by a productive life.

Spiritually young people have a lot to offer and are desired among church people. They are full of ideas and vigor that can infuse many ministries. Youth pastors can relate to the next generation because just a few years back, the same problems existed for them. By now, childish things are put aside, and their faith is strengthened day by day. Spiritually young people desire to discover the deeper teachings of God's Word and put what they learn into action. This demonstrates to the world that God is still on the throne. This season in a person's life can, however, look like taking one step forward and one step back. Learning is still the number one thing that needs to occupy us. In this stage, we are in danger of becoming stagnant and satisfied that we have arrived. After all, we are living the Christian life.

Not so fast; there is still more in store for us: the abundant life God wants to give to us where we are finally able to follow Him fully. Our heavenly Father is wise and knows all of our life's ups and downs. In this stage, very difficult circumstances cannot be handled well, and for this reason, we must all strive to reach the last level, which the Bible identifies as the Spiritual Mature Stage or the Father Stage.

> So Christ himself gave the apostles, the prophets, the evangelists, the pastors and teachers, to equip his people for works of service, so that the body of Christ may be built up until we all reach unity in the faith and in the knowledge of the Son of God and become mature, attaining to the whole measure of the fullness of Christ. Instead, speaking the truth in love, we will grow to become in every respect the mature body of him who is the head, that is, Christ. (Ephesians 4:11–13, 15 NIV)

Yes, maturity: This is what I long for. Have I arrived? Do I display this kind of faith and depth in my walk with the Lord every day? Not really. I still struggle, and the very moment I realize I live in the realm of the mature, I will surely fall because pride has triumphed again. When I live the spiritual mature life and face trials or extreme difficulties, I'm able to fully trust God with it all.

Our heavenly Father knows that only the spiritual mature life prepares us for what life will bring our way. After his horrendous trials and suffering, Job, the Old Testament patriarch, realized who God really is. What a treasure to know God in such a way, that no matter what He chooses for our life, or whatever we choose for ourselves, we give Him the rightful place: the center of our life. We give Him his rightful place on the throne of our hearts. This place of honor belongs to God, and we should not be afraid to allow Him to establish Himself there. An individual in the

Spiritual Mature Stage has complete contentment in all circumstances. Their source of strength is found in Jesus alone. These individuals are future minded, not past oriented. Mature people accept the fact that all things work together for their eternal good.

We must have a desire to grow for the purpose of being mature. Each one of us may start off with great exuberance, but we may eventually lose our zeal. There is also the danger we become satisfied with where we are and therefore become stagnant. Just like the Dead Sea, which has only inflow and no outflow, it is dead. In the same way, if we stay at the same place and believe we no longer need to grow spiritually, we are ineffective for God. We need to be like the Jordan River, which has inflow and outflow. This means we fill ourselves with God and His Word, and then give out to others in need, to those who do not know Him yet.

When we examine the life of Paul, he shares with us often that he felt he was not mature enough, and he kept on striving to improve his relationship with his Savior (Philippians 3:12–14). Some of us have come to the conclusion it is too much effort to grow in the Lord. We have lost our hunger and thirst for knowing God and settle for less.

When my husband was a pastor, this statement led me to challenge the ladies at the Bible study I was leading. I asked them to visualize themselves sitting on a chair as they evaluated their spiritual condition. Would they see a spiritual infant or a mature person? I still remember the looks on their faces: stunned, puzzled, and at the same time, curious. What would such an activity produce or show them?

Finally, one lady said in a soft voice, "I would see an infant sitting in my place."

Her evaluation of herself revealed to the group that she was spiritually in the infant stage, having even grown up in the church. This describes countless believers who have fallen by the wayside because they did not get the proper nourishment from the pulpit or a Sunday school teacher. If the church or a study group provided real spiritual food, then I believe spiritual growth would be possible and actually encouraged. Each person can choose to feast on the things of God or live in a land of famine and accept the consequences of that decision. Taking inventory at the end of each day reveals whether we fed the body or the spirit. We must remember, in order to reach the Spiritual Mature Stage, it will take time and effort on our part. Only then can we be equipped to discern between good and evil.

Now, the question we all need to ask ourselves is, how old are we spiritually? Once you have identified your spiritual age, seek God and ask Him what next steps you need to take to continue your spiritual journey.

When the Heart Was Spiritually Abused, Then What?

You may have heard the terms "spiritual abuse or having been victimized or deceived" or you may not know what it encompasses. Sad to say, this is more common than we would like to believe and takes place behind closed doors, in the church setting, in the home, by believers, and the list goes on.

Let me begin by giving you a definition of what spiritual abuse is and what it looks like. It takes place anytime someone misrepresents who God is or does not tell the truth about God, as written in the Bible. These false teachings are lies about God and become the new truth for us, damaging our ability to respond in a right relationship with God. In essence, God or scripture is used to control us, attack us, put us down, or even shame us. They are used to set a standard of performance that can only be attained by completely obeying a set of rules and moving into a performance mode. Often these rules were never given in the scriptures. They are human-made for the purpose of making us conform to someone's private agenda. God and His Word are also used to shun people if they do not conform. This gives us no option other than to withdraw emotionally.

The results are devastating, and we see it over and over again. Spiritually victimized individuals simply cannot connect with God on a heart level. Praying is almost impossible. Reading God's Word is very difficult. Sitting through a sermon is torture. Attending a Bible study is out of the question. They do not know who God is, and they certainly do not know who they are in Christ. The best this person has to offer God is to connect with Him from the head in a logical, factual, unemotional type of worship. They have established an intellectual belief system about God but never achieve a heart connection with Him. Outwardly, these people become pretenders, having convinced themselves they have a heart connection with God. They have never felt God's love in their heart for themselves.

People are sometimes so forced with scripture they cannot enjoy reading it. If that is the case, I offer them a temporary bridge that leads them back to God. A bridge is a means of stimulating the longing in their heart to unmask the lies and build a new truth. A bridge can be in the form of a good book. When I recommend a book, I reach for those that demonstrate an individual's high level of spiritual maturity and show readers the steps they need to take to put them on a different path. Some of my favorite books are missionary biographies. These can include just about anything: how the call on a person's life was received, what steps were taken to engage in God's bidding, what hardships had to be overcome, the deep faith that allowed them to continue the mission God had for them, and so on. The book needs to motivate the reader to find the true God, who meets the needs of people and reveals Himself in awesome ways. These books were written from personal experience of traumatic circumstances. What do I mean? Men and women (sometimes parents) have written books about their struggles and have recorded how they moved from trial to triumph, from a mess to a message. These individuals were often thrust into life events they never anticipated, situations that God, in His infinite wisdom, selected for them. When we read about a wounded person, and we carry similar wounds from hurtful events in our own heart, we can experience an instant connection with them and their journey of healing. This can create a longing for our own healing.

In the recommended reading list, (in the back of the book) you will find some of my favorite books I reach for when I need a bridge. There were moments in my life I discovered how God has provided for others, how miracles are still a part of God's plan. Of course, the Bible is full of miracles and stories of individuals who received a special touch from God. A person who was spiritually abused cannot accept what the Bible has to say because the stories in the Bible have been distorted by others for their personal gain.

One day, a young woman came into the office, seeking help. She was in a bad way. Countless abuse issues of every shape had been forced upon her, and the spiritual abuse she had to endure disconnected her from a loving heavenly Father. The term she used to describe her home was profound; she called it a "house of terror." For her, past church experiences were not good memories. Even still, she felt anger flowing toward her from the pulpit. The words the pastor spoke sounded very much like her father's words, and new arrows constantly buried themselves deep in her heart. She had transferred what her earthly father said about her to the rest of the people sitting in the pews. She automatically believed that the folks all around her saw her the same way her father did. Church became a place to be feared, and shame constantly accompanied her. Because of false beliefs instilled in her as a very young child, she had no foundation of who God really is.

Without realizing it, she had transferred all of her conflicting emotions upon God and saw Him the same as she saw her earthly father. All she could remember was that the Bible was used to hammer the message into her heart. God must punish her because she is an evil child who does evil things. Only a severe punishment, like a stoning, would clear her from her wrongs. No wonder she wanted nothing to do with God's Word. It started with her earthly father and with a God who seemed equally as harsh and rigid. Her dad could never accept her, and she could not see how God would ever accept her.

Some see God as a loving Father and a faithful friend. Others see God as unloving, uncaring, punitive, and distant. How can God have so many faces? Were these faces put on God through misunderstandings and false expectations of His children? Or were these faces put on God by our earthy parents or others misrepresenting God? A false picture is so often all that is left of who He really is. Do we limit God with our own perceptions or assign Him a level of compassion equal only to our own? Sometimes, our faith is colored by the view of God of an earthly father, mother, pastor, believer, or friend. It can take years to finally discover the truth of who God really is. Of course, if we incorporate prayer into the process, discovering the truth can happen rather quickly. Jesus will reveal Himself to the person seeking Him.

Resolving Spiritual Abuse

Individuals who have been spiritually abused borrow the Good Shepherd's dress code. They are always proper and avoid drawing attention to themselves. They borrow His voice by being politically correct but don't really know the heart of God. It all becomes a show. They learn to act a certain way and behave like they have it all together, pretending to be close to God. The sad truth is, because of the way God was presented to them at some point, a false picture and belief system is now their truth. The result is they have learned to hide their real selves and continue to struggle to survive in this Christian world, always keeping God at a distance.

How do we begin to resolve spiritual abuse? Similar to the other violation issues, this may take some time. A good beginning would be to write down all the things that happened in your life. Make a list. Write down and identify the spiritual abuse and the damage you received from others. Begin by identifying the individuals who have used God or the scriptures to control you or jot down how certain events connected to spiritual things made you feel. Spiritual abuse can come in the form of being attacked or belittled in the name of God and His Word.

While making a list, you may discover others who have put you down or shamed you in some way. The key is to be specific and honest about what happened and name the individuals who committed these acts. One other area that needs to be explored is whether God or His Word was used, at any time, to set a strict standard of how you were expected to behave or perform in order to be accepted. In other words, what human-made standards (not found in the Bible) were forced on you? One last item is to identify if God or His Word was used to shun you. Shunning is when others emotionally or even physically withdraw from us. This is often done because other people's interpretation of the scriptures is contrary to the truth.

This resulting list will be a valuable tool to guide you through the prayer process. All the issues are collected in one place, and when the time is right, you can remember the issues that were uncovered. You need to take these spiritual deceptions to Jesus in prayer, for the purpose of seeking His healing. As already mentioned, add the names of the persons next to the list of offenses: Who did the damage? How did this make you feel? Not only do we need to talk to Jesus about the real truth about Himself, but our heart needs to move in the direction to eventually forgive the people who have hurt us.

When the time is right, consider going to Jesus in prayer. Bring Him into every aspect of your life, especially into the list you have made and the issues you have identified. We should never rush this important step. Not only will we be talking to Jesus about the spiritual abuse issues we have experienced and identified, but we also want to ask God to show us the pain and damage this created in our heart. Sometime during this prayer time, the heart needs to make an important decision: Am I ready to forgive each person from my heart? As already mentioned, it is for this reason that we slow down and take one issue at a time to prayer. If we bunch everything together, we will not achieve true freedom in our hearts.

Forgiveness is the most difficult command God gives us. If it were not for the example of His Son, Jesus, we would not know how to go about it. When Jesus was taken up to be crucified, forgiveness was already on His mind. There was a moment when everybody present could hear the voice of Jesus saying, for all to hear, "Father, forgive them, for they do not know what they are doing" (Luke 23:34a NIV).

Volumes have been written by others to teach us what forgiveness is all about, but we still struggle. One reason we struggle is because, if we have to forgive, most likely we were hurt by words, actions, or unkind deeds. Our human nature dictates to us this response: We got hurt, now we want to hurt back in order to get even. I have met many people who had sleepless nights, thinking about revenge. Revenge will never bring healing to the heart. Only true forgiveness can restore the peace we so desperately long for. Personally, for me, forgiveness is to choose to willingly release the person into God's hands. By releasing them, I forgive them for the pain and the consequences they have caused me. My heart knows and trusts that one day, God will vindicate me.

> Do not take revenge, my dear friends, but leave room for God's wrath, for it is written: "It is mine to avenge; I will repay," says the Lord. On the contrary: "If your enemy is hungry, feed him; if he is thirsty, give him something to drink. In doing this, you will heap burning coals on his head." Do not be overcome by evil, but overcome evil with good. (Romans 12:19–21 NIV)

We long to be vindicated, to be avenged, and to inflict just punishment on people for the wrongs they have committed against us, wrongs that ultimately damaged our heart. In essence, this would be an act of retaliation, getting even, settling the score, so to speak. Yet God asks us to forgive others like He has forgiven all of our wrongs. He then asks us to provide for the person's physical needs. If we pay back, we engage in the same evil practice as the person who hurt us. Forgiveness is handing the person over to the Lord. He decides on the punishment and consequences. In my next chapter, I will dig deeper into this principle. In my own life, I made a difficult decision to forgive those who had deeply hurt me.

Here is one sample prayer I might pray with the woman I mentioned earlier, who came into our office: "Jesus, my dad constantly criticized and rejected me if I didn't do everything perfectly, according to how he interpreted Your Word. He spiritually damaged me by forcing his beliefs on me. Jesus, are You like my dad?"

It is important that you pause after each question and give Jesus the opportunity to speak to your heart. The way Jesus speaks to our heart differs from person to person. He can give you a picture that specifically relates to what you just asked Him, or He can give you a portion of scripture that communicates what He wants you to know. At times, there is just a knowing inside because the answer is placed by Jesus directly in your heart. There are times when a song is given, and the words of the song answer what is asked. Jesus is so personal. He knows exactly what you need.

Together, this woman and I continued, "Jesus, how are You different from my dad? I have no idea who You are, or who I am. Could You speak to my heart and let me know the truth about You?"

In prayer, we can ask Jesus anything our heart longs for. He will prompt our hearts by placing His truth over the lies that have ruled our hearts. During the prayer time, keep checking with your heart to see if it is beginning to fill with compassion for the person who created the hurt and wounded your heart. You can begin the forgiveness process anytime you are ready. Releasing the person who committed the spiritual abuse is a vital step in bringing freedom to your heart.

The lady I was praying with melted in the arms of Jesus, and when I felt the time was right, I led her to speak these words, giving her the opportunity to decide if she was ready to forgive: "Jesus, have I ever forgiven my dad for ...?" (If you or the person you are praying with is ready, continue on.) "Jesus, today I choose to forgive my dad for giving me a false picture of who You are, for using Your Word to force me to fear You and believe You are an unloving, harsh God who does not love me. My heart believed I had to be perfect. Today, I choose to release my dad to You. I want to forgive him, from my heart, for the pain and consequences he has caused me. Jesus, will You begin pouring into my heart all the good things You want to give to me and fill my heart with Your love and peace?"

While you pray, God will perform the miracle of healing and set you free. Your heart will feel lighter, happier, and for the first time, loved by Jesus.

If someone was spiritually abused by a pastor who misrepresented God in such a way that He was seen as a punishing God, sending everybody to Hell for not living a perfect life, we can pray something like this: "Jesus, I was damaged by Pastor _____ who constantly used his message to make me feel that You want perfect obedience, that I do not measure up to Your standards. What did that do to my heart? Jesus, I struggle to pray and read my Bible. When I pray or read my Bible, I see the face of my pastor and hear his accusing voice. Can you disconnect all that and take these images out of my heart? Jesus, does Your heart hurt because I can't pray or read Your Word without emotionally blocking You? What kind of relationship do You want with me? Do You want me to perform for You or do You want me to feel loved and believe in my heart I am who You say I am? Jesus, can You heal my heart so I can emotionally respond to You in prayer and in reading Your Word? How would you do that?" You also could ask Jesus to place a new love and desire for reading His Word in your heart so you will be able to go to the Word directly and see for yourself what it has to say about Him.

Keep praying and connecting, and eventually, you will feel the love of God as never before. Just having a conversation with Jesus and letting Him tell your heart what He has to say is all you need to do. Little by little, something will change in your heart, and a longing to discover the true God will spring up. This inward change is so powerful; it's actually visible in your face. Peace and rest now appear on your countenance. Jesus was brought into all the issues previously identified, and your heart is filled with good things. It was Jesus who took the pain away and took it out of your heart and then replaced the pain with good things.

One day, a woman I was having prayer time with asked me if she could use the restroom. After a while, she returned, only to ask once again to be excused again. I started to worry, wondering if she was ill or what was going on. Then, after her third trip to the restroom, she burst out, "I cannot stop smiling. I just have to look in the mirror and see my smile. Everything has changed. My heart never felt this good or this light."

Praise God for the miracle of a heart changed.

After you receive healing from spiritual abuse, the way is open to freely explore Christ. Eventually, you will realize your full potential to grow and mature.

A Picture of Spiritual Deception

As already mentioned, spiritual deception is a reality in many homes, in churches, and in other circles. Countless individuals have experienced false teaching, and even entire congregations have been betrayed by individuals who were imposters of the true gospel. A false picture of who God is was presented, resulting in a misrepresentation of His attributes and character.

This practice is not new. You see, our enemy, Satan, is cleaver. He repackages the truth with just enough lies that we believe not the truth anymore. From the beginning of time, his methods have been the same. If Satan allowed too much of the truth, most people would discern the falsehood and not follow what he's presenting. The following is an example of what Satan has in mind for deceiving people, especially the ones belonging to a household of faith.

Many years ago, I saw a movie set in a small village in northern Sweden, at the turn of the century, circa 1896. This unique film portrays a clear picture of how apostasy from the truth to a false belief system can happen in an unexpected way. The title of the movie was *Jerusalem*.[3] The main characters were members of one family. The older son ran the church in a small village for a long time. At some point, he leaves the village to work at the family's sawmill, and while he is away, the village is without a church leader. An American evangelist steps into that vacuum. He is an elegant preacher, full of spirit and messages about "fire and brimstone." Not only is he a very charismatic preacher, he also heals individuals through the laying on of hands.

Eventually, this man convinces the former preacher's sister to take over the family farm and ministers out of her living room. He also convinces some of the people to sell their farms and move to Jerusalem, with the goal of getting closer to God. Some of these farms had been in their families for hundreds of years. All the proceeds from these sales are given to the preacher, and before too long, some two dozen villagers find themselves on a journey to Jerusalem with that preacher.

Their arrival in Jerusalem was not like anything that this small band of believers could have imagined. Immediately, their families were separated. Husbands and wives were taken to separate areas of the large compound and had to sleep on hard cots. Even the children were taken away and cared for by strangers. Not even at mealtimes were the families allowed to keep company with each other. The food consisted of only soup and bread.

What can we learn from this story? You may say, "This could never happen in the twenty-first century." Not so fast. The lesson to take away from this film is that this *can* happen. It has become a reality for individuals who did not stay close to the true faith. Throughout the movie, friends and neighbors pleaded with their fellow villagers, telling them God can be worshipped here, that they didn't have to sell everything and move to Jerusalem to be closer to God. They did not listen.

Today, there are voices that beckon individuals to believe lies, false doctrines of who God is. In my case, the truth was twisted just enough to make me believe this was the gospel truth. I never actually thought to challenge what I was being taught. My spiritual mentors had attended seminaries for years. They had prepared themselves to proclaim God's Word. These spiritual advisors and teachers were ordained by a denomination common to society, had graduated with prestigious honors, and were thereby declared fit to teach the Bible. Surely such individuals were teaching the truth, or so I thought.

Yet even as a child, I could never shake the feeling that all the teaching I received was somehow superficial. There was no joy or peace in anyone's life to give testimony to God's presence. My spiritual leaders were consumed with instructing me in what was acceptable behavior and dictated a set of dos and don'ts. This was called worship. I learned that worship was to obey the rules, nothing else. As a child, and later as an adult, I had no desire to follow more rules, nor did I want to memorize prayers and offer them to people who were like me, flesh and blood. I never fought the system. I simply endured and bade my time until I could say, "Farewell," to that chapter of my life.

Why Is Spiritual Growth so Hard for Some of Us?

Let me follow this question up with another question equally as important: Why do we resist spiritual growth? I believe the answer is this: It requires an inner change, when outwardly, we want to remain as we are. Our thinking is this: it's our right to stay angry at the person or the circumstance.

Spiritual growth includes knowing you will wind up with something you don't want: forgiveness, instead of holding on to unforgiveness. It also urges us forward to a place we have never been before: forgiving when it seems impossible. Inside, we feel uncertain and uneasy, and our struggle begins in earnest. Our natural thinking wants what we perceive to be just and fair. With this kind of thinking, forgiveness is impossible.

Forgiveness cannot be achieved by learning something new; it only comes when we become new ourselves. How can it be achieved? The old person, with our way of thinking, needs to die in order for the new person to be born within. Our angry, negative feelings must lose their power. We carefully stack up all the wrongs the person did to us into a high wall. This wall must come down. How do we do this? We do this by not looking at all the stacked-up charges but by looking at the person, instead.

Forgiving others is always in our best interest, even though it does not seem so at first. When we were children, we were taught not to fight or attack or call others bad names. As adults, we also refrain from doing these things. However, when we are wronged as children or adults, we somehow want to get back at the person who has hurt us, to get even. We do that by natural impulse. If you don't get back at your offender, you stuff your hurt and all your anger. This means you don't deal with it. If you do get back at the individual, you may do it with gossip, by slacking off at work, or something that hurts the person indirectly. This relational war goes on forever because you never feel the score is settled.

Legalists focus on the negatives of others and cannot imagine forgiving anyone. Over time, their negative behavior becomes a habit of life, and they no longer see the positive and good in others. The result is a hardened heart. A spiritual prison is created inside the heart, and the soul cannot see out. All you know is, "An eye for an eye and a tooth for a tooth." Restlessness takes over, and you are consumed with the offender, when in reality, you consume yourself. These same feelings also transfer to the person of Christ. We get cold toward God because, after all, He should punish the evil done to us.

Each of us also carries our own list of unpardonable sins, and so we condemn ourselves. In our head, we know we are forgiven, but sins from the past still lock us inside. Gradually, unforgiveness becomes aggressive within us, like a cancer in the spirit. If legalists want to please others, they pretend to be ready to forgive. In this same instance, this kind of forgiveness is mechanical and from the head, not from the heart.

When we consider forgiveness, we are faced with a new set of problems. We realize we have to surrender or give up payback, bow down, lose. I don't want to lose. Nobody does. But is forgiveness really losing, or is it gaining? Holding on to unforgiveness means we remain a prisoner of our own making. Choosing to forgive sets ourselves free. Which one is more difficult? Which one looks better to you?

A Practical Plan to Grow and Mature Spiritually

I want to give you some practical tools to begin the process of growing in Christ and maturing in your spiritual walk with Him. There is no right or wrong about where you should begin, or what you should do, because your journey will be your own personal experience with God. Everyone has a preference of how they choose to grow and mature in their faith. The following are guidelines for you to consider; you may come up with others not mentioned here.

One way to grow spiritually is to get God's Word into yourself as much as possible. Several years, back I had the privilege of counseling a young lady. As she sat in my office, her face revealed a puzzled look. Before too long, it became evident she did not have a relationship with Jesus Christ. I have often had the privilege of sharing my personal testimony and the gospel with my clients, for the purpose of leading them into a personal relationship with God. This young lady was ready, and with a simple yet sincere prayer, she invited Jesus to come into her heart and be her Savior.

From that moment on, she was determined to get as much of God's Word into her life as she could. She plastered her apartment with scriptures God pointed out to her. Not only did she saturate herself with God's Word, she attended every Bible study available and submitted herself to a discipleship program. She almost seemed to live and breathe the words from the Bible. In essence, she surrounded herself with God. Within a year's time, you would not have recognized her.

The Holy Spirit cannot bring to memory what we don't know. To reach the Spiritual Mature Stage, there must come a time when we literally compare ourselves with scripture because His will never leads us contrary to His Word. One way to reach this milestone is not only by reading the Bible, but by letting the Bible read you.

Recently I heard the phrase, "What if we treated our Bible like we treat our cell phones?" We carry our cell phones everywhere and never let this supposed lifeline out of our sight. What if we flip through our Bible while we stand in line in the grocery store or wait for the bus? Before we knew it, we'd be a walking gospel.

One other area that must be developed to reach the spiritual mature life is learning to engage in a vibrant prayer life:

> And pray in the Spirit on all occasions with all kinds of prayers and requests. (Ephesians 6:18 NIV)

Scripture is filled with examples of individuals praying to God. These people prayed in good and in bad circumstances. Like me, most of us have to learn how to pray. Praying from the heart with passion will take time and comes from knowing God on a personal level. Praying what God wants is something that takes practice and patience. Discovering God's will can only be achieved by listening to His voice. God has a master plan in mind for us, and contrary to our beliefs, He does not play hide-and-seek with us. God's desire is to reveal His will to us because this is where He needs us to be.

There was a time in my early years of walking with the Lord when knowing God's will for my life was a rather frightening thought. In essence, I was afraid of surrendering myself to God. If we are honest with ourselves, this is exactly the case. My belief was God is so restrictive, and I would have to give up a lot of my activities and pleasures. Now I know God's will for my life is a good thing, not to be feared. Yes, God's definition of what is good for us is different from what we may envision. We may believe that getting everything we want is for our good. God's idea for our good is to form our character, to fashion us to be more like His Son, Jesus, every day.

The last area I would like to mention is that God uses our circumstances in the growing and maturing process. His desire is for us to completely surrender ourselves to whatever is going on in our life. As already mentioned, one of my favorite activities is reading a good book, especially when I can immerse myself in a biography. There, I can read how God has used circumstances in people's lives to bring them to a crossroads where a choice had to be made: to either follow God or take matters into their own hands. When we read, for example, of prisoners tortured and treated inhumanely, and that they are still able to sing and praise God, our hearts long for that kind of fellowship. Yes, at times, we must pick up our cross and whatever that represents. God may want us to carry it publicly and trust Him all the way.

When difficult times come into our life, a decision has to be made. What we choose will determine if we move in the direction of reaching the mature life. Maturity can be costly and requires much, yet the reward is great. Don't get me wrong: I'm not ready to jump up and volunteer for a tough assignment from God, but if He chooses to allow this in my life, I pray I have reached a level of maturity that will allow me to stand firm and finish strong.

A careful study of the Bible reveals to us the principle of sowing and reaping. Four lessons are to be gleaned from this teaching. The first two are cause and effect (or result). The last two are blessing and peace. Let's unpack these for a bit. Not to make things complicated, a cause is simply the action that will create an effect. For example, if I am the cause of creating strife between two people, the effect will be that these individuals most likely will alienate themselves from me. On the other hand, if I become a blessing to two individuals, a relationship of peace will be fostered between us. I can choose one, but I also must accept the other. If I change what I do, the results will also be different.

Moving toward maturity is necessary to fulfill God's purpose for us. His purpose is for us to change the world. In essence, He wants His Kingdom to be reflected in us. God will let us sit in our circumstances with the purpose of getting us closer to Him, to give us a wake-up call and move us along. If God had not allowed persecution to happen in Jerusalem while the disciples huddled together, the gospel would not have gone out into the rest of the world. God has chosen you and me to represent Him on earth by becoming a picture of Him for the world to see.

It is not the pastor's job to mature us, though he can help by giving us opportunities to attend Bible studies and by feeding us with God's Word. The final responsibility and privilege rests with the individual, you and me.

How to Reset Your Spiritual Heart

1. Be completely honest with yourself and determine what your current spiritual stage is.
2. Evaluate your relationship with God. Does He look and sound to you like your dad, who always criticized you and gave you disapproving looks? Is God like a person who deeply hurt and wounded you? Talk to Jesus in prayer about all of these unresolved issues, and follow the steps recommended in chapter 3.
3. When you are ready, forgive the ones who have wounded your heart. Unforgiveness will affect your life. In the parable of the unmerciful servant (Matthew 18), Jesus lets us know the one who did not forgive was turned over to the king's torturers.
4. If at any time your heart was spiritually damaged by a pastor, leader, or believer, go to Jesus in prayer and grant forgiveness.
5. Become a part of a small group or consider asking God to bring one person, who is more spiritually mature, into your life to disciple or mentor you.
6. Pray and seek the face of God to direct you to a ministry of His choice. We must make ourselves available to God at any stage.
7. Select reading or viewing material that fosters and encourages growth and has the potential to challenge you to strive for the same. Never neglect the Word of God by excessive reading of other materials. Only God's Word has the power to transform a heart.
8. Fall in love with the Jesus by using a Bible program on your electronic device. Or use a Bible concordance and do a topical search on the word *love* or *compassion*. Record your favorites in a journal or memorize some of them. Instead of reading the Word, opt to listen to the Word using a software program. My favorite Bible app is biblegateway.com.[4] It is very user friendly and gives you many free options to enjoy God's Word.

9. Bring God into all of your daily activities. Jesus wants to hear from His kids. When you misplace your phone, ask Jesus to show you where it is. Train yourself to go to the fountain of truth, God or His Word, if you are not clear on which direction to go in your life.

10. In your growing and maturing process, include music and other spiritual aids to center yourself in Christ.

11. Establish your spiritual safe place as you engage in the M&M method (you will read about this in chapter 6).

My Personal Love Relationship with Jesus

It now has been decades since I first said yes to Jesus. So much has changed that I don't even know where to begin. The little church we found while searching through the Yellow Pages became our place of worship for the next ten years. Each Sunday, we entered the mortuary, full of life and expectation as to what we would learn that day. As the congregation grew in number, we eventually conducted our worship services in a proper church building. But I realized a building was not required to have church. People are the church.

By that time, I had asked Jesus to disconnect my vow "never to attend church again." As mentioned earlier, this vow came from having no connection with the god that was presented to me while growing up. I greatly feared the god my church presented to me. I did not want any barriers between me and Jesus, and one day while I was praying, I brought Jesus into this area of my life and asked His forgiveness for making this foolish vow. As always, He restored me, and more freedom and peace came into my heart.

The church building was no longer a frightening place, filled with gloom and doom. I actually looked forward going to church, praising God with others collectively, and learning about Him. My eyes were opened to who Jesus really is. I understood I could go directly to Jesus for all of my prayer requests, needs, or whatever my heart wanted to say to Him. My spirit was elated.

There was one area where I struggled for a long time: I had no idea how to pray. My spiritual advisors from childhood taught me that God was not to be approached directly, so I had difficulty relating to God. Believe it or not, I was able to recall some of the prayers I had memorized; this was pretty much all I knew about praying. I had no idea what I would say to God or how to talk to Him. Would He even listen? So for the first years in my newly found faith, I satisfied my need of getting to know God by reading my Bible. To my surprise, I discovered, in God's Word, when people prayed, they were not always kneeling. Some of them raised their hands, while others lay prostrate before God. Oh, how I longed to know God so intimately that I would be comfortable and free to worship Him this way.

If it had not been for my friend, who met with me on a consistent basis, my spiritual journey would have moved along at a snail's pace. But with her help and assistance, I was able to understand spiritual principles and began living that new life of mine. There were isolated times when I was confronted with my spiritual upbringing, and I wrestled with past unresolved memories of my early church days. Never in all of my wildest dreams did I ever consider that I had experienced spiritual abuse, not in a drastic way, but enough that my picture of God was distorted.

I had to admit to myself I had become a puppet of some sort. I did what I believed was acceptable, learned how others talked or related to each other, and copied other people's spiritual knowledge. For the longest time, I was unable to live my new life publicly or incorporate this new kind of worship at a church service. One time, when I was alone, I practiced talking to God from my heart. I felt silly, and it was so out of character that I gave up on the idea. I longed to experience God. I wanted to feel His love.

One activity was always awesome; during this activity, I could truly enjoy God and feel His presence. This was song time. Whenever I sang, my heart resonated with God. When the memories from my childhood would flood my heart, I could soothe my heart by singing new songs to Jesus. God eventually used these spiritual songs to reveal Himself to me. My heart was especially tuned to the words of these songs, and I memorized many new ones with the purpose of giving them back to God as an offering of praise. This was the beginning of my prayer life taking a turn for the better. Not only would I sing for Jesus, but in some way, Jesus sang with me, and this felt like I was praying.

I never felt the need to resolve the spiritual abuse I experienced while growing up, yet in my heart, I still feared God. I felt unworthy and out of sync with Him. When others made certain comments about their relationship with God, I often felt judged, criticized, and shunned in some way. I became a good pretender, and had it not been for my dear friend, I would be completely satisfied living that false spiritual life.

It was not till years later my heart urged me to address my spiritual past and my ongoing struggles with God. In order to finally have a close, intimate, relationship with God, I had to bring Him into this area of my life. I set aside a day, determined to spend time with Jesus, and invited Him to have full access to this part of my life. I was fully prepared for God to perform heart surgery on my spiritually wounded heart. I asked Him to reveal to me if anything I had experienced in the past had created damage in my heart.

While I was in prayer, I was brave enough to ask Jesus questions to which only He would have the answers. I realized He saw me at every stage of my life, heard all the words I've ever spoken, and knew all of my thoughts, especially what was in my heart. No longer did I want to go on pretending and lying to myself that my relationship with God was awesome. I needed to get to the bottom of the matter. Why was my heart so void of feeling that I couldn't truly experience God?

The longer I prayed, the clearer it all became: Jesus let my heart know that what I had learned about Him was a false representation of who He is. In addition, I had transferred the behavior of my dad to Him; eventually, God and my father looked and sounded the same to me. My heart understood that the god others had created for me was a stern and unloving god who never had time for me. He did not care about me and just put up with me in some way, and eventually he would send me to a place where I would spend eternity, away from him, forever. I was so wrong, because now my spiritual eyes were opened. God does not sent anyone to hell; we send ourselves by not believing in the Son of God, Jesus Christ. God was not anything like this. For the first time, His love filled my entire heart and being, I truly overflowed with all of His goodness. Not only did I feel His love, but I also knew it was real.

From that day on, my relationship with God was different. Everything changed inside of my heart. During my prayer time, Jesus spoke directly to my heart and gave me the real picture of who He is and how much He cares about me. Right after my personal encounter, the Bible seemed to come alive, and my prayer time changed. The picture I once had in my heart no longer had any power over me. It had been transformed into a new picture.

One night, something I'll always treasure in my heart was given to me by Jesus. In a dream, I was walking down a street, when all of a sudden, I was taken up by a whirlwind. The wind was gentle and very warm. It almost felt like I was being wrapped up in a warm blanket. I felt a presence and instinctively knew it was Jesus. I wanted to stay in this place forever, but all too soon, Jesus let me know it was not my time, and I needed to return. This encounter is still with me, as if it happened yesterday, and whenever I feel negative thoughts or if hurtful memories want to steal away some of my joy, I go back to this place and immediately feel loved and cared for.

I was never taught you could ask Jesus for pictures, but this is exactly what He did for me. I had read about people having dreams about Jesus, but I never believed this would happen to me. I was wrong. God has done this for countless others I've had the privilege of praying with. The pictures or dreams are always very personal, direct messages from Jesus Himself. You are familiar with the word *priceless*? Well, this is exactly how I feel, that my pictures and this dream from Jesus are priceless, especially the picture already shared with you, of the large, beautiful, jeweled heart. Even in this world, if anyone would ever receive a large jewel like this, it would be simply overwhelming. Jesus wanted to give me the message of how valuable I am to Him, how much worth I have in His eyes, and how beautiful He created me.

As my personal spiritual journey continues, I realize I'm free in Christ. He is in charge, and this suits me very well because when I was in charge of my life, it was a disaster. My future would not have been anything I now experience. Today, I understand the Tree of the Knowledge of Good and Evil in the Garden of Eden. This tree did not look like bondage to Adam and Eve; it looked like freedom, in the same way sin looks fun and exciting and not like bondage at all. Yet I was in bondage to sin for many, many years. Now I have freedom in my heart, and it's priceless. Each and every one of you can have it. Having inner freedom doesn't even come close to all the other freedoms we enjoy. It resides deep within the heart. I had lost the songs I had sung. Life and the choices I made simply drained them all away. Now my heart sings a new song to the King of Kings and Lord of Lords, as I eagerly wait to sing in His presence.

In the meantime, I strive to continue in my growing and maturing process, to be Christ-like and show off God and impact my world. Jesus taught us about the kingdom of God. His desire is to have the kingdom in our own life, here on earth. God does not dwell among us; He lives within us. You and I are pictures of God to the world. What the world sees in us is often their first exposure of who God is. It is God's heart the world needs, and you and I can be the visible representative of God here on earth, just as Paul admonished the believers in Thessalonica. He wrote these words:

> For you know that we dealt with each of you as a father
> deals with his own children, encouraging, comforting and
> urging you to live lives worthy of God, who calls you into
> his kingdom and glory. (1 Thessalonians 2:11–12 NIV)

CHAPTER 5

GOD WANTS US TO GROW
AND MATURE SEXUALLY

How can a young man [or woman, I add] keep his way pure?
By keeping watch [on himself] according to Your word
[conforming his life to Your precepts]. (Psalm 119:9 AMP)

When God laid it on my heart to flesh out how He sees a person completely whole in His sight, I never thought to write anything about sexuality. The reason is simple. I did not believe God included this topic as an area in which we were to grow and mature. Sexual maturity is a term most of us never even think about. Some of us may say this happens naturally, so we really don't have to worry about it. Do you believe this is true? Could it be, many of us have never truly had the opportunity to grow and mature sexually, and for this reason, we struggle in this area?

How wrong I was. God is the Creator of our sexuality. Even now as I write, I realize the impact our sexuality has on our wholeness and quality of life. Everything seems to come together in our sexual life. Our physical body is engaged, our emotions are aroused, and findings have confirmed even our spiritual being is connected in some mysterious way. All these areas meld into one, and this makes our sexual being a powerful force.

In my lifetime, I have seen too many hurting individuals, along with entire families, whose lives have been impacted by never having the opportunity to fully grow and mature in their sexuality. Many of these people had their sexuality awakened at a time in their life when the top priority should have been playing and going to school. They were violated in the sexual area, and everything changed. In today's oversexualized culture, marriages, families, and churches are under attack to overwhelming proportions. The influence of pornography starts at an age that is creeping lower due to the internet. Many individuals are hurting in their heart due to the impact of porn in their personal life or in the life of a loved one.

For several years, I homeschooled my children. I decided to read the Bible with them from beginning to end. When my twins were in the fourth grade, I figured this was as good a time as any to begin our reading. Things went along just fine till we reached passages that required a great deal of explanation on my part. These were related to immoral sexual behavior. Immoral behavior is measured when there are certain standards or laws, and the sexual activity violates these standards or laws as recorded in the Word. God's standards and laws on sexual behavior are clearly spelled out for us in scripture. After some time, I made the decision to wait a few more years till my children were at a more appropriate age, where they could benefit from the full spectrum of what God wants us all to know; when they would have a better understanding of sexuality, and I could effectively explain to them what immorality is and how it violates God's principles and standards.

As with all of the other subjects, we need to begin with God. He is the source of all truth, and He is the person we go to for knowledge and understanding in any area. The Word of God is a clear, permanent record that was given to assist us in living what we affectionately call "the Christian life." In actuality, the true meaning of the word *Christian* is "Christ follower." A person who is committed to the teachings of Christ and all of His promises will apply these truths into their daily lives, thereby amplifying Christ's example.

God has a lot to say in the scriptures about sexuality, and for this reason, it is important to know His perspective on the subject. Have you ever explored God's Word on the topic of healthy sexuality? Do you fully know His will in this area? I never had the idea till I finally made it a priority to get to the bottom of it all. I found God gives us guidelines about sexuality in Leviticus, as well as in other books of the Bible. Here we can read and clearly understand the dos and the don'ts. Then throughout the Bible, we read of warnings against certain behaviors that are considered sexually immoral, those we need to stay away from. Why? Because if we engage in sexual immorality, we actually defile ourselves:

> "I have the right to do anything," you say- but not everything is beneficial. "I have the right to do anything"- but I will not be mastered by anything. You say, "Food for the stomach and the stomach for food, and God will destroy them both." The body, however, is not meant for sexual immorality but for the Lord, and the Lord for the body. (1 Corinthians 6:12–13 NIV)

God wants us to know what He has in mind regarding healthy sexuality. He also has included in His Word many accounts of how this wonderful gift from Him has been abused throughout history.

In the account of Creation (Genesis 1:1–28), we read that God included His purpose for our sexuality when He created us male and female. Each one has his or her own reproductive parts as needed for procreation, and these are vital, essential parts to guarantee the survival of our species. When God created Eve, He fashioned her into a perfect female genetic counterpart to match Adam's male genetic part, for the purpose of being able to reproduce. God commands Adam and Eve to be fruitful (Genesis 1:28).

In the scriptures, we read that as humankind began to populate the earth, people eventually moved away from God's pure design to a perverted view of sexuality. We're not given the details of these perversions, but we do read specific instructions from God about activities we need to stay away from. One of these examples is recorded for us in Genesis. Angels arrive in Sodom to visit Abraham's nephew, Lot, and he takes them to his home to spend the night. We read the following:

> Before they had gone to bed, all the men from every part of the city of Sodom—both young and old—surrounded the house. They called to Lot, "Where are the men who

came to you tonight? Bring them out to us so that we can
have sex with them." (Genesis 19:4–5 NIV)

The inhabitants of the city were corrupt, and for this reason, God
destroyed not only the city of Sodom but also the city of Gomorrah.

Later on in the book of Exodus, we read that God entered into a
covenant relationship with the Israelites at Mount Sinai. His desire was
to set these people apart, to live a life so pure it would be a reflection
of His holiness to the entire world. God knew the nations surrounding
the Promised Land were engaging in all sorts of sexual behaviors He
considered an abomination. If Israel obeyed God's commands, the words
written down by Moses, He promised to bless them abundantly. But if
Israel chose to embrace and follow immorality, like Egypt and Canaan,
they would fall under God's curse. Obeying God and remaining sexually
pure would demonstrate the holiness of God to the world, and it would
also result in the fulfillment of God's promise to them: enjoyment of health
in their physical, emotional, spiritual, and sexual life. The same mandate
applies to us today. God has not changed His mind on sexual behavior, as
outlined in the book of Leviticus.

As always, God has it right. What He says always works best for us.
For this reason, we can and must get our instructions from God on any
topic. Who else on this earth would qualify to give us the pure, intended
message on why we were created as sexual beings? How do we handle the
responsibility of this powerful gift, and when is the right time to engage
in sexual activity as God intended? Our enemy, Satan, knows God's intent
for sexuality, and not for one minute should we believe that his agenda is
the same as God's. He never has the same purpose in mind. He wants to
destroy the good things God has provided for us.

No Longer as God Created Me to Be

From the moment I was born, I struggled with my sexuality. As you
know, my parents wanted me to be a boy, and my little heart understood
the rejection it felt. I disliked being a girl, and the way my father made
comments about my features did not help me in the least to accept my fate.
In many ways, I felt like I came from a different planet. Since I was born a
girl into a household full of girls, it should seem natural to be comfortable

being a girl and to embrace my sexuality as a normal thing. But this was not the case, and for years, the puzzle just did not come together for me.

My sisters seemed to enjoy the whole experience of being girls and all that came along with it. They loved to put on fancy dresses and stare at themselves in the mirror for hours until their makeup was just right and they looked perfect. For me, grooming was a quick affair: Jump in the shower, put on my shirt and pants, comb my short hair; I was ready to go. My mom insisted I wear dresses on Sundays and, of course, the scratchy pantyhose that came along with this ordeal. I felt very uncomfortable and, in some way, believed my mom was torturing me by making me wear all of this unnecessary clothing. The instant I came home from church, I cast off these offensive items and got into my usual attire. What a relief. I felt my body could breathe again.

During my growing-up years, the topic of sex was taboo. My parents were wrapped up in their own issues and never talked with us things that concerned us. This included the subject of sex. It was as if sex didn't exist. So I fumbled along with the physical changes that came along with my sexuality. Nobody talked about anything; nothing was ever explained to me. I figured it was just not important. Because of the dynamics in our household, I dared not ask my mom any questions, and my sisters never talked about sexual things, either.

Actually, I could never figure out if the subject was evil or good. If it was considered evil, it would make sense to stay away from it, as far as the east is from the west. If the subject was good, then it should have been discussed at some point in my younger years. There were some indirect references to sex. Every now and then, my mom would declare she felt like she was being taken advantage of every time my dad would have sexual relations with her. Later on, after I had moved out of the house, my mom often said she had never wanted any children. I figured the reason she let out this bit of information was to share with others that the less she was physically involved with her husband, the less the chance she had of getting pregnant and having another child.

As I grew up, my curiosity about sexual things increased. I wanted to know what everybody talked about behind closed doors. The topic of sexuality was treated like the plague. In the annals of history, we read about towns that were infected with the plague; people avoided them, so as not to catch this deadly disease. Was sex something to be feared and avoided, or was it just not talked about? If not, why not?

Then there were awkward moments when a teacher was supposed to talk about sex and teach us what we needed to know. These talks were even more confusing. They concentrated on the actual physical parts needed to produce a child. We had to watch films about how a baby developed, but this did not give me any information on the subject of sex. Not one of my teachers ever spoke about the consequences of having sex before marriage, the possibility I could contract a sexually transmitted disease, or the horrible emotional pain that would linger after having giving myself to many men. She never mentioned anything about healthy sexuality or what "pure" means.

This left me with sex still being a deep mystery, and I constantly asked myself these questions: Is sex just knowing how to have children? Is this all God wants us to do with sex? Later on, I did put the pieces together and learned what God had in mind when He created us. God created us as sexual beings, and His desire was to create us male and female. He placed a healthy appetite for sex in our DNA. He approves of sex. It is His gift to us, to experience physical and emotional closeness:

> As for you [meaning humankind], be fruitful and increase in number; multiply on the earth and increase upon it. (Genesis 9:7 NIV; this refers to engaging in the act of marriage to have children).

> I have come into my garden, my sister, my [promised] bride; I have gathered my myrrh along with my balsam *and* spice [from your sweet words]. I have eaten my honeycomb with my honey; I have drunk my wine with my milk. Eat, friends; Drink and drink deeply, O lovers." (Song of Solomon 5:1 AMP; Solomon speaking to his bride after the act of marriage)

If you truly understood the metaphors presented in the Song of Solomon, along with their meanings, you might close the book, look at the front cover, and double-check the word inscribed: "Bible"? Yes, God created sex not only for having children, but for the enjoyment of one another.

When I was still living in my parents' home, I always preferred behaving, dressing, and presenting myself very much as a boy. This was, after all, my father's wish: to have a boy. I did not want to flaunt myself as a girl in front of him, and this seemed to make his rejection of me somewhat easier. My father's constant teasing and inappropriate word play made me feel ashamed and very uncomfortable. I had no idea why he said these things to me. He said them repeatedly, over and over again, throughout my life. I finally came to the conclusion I just was an awful creature, and anyone was entitled to do with me as they wished and talk about any way they wanted.

One day, I finally realized why my mom always told me that all I was good for was to be a prostitute, and why my dad made such crude remarks concerning my physical body. What happened to me on that fateful day cemented a lie in my heart and twisted my sexuality for years to come. I was looking in the trunk of my father's car and discovered his pornographic magazines. They were right there, for all eyes to see. It almost seemed as if my dad wanted me to find them, to let me know his idea of how a woman should look. I knew about these magazines because the boys at school talked about them all the time. My curiosity was sparked, and I wanted to see for myself what these boys and my dad looked at.

As I leafed through the pages, I was horrified at what I saw. Actually, the seductive poses and alluring pictures of the women did not impact me at all. What horrified me were the beautiful faces, the flawless bodies, and the feminine appearance of each woman on the pages in front of me. I tossed the magazine back into the trunk and slammed it shut.

A few days later, I was home alone and wandered into my parents' bedroom. My plan was just to look around, not really snoop, but just to explore the room, which was off-limits to me. There were times my mom would order me to get this or that from her nightstand or dresser, and I would quickly run and do her bidding. It did not bother me not to have access to my parents' bedroom. After all, I enjoyed my privacy when I was in my own bedroom.

On this particular day, however, I had an inner urge to go and see this mystical world up close. This room held some kind of secret, I thought, so

I went ahead and opened the door. The first piece of furniture I saw was the massive bed. My mom told me I was born at home, and now I stared, as if for the first time, at this bed where I was not only born, but most likely conceived, as well. The idea that my parents were sexually involved repulsed me. In my mind, I tried to answer some questions: Was my dad drunk the very night I was conceived? Would my mom later declare that, once again, she felt like she was taken advantage of by my dad? Another thought came rushing into my mind: *When my dad would have sexual relations with my mom, would he think about the women from the magazine?* My stomach churned. I was repulsed and ashamed of my dad, and a deep sadness settled in my heart. I felt like I had lost something.

In my parents' bedroom was a full-length mirror. I walked over to it and took a good look at myself, fully dressed, from top to bottom, and examined every inch of my body. The pictures I had seen in the magazine a few days earlier began rolling through my mind. I was about eleven years old at the time, and suddenly it hit me: No wonder my mom keeps telling me I am ugly, good for one thing only, and that I will one day stand on the street and sell my body as a prostitute. It's true. She's right. I don't look anything like these women or these young girls. If my dad looks at these women, and he is after all a man, no man will ever look at me or desire me. Now I knew why my dad used crude remarks concerning my unsightly body. He was just pointing out what I really was: not lovely, not beautiful.

My heart panicked, and I saw my future fall apart right in front of my eyes. A deep sadness gripped my heart, and all I wanted to do was to crawl into a corner and never come out again. By this time in my life, one other sexual event had distorted my sexuality. It refashioned my mind about sexual things and damaged my heart. My thoughts about sexuality were completely warped and distorted.

As I stormed into my bedroom, my mind flashed back to a day when I was about seven years old. What happened to me then had drastic consequences in my life and led me to make terrible choices. Satan, the opportunist, held me in shackles for years. Another girl brought me into her bedroom and touched me and encouraged me to touch her. In my mind, I knew what we were doing was wrong. Shame, guilt, embarrassment, and feelings of being utterly exposed and extremely vulnerable washed over me, all at the same time.

On the other hand, my heart felt so lonely. These secret meetings continued for some time, and in some bizarre way, my heart no longer felt neglected and alone. The love I was given was inappropriate. Not only was my sexuality awakened way too soon, but my feelings toward females changed, as well. I became very aware of my same-sex attraction, and this led to future choices and activities. I felt so much guilt, and for years, a great battle raged within my heart. But the battle inside of my heart to forgive or not to forgive this girl and myself was greater still. Somewhere deep inside, I kind of knew I had to forgive her for leading me down the wrong road, for using an emotionally neglected girl and introducing her to inappropriate sexual practices. It required God to meet me deep down in my heart, and this did not happen until many years later.

I did not know at eleven years old, as I stormed into my room after my secret visit to my parents' bedroom, that later, on two more occasions, my body would have to endure being inappropriately touched by others. First, when I was thirteen, a man sexually abused me while I was delivering a meal to his house. I felt so trapped. There was no way out for me, nobody to help me escape. While the activity went on, my future rolled before my eyes once again.

So this is what it feels like to have a man just do whatever he wants with you. These were my thoughts. From that day forward, every time I was in the presence of this man, my heart constricted, and the shame just about overwhelmed me. Who could I tell? Who would believe me? Who was my protector? The voices were silent, and my emotional heart hid further and further back in the dark attic corner, shivering and crying, wanting it all to stop somehow.

After graduating from school at the tender age of fifteen, I attended nursing college. I lived life as if there was no tomorrow. Beer, wine, and hard drinks were my best friends. I often found myself with someone, anyone, at a bar drinking the night away. By that time, I gave myself sexually to whoever wanted to have me. It never crossed my mind that this was wrong. The shame was replaced by numbness, and a kind of tuning-out went on at the time.

One night, a bar owner asked me to come up to his office. I didn't give it a thought. After all, these people were my friends, and he probably just wanted to talk. The moment the door closed behind me, I knew what his real intentions were: to humiliate and embarrass me. The sexual acts he performed in front of me while I stood there, exposed, frightened me so much, I believed my very life was in danger. That day, I lost all feeling, and my heart turned to stone. I went through the motions as I continued with my wicked sexual life. My future was set, and from here on out, I would choose accordingly; there was no turning back.

The men I gave myself to promised to care for my heart, but in the end, they only used me to satisfy themselves. My life became a cycle of sex, and rather than stand on the street and collect money from men, I just gave it away for free. I could not bring myself to admit that no man would actually pay for my services. So I just gave it away. I could not risk being without a man.

These parts of my journey have been the most difficult to tell. The events that happened to me changed everything from what God had planned in the area of my sexuality. When all these things occurred, I made a vow in my heart to never, ever tell a soul about what had happened to me and what I had done. The shame, guilt, and sorrow for the choices I had made were too great, and by this time, I hated who I was, the horrible creature I had become. My mind and heart were so confused.

As life went on, I could no longer differentiate whether I was actually the victim or the instigator. Satan really used my pain to destroy me. He distorted the facts in my mind, accused me as the guilty party, and filled my heart with fear. It was best to take my secrets to the grave with me. Shame kept me from getting help from anyone. Who could I trust with my confusing story? And who would believe me in the first place? I was no longer what God had created me to be, and sex became my substitute for relationships.

The Sexual Developmental Stages

Contrary to what you may have been taught, sexual development has several stages, beginning with early childhood and continuing to the time we leave this earth. As a child begins to grow and mature physically, emotionally, and spiritually, the sexual process goes on behind the scenes, mostly unnoticed. Our sexuality, however, also needs to grow and mature to be whole and to fully enjoy this part of our life.

Developmental stages are defined by milestones. We achieve these milestones as we move from one level of achievement to the next. The final goal is to be fully mature in this area of sexuality. Just as children can recognize Mom and Dad and learn how to walk, they will similarly experience their own connection with their body and sexuality. I would like to briefly draw your attention to these milestones or stages. The development of your sexual health depends on how you handle each stage.

The Infant and Young Toddler Stage

When we talk about development and stages of our sexuality, we need to begin at the Infant and Young Toddler Stage. An infant is considered to be birth to one year of age, and the Toddler Stage follows. During this period of time, we experience positive physical contact by being held, kissed, snuggled, and tickled. Infants and toddlers are probably the most held group in the sexual development stages because they are unable to help themselves. Feeding, changing diapers, and holding the infant and toddler are all activities involving some kind of touch. If these touches comfort the child emotionally and physically, then the experiences produce a connection and a bond. If the bond is established early a solid foundation for sexual intimacy down the road will be the outcome. A good foundation is needed and is very important in creating a healthy sexual life.

Before I continue with this subject, I would like to take a quick look at three heart connection points so each of us can familiarize ourselves with how to establish this foundation. Healthy sexuality depends on how well and how tight we are connected emotionally with others, especially when we are very young children.

The Three Heart Connection Points

You may have heard the expression "attachment bond." This connection is formed while babies are in the womb. This is an emotional bond the baby forms with Mom, and at the same time, Mom establishes one with her child. This happens even before she holds her baby for the first time. If at any time, Mom has thoughts of not wanting the child, or the child hears voices outside of the womb expressing they are not wanted or wished for, the unborn child may no longer be able to form an emotional connection.

This can result in bonding difficulties with Mom and Dad and a lifetime of struggling to connect with others emotionally.

In most cases, moms and dads form a deep emotional bond with their infant. This is done in a very natural way, with no instructions, and it's actually quite simple. We cannot, however, stop bonding at the infant and toddler stages. You may ask why we need to form attachment bonds at all. Do we need to connect our emotional heart to someone in the first place? You see, God placed in our hearts a deep need to be connected emotionally on a heart level with someone. Children, kids, teens, adults, and even seniors have this deep need inside of them. What is the purpose of having an emotional connection with someone? The purpose of giving ourselves emotionally and completely to someone is that, in turn, the other person will want to establish the same emotional connection with us. From the first day we were born till the last day we leave this earth, we need a person to emotionally connect with us. There are three connecting points we need to apply in order to achieve this heart connection.

Have you ever heard the expression, "I give you my whole heart"? What does it actually mean? It means you have chosen to emotionally connect with the person. You have formed an attachment bond, and now you are one with them. Isn't this what we long for when we get married? So what are the three connecting or bonding methods we need in our lives? Keep in mind that we only receive them in the very early stages when we are infants and toddlers.

If you have the blessing of being a parent yourself, or you have the privilege of caring for someone else's child, you'll find yourself doing these three things naturally, without even thinking. The first connection point is when we hold another. We hold babies all the time, and when we hold a child, he or she feels you, and you feel the child. The simple act of connecting this way involves touch. The closeness you both feel will be accelerated if you allow your heart to come to the little one you are holding.

What does it mean to allow your heart to come to the child? Let me give you an example: When I held my children in my arms, I thought specific things like, "Thank you, Jesus, for allowing me to be a parent. Fill my heart with love. I want to nurture this child. He is the most important thing in the world to me." In essence, I was celebrating the child in my thoughts. These thoughts warm and fill our heart, and in return, warm and fill the heart of the child. This, along with holding them, establishes a connection. When you add positive thoughts in your heart, the touch is magnified many times over.

The second way we connect emotionally while holding another is by looking deep into their eyes. This is exactly what we do when we hold an infant. At first, this can be a bit challenging because the lights and the ceiling fan are more interesting to them than you are, but that will change if you initiate the eye contact. Once the eyes have locked, the connection is made. This activity can relax both mother and child to where time almost stands still. Again, just as we continue with touching or holding, the thoughts also need to continue reaching the heart of the child in order to give more power to the activity.

The third way we connect with an infant is by talking to them. So now we are holding them, looking into their eyes, and our voice becomes the soothing, warm connection that both need. When my kids were little, I held them close to my heart, looked into their eyes, and told them all the things I wanted them to hear. I said, "Look at your long eyelashes; you are beautiful, my little princess." I saw the joy on my children's faces as I held them in my arms. I was often surprised I did not get an answer back from my kids because we were so engaged with one another, truly connected on a heart level. The enjoyment we receive from this activity is priceless because in those moments, we achieve a heart connection.

Any one of the three heart connections can be done separately; however, if all three are administered at the same time, the bond is very strong. The heart will not only relax; it will enjoy and feel at the same time. I have often recommended this prescription to my clients: to take three pills each day, that is, to enjoy, to relax, and to feel.

Here is a quick summary of the three connection points:

- First: We need to be held by someone who loves us deeply, and together we can let our hearts naturally come to each other. In these moments, we not only feel loved, cherished, and valued; we have a much deeper emotional connection with each other. We literally feel each other's hearts.
- Second: We need someone who takes the time to look deeply and honestly into our eyes, and we, in turn, need to do the same to

them, for the purpose of having an intimate heart connection. Only then can the heart truly relax. It's almost like seeing into each other's soul. This connection is beyond description.

- Third: We need to connect with someone by talking with them in a soothing voice, so we can enjoy each other's company.

If we utilize these three connecting points throughout our whole life, we will not get lonely, feel rejected, or struggle with depression. We will feel chosen, paid attention to, joined together, and treasured.

Did my parents connect their hearts to mine, using these three connection points, when I was an infant and young toddler? Did I connect my heart to theirs? My answer: "Most likely, not." I'm sure I was held and all of my physical needs fulfilled, but was I truly nurtured? Nurturing is not only to take care of someone's physical needs; it also includes connecting on a deep emotional level. It's like a link we establish with another person because we feel totally one with them. As already mentioned, this linking process starts while we are still in the womb.

When my mom was pregnant with me, she was in her late thirties. Having another child was a challenge, indeed. The main issue wasn't being pregnant; another child was not in her plans. The news of her pregnancy was only celebrated by the possibility I would be the boy my father longed for. After I was born and the doctor announced my gender, the celebration stopped. As already stated, Jesus revealed to me many years later that my heart was actually wounded while I was still in my mother's womb. Why was my heart damaged and filled with pain before I was even born? Jesus laid it out for me to see. I was rejected in the womb, and then I was rejected after I was born. My heart could not emotionally link with my mom's or my dad's heart, so the three of us continued our relationship with detached hearts.

The Toddler, Preschooler, and Kindergarten Stages

During the Toddler Stage, it is not uncommon to see little ones touching their private areas while having a diaper change or enjoying a warm bath. Toddlers love to run around naked, in a true sense, they celebrate unashamedly the freedom of who God created them to be. These early explorations are a vital part of children getting to know their personal, private parts. The reaction from the adult will set the stage for how children view themselves and their sexuality. If parents use a harsh voice or discourage this activity, or if their facial expression shows disapproval, their child's first lesson in sexuality is already distorted. On the flip side, if parents don't act angry or surprised, it fosters a healthy acceptance of the child's sexuality. The best way to handle these kinds of happenings is to gently remove the child's hand, distract the child, and offer a different activity.

You may remember a time when your parents told you no in response to something you wanted to do. You may not have taken the no seriously, or you may have wanted to obey. Another response will often take place: The no can spark curiosity, and the child then seeks to discover the mystery behind the command. The longing to get to the bottom of why an activity is so strictly forbidden can actually push a child in the direction that is being avoided.

If sexual abuse of the child has taken place while in this stage of life, most parents will not understand their reaction: tears, sudden withdrawal, or shy behavior. Instead of exploring the depth of the meaning of these changes in behavior, the situation will be handled very practically. The child is considered to be going through a phase, and this will not allow the truth to be found out.

Years ago, when I taught children's church or Sunday school, I could almost always identify the kids who had been sexually molested. I would take them aside at times and just let them talk. I wanted them to know there are safe people who can be trusted, people who can advocate for them and call for help. When sexual misconduct was disclosed, I notified the authorities. I would present the child's case as best as I could, so that the sexual activity would stop and the child would have a safe place to live.

During the Toddler Stage, children become aware of being male and female for the first time. This awareness is referred to as gender identity, where children accept the fact they are either a girl or a boy. Parents offer activities to their children to foster their maleness or femaleness. As the child transitions to the preschool years, parents should teach them about keeping their private parts to themselves and not to expose them in public. They should also understand that under no circumstances should anyone, including a family member, ever touch their private sexual parts.

Preschoolers look to their parents for instructions and hear in their voice, or observe their body language, how the parent views sexual things. If parents were sexually violated, their sexuality is not on the course God designed for them. Actually, their whole identity has changed, and now their view about their sexuality runs backwards. These parents may scold or smack the hand of the child, or say harsh words, if they find the preschooler touching themselves on their private areas or if they want to run around the house naked. Children will then feel ashamed, not because they did anything shameful, but because Mom or Dad humiliated them, thereby creating these new, confused messages and feelings.

As time progresses, children will become curious about where babies come from, especially if they see their mommy pregnant with a new family member. It is wise to stick with the truth and give enough information as is appropriate to the age of the child. If the child is still very young, you could say, "Because Mommy and Daddy love each other very much, another boy or girl will join our family."

I cannot really remember if I was allowed to freely express and discover my sexuality, or if I was chastised if I ever ventured to touch my body or run around the house naked. It is my guess I was not cuddled, kissed, or held just for the joy of it when I was an infant, toddler, and kindergartener. By the time I reached the Kindergarten Stage, I had learned that sexual things were taboo in our household, not to be mentioned or talked about. The body was just a vehicle in which to live on this earth. I had no idea what sexuality was all about, and I was actually frightened to have anyone see me without clothes.

When my children were in this stage, the question as to where babies come from arose. Both Mike and I wanted our kids to learn about their sexuality as God had intended it, and we came up with the following solution to sharing God's plan with them.

Prepare the Way for the Truth: A White Box from God

In the beginning, when our children's curiosity became obvious, we took each child aside separately in a relaxed, comfortable setting and introduced them to God and His plan for sexuality. Because we have twins who are a boy and a girl, we chose to give the instruction as related to their gender. Realizing all kinds of questions could come early on, my husband and I came up with a plan to delay the truth but always be straight and honest with them. When the time came and we could no longer delay the talk, we went ahead without trepidation. I spoke to our daughter, and Dad had his conversation with our son. Both children, however, felt comfortable coming to either one of us to share what was said during their private sessions with the other parent. It has been many years since then, but I will do my best to recollect our conversations with our kids.

After we found a good spot where we would be undisturbed, I began, "I'm so glad you want to know where babies come from. I cannot wait to tell you everything God wants you to know on the subject. You see, this is all in God's plan for your life and one of the gifts He will give to you. But gifts are special things, and we don't get them all the time. This gift from God will be given to you at just the right time. You will need to wait a few more birthdays to be ready for this special gift. But don't worry; God will not forget."

By now, my daughter was excited. After all, it's not every day we receive a special gift from God. Your talk about sexuality will go much better if, at some point, the child has been introduced to Jesus. Our children saw us praying, going to church, and reading the Bible, and we read many Bible stories to them. God was a natural part of our life, and it was easy to bring Him into this important conversation. After all, it was God's idea to create us as sexual beings in the first place.

At this point, our daughter waited expectantly for what would come next. Carefully choosing my words, I continued, "When you are all grown up, you may want to get married. One day, you will meet a young man, and you will not be able to imagine ever being without him. The two of you will want to be with each other all the time. Eventually, he will ask you to be his wife, and the two of you will get married. You know, at every wedding, the bride and groom receive many presents. You and your new husband will also receive many gifts, and on this special day, your wedding day, God will give the two of you His special present. The present He has for you will sit on the table with all of the other gifts. It is a bright white box tied with a beautiful sparkling white bow. Can you imagine? This white box is from God, and it is for you and your husband to have and to enjoy for as long as you are man and wife."

At this point, we talked about what happened at our wedding, the gifts we received and the fun we had opening up all the packages. I also included God's Word in our conversation by reading the account in John 2:1–2 (NIV): "On the third day a wedding took place at Cana in Galilee. Jesus's mother was there, and Jesus and his disciples had also been invited to the wedding."

For some reason, her quest for an answer to the original question was forgotten or no longer needed. Knowing that God would prepare a gift for the couple and give it to them at their wedding seemed to be more exciting.

As time went on and my children grew older, the old curiosity was sparked again. By now, my kids were in their elementary grades, and they needed to know more about that white box. This time, the box became the focal point of the conversation, so the dialogue continued where we left off.

I said, "As the wedding celebration slows down a bit, you and your husband will begin opening your presents, but this beautiful white box sitting on the gift table will not be unwrapped for all eyes to see."

"Why not?" my daughter asked. "Don't the guests want to see the gift God gave to us?"

"I don't think so," I answered. "You see, this gift is different from all the others; it needs to be opened by you and your husband in private, when you are alone with each other."

I went on to explain, "The people at the wedding who are already married received their own white box from God. They know what's inside. All of the single people have to wait for their own wedding to receive their special gift from God, just like you and your husband had to wait."

Again, my daughter focused on this mystery gift and its secret contents, yet she was satisfied with the information I had provided. Was it the word, *secret*, the secret that the box held, the reason she did not press for more information? Or perhaps she was satisfied with the anticipation of receiving this box, and that caused her to be willing to wait for the answers. I was pleased we would have another conversation at a more appropriate time when her ears and her heart were ready to receive the full information. Still, the puzzled look on her face revealed it would not be long before she needed to find out about the real contents of this white box.

When my kids reached their tweens, just before their official teens, the physical changes in their bodies became evident. It now seemed time to finish the story of the white box from God. For some reason, the children were mature and fully capable of understanding the next step and knowing the depth of what God would be giving them.

Again, we spoke to our children in a private, relaxed setting. Once again, I picked up the story where we left off. The wedding activities are over, and the bride and groom are ready to retire to their private room with the white box in hand.

I spoke these words: "Can you imagine how exhausted you two will be at this moment, after all the months of planning and preparing for the wedding? The day has finally arrived, and the excitement of now being husband and wife will linger on. The time has come to leave the party, where lots of people have wished you well and cheered you on. They saw you cut the cake, became teary-eyed as they watched your first dance, and witnessed the two of you giving each other lots of kisses. What a whirlwind of activity. Now it is just the two of you, together, beginning your honeymoon. Your mind is still processing the day, and like a blender, it's all mixed up. You are both overwhelmed by all the gifts you've received, but never for one moment have you forgotten the special white box you brought with you to the room. It is now sitting on the table, waiting to be opened." The moment to reveal its contents came.

Purposefully, honestly, with an unashamed voice, looking into my daughter's eyes, I unfolded the act of marriage between a husband and wife. The mystery took on new meaning because now the gift was open for her to see and understand.

How beautiful it was to walk with our younger children on this journey, a journey we had not taken with our older child. Not only were we able to explain the act of marriage to them, but we also shared with them about their own development in the sexual area. From the moment we revealed the gift from God my husband continued to take our son aside and instruct him on what he could expect in the future as to the development of his body. In the same way, I shared with our daughter the changes she needed to be prepared for and explained what her future would hold as her body continued to change.

Having the opportunity to describe our sexuality on this personal level is very rewarding, indeed. Never did I dream it would be this easy, especially since my upbringing was not anything like this. Were we perfect parents? No, not at all, but our intentions were to be honest with our kids, no matter what the subject.

Sometime later, our son came to me and asked me a very important question: "Mom, if I decide to open up God's gift before I get married, what will happen to me?"

I stopped everything I was doing, looked into his eyes, and said, "Son, I want you to remember two things. First, God always loves you, no matter what. Second, I will always love you."

I also shared with him the principles of asking God to forgive him and to forgive himself. After our conversation, the reality of his question really hit me. I was grateful this subject had come up, and I could once again point my son to God.

The Elementary Stage: Ages Six to Ten

In this stage, media and the social environment begins to influence, shape, and have a role in your child's life. If adults have not become a trusted and reliable resource, information will be gathered from other venues. Children will seek information about sex, reproduction, and male and female differences from outside sources. Anytime outsiders become consultants on the subject of sexual things, chances are the information will be sketchy, inaccurate, and of a person's own interpretation. This creates a false picture of what God planned for our sexual being.

During this stage, our children will be exposed to bad language at school, from friends, TV, and adults. When they hear these words and phrases, they will most likely repeat them without even knowing what they actually mean. Kids learn from modeled behavior and are like little copy machines. Parents should feel comfortable enough to explain a bad word without having to go into detail. Let children understand why you don't want them to use these words.

It's possible your child will have peers who tell jokes and poke fun at one another. Children can actually be deeply hurt if the fun was directed at them and pointed specifically at their sexuality. These off-color jokes, laced with references to body parts and their functions, are very inappropriate and distasteful. Adults need to continue to be good role models and steer their children to a more appropriate fun group. Your child's natural curiosity is not an evil thing. It is wisely planned and designed by God Himself.

When I reached this stage, my little ears heard bits and pieces of how sexuality and sexual activities were viewed. My mom declared sex as the duty of a wife to be endured, something we have to do if we want children, a necessary evil women just have to get used to. As mentioned previously, I never enjoyed my body and my sexuality because I knew I was supposed to be a boy. My first experience of having been sexually abused took place in this stage, and everything about my sexuality changed. Deep shame and confusion filled my heart. I could no longer stand the thought of being exposed by anyone, and my blanket became my best friend, comforting and soothing my hurting heart. From this day on, my sexuality was completely twisted and headed in the wrong direction.

The Puberty Stage

There comes a day when puberty comes knocking at the door, and your child's world changes. Children know, without consulting their parents, something important is happening in their body, in their life. At the same time, these drastic changes are a bit scary. All of a sudden, their physical body begins to change right in front of them, and young boys and girls wonder if these changes are normal.

Kids, especially teens, compare themselves to their peers. If this outward transformation does not happen to their bodies at the same time it happens to other kids their age, they can get very anxious. Parents need to understand and dial into the heart of their growing child by listening, supporting, and offering gentle words of comfort. Our world is filled with many people, and each one is a unique individual, handcrafted by God Himself. This is a good message for the parent to offer at this time.

If children are prepared to expect these changes, all there is left to do is teach them how these changes relate to the future. After all, these changes can impact their life, as now the body of a girl is ready to conceive and carry a baby. The body of a boy is able to father a child. It is very important your teenager has a good understanding of these changes. If your child is sensitive, shy, embarrassed, or intimidated, take the initiative and begin the dialogue.

In our day and age, changes to the body seem to occur earlier than they did for our grandparents. Nine-year-old girls start their monthly cycle, and eleven-year-old boys are growing facial hair. This gives us all the more reason to talk to our kids about sexual things early on. Don't leave the sex talk up to the school system. It is your privilege to be the one to introduce your child to the marvelous world of their sexuality.

Puberty was filled with shame and embarrassing thoughts for me. By now, my second experience of having been sexually abused had become part of my already hurting and damaged heart. I hated sexuality and all it stood for. I hated my life and could no longer bury the images of my sexual activities. My heart hurt, and my self-image was anything but good. My resolution was to just go ahead and do whatever I wanted sexually, because I was used and exploited, second-hand goods. My mind could not wrap itself around the thought that sex might be a wonderful gift from God. Sex to me was something others just took, or I gave without strings attached.

The Final Stage: Sexual Maturity

Exactly when we reach the stage of sexual maturity cannot really be calculated in years. It is a process similar to the way the Bible identifies our spiritual age, by identifying various spiritual stages. As already mentioned, these stages are mile markers that help measure the process till the final results have been achieved. Puberty can actually be considered as the Sexual Mature Stage because males and females can now reproduce; however, just the ability to reproduce is not a sign of sexual maturity. Maturity also entails responsibility, and in the area of our sexual being, this is quite another story.

Our sexual desires and appetites naturally awaken when we are old enough and our body comes to full maturity, in the physical sense. We all have a natural sex drive, or none of us would want a mate. This strong drive has to be fulfilled by someone. Only in the marriage covenant are we to fulfill our each other's sexual needs. As a single person, you need to have a lot of self-control. It is for this reason Paul warned that not everyone is able to stay single and also pure at the same time. He said it is better to marry than to burn in the flesh. Everyone is responsible for placing their sex drive under God's control; otherwise, we will succumb to our sexual passions and get involved in sinful practices. Paul wrote about this to the Corinthian church, when he said:

Now to the unmarried and the widow I say: It is good for them to stay unmarried, as I do. But if they cannot control themselves, they should marry, for it is better to marry than to burn with passion. (1 Corinthians 7:8–9 NIV)

When young Joseph was at Potiphar's house, he was a fully grown man with the natural sex drive God had given him. Potiphar's wife longed to be with Joseph and wanted him to go to bed with her. She made advances toward Joseph daily, but he resisted. He made it clear she was not for him because she was another man's wife. Well, that did not mean a lot to Potiphar's wife. She was determined and set on her course. One day, she would not take no for an answer. What did Joseph do? He fled the house; he ran away. Did he not feel the need to have sexual relations with Potiphar's wife? Yes, he probably did. He was a healthy male, after all. Then how could this young, healthy male resist her offer?

…because you are his wife., How then could I do this great evil and sin against God [and your husband]?" (Genesis 39:9b AMP).

Joseph knew something we have forgotten. He did not cave into his sexual desires because his heart was set on pleasing God. By holding fast to God, he was not only able to resist; he was able to set aside his personal feelings and needs. This is self-control in action. Self-control is needed for unmarried individuals. They need to be self-disciplined and trust God rather than give in to sexual passions and desires:

It is God's will that you should be sanctified: that you should avoid sexual immorality; that each of you should learn to control your own body in a way that is holy and honorable, not in passionate lust like the pagans, who do not know God; and that in this matter no one should wrong or take advantage of a brother of sister. The Lord will punish all those who commit such sins, as we told you and warned you before. (1 Thessalonians 4:3–6 NIV)

By the way, intercourse outside of marriage is not the only form of sexual immorality God had in mind when He commanded us to stay away from immorality. Sexual immorality includes all stimulation that involves our sexual parts. We must rely heavily on the influence of the Holy Spirit in our life. Self-control over our sexual desires and passions is not an easy task, but for most of us, this is only a temporary state, as we seek to marry and enjoy sexual activity with our spouse. For some, the single life is a permanent choice, where celibacy and self-control have to be established. A deep intimate relationship with God is a must in order to stay focused on Him and bring glory and honor to His name. Only then can we overcome our natural sexual desires.

One day, we will give an account to God for all of our activities. Believers in Christ Jesus know God has already forgiven us. We are, however, commanded to confess our sins before Him (1 John 1:9). Confession is simply being in agreement with God about having violated His moral principles and admitting that we have sinned. We also need to forgive ourselves and make a new commitment to stay pure and live within the boundaries God has set for us. Sex was given to us by God for procreation and for pleasure. On the other hand, it is not self-seeking. It is designed to meet the other person's needs. God instituted marriage when He created people with male and female sexuality (Genesis 1:27). He alone possesses the authority to define marriage and determine the proper use of sexuality. He intended that all human sexual relationships take place exclusively within the bond of marriage. It is a lifelong union between a man and a woman.

By this time, I had been sexually abused for the third time and did not have the opportunity to reach the Sexually Mature Stage. For years, I remained the little girl struggling with sex and all that comes along with it. It had become the same as it was for my mom: "Sex is something we do because the man needs it." There were brief moments in my sexual life, especially after I was married, where I saw a glimmer of how beautiful and rewarding a healthy sexual life could be. I failed to grab hold of it, however, and it slipped away from me. After Mike said, "I do," he had no idea of my past and the damaged little girl he had now inherited. Without knowing my issues, he was always a gentleman, seeking not his own pleasure, but desiring to meet my needs. If only my heart could engage, but it was so far away.

When God's Gift Is Violated

Sex is not about taking but rather about giving. When people have been sexually violated, a lot has been taken from them. They have been robbed. Everything about their sexuality changes, and the devastating effects linger for years. The suffering is like a deep pain they carry all alone in their heart. Neither medicine nor ointment can cure it. Not even the loving, caring hearts of precious loved ones can reach it. For this reason, most sexually abused people keep the events a secret, hidden deep in their hearts, believing this is the best way to handle what happened. Sharing the horror of the experience seems like a big risk. Explaining what they felt and describing the aftermath is even more challenging.

Anytime we experience damage from another, pain is created in our heart. The following abusive situations have been identified as the greatest kinds of pain you may endure:

The number one pain a person can experience is torture of any kind. This includes satanic rituals. Years ago, I had the privilege of sitting down with a lady who was forced to participate in this kind of activity when she was a little girl. This involvement created a severely damaged heart, and at the beginning of our time together, it seemed impossible that her heart could ever be healed. The inner pain from her past haunted her day and night, with no peace in sight. Her healing journey started the first day we spent together as she gave her heart to Jesus; however, her battle to stay free spanned several years. The enemy was fierce. He had convinced her heart she could never be forgiven for all she had done. He had hijacked her mind by holding her thoughts in constant terror of past memories. For some time, she continued to struggle to set aside the knife she had been using for years to inflict deep wounds to her body. In many ways she was like a prisoner longing to be set free. Before Jesus came into her life her past had become her future. But Satan forgot something. She now belonged to Jesus:

> Little children (believers, dear ones), you are of God *and* you belong to Him and have [already] overcome them [the agents of the antichrist]; because He who is in you is greater that he (Satan) who is in the world [of sinful mankind]. (1 John 4:4 AMP)

The second worst pain people can experience is to have their life threatened. For example, if someone were to hold a gun to your head or threatened to kill you, or if you were in a war or found yourself in a hostage situation, to name just a few. This painful event is seared into your memory, and if God does not meet you deep inside in your heart, a life of extreme fear and anxiety in in your future.

I have listened to people who were able to recall their ordeal years later, and they were still literally shaking, extremely anxious, and restless. Memories of someone wanting to kill them could not be processed and didn't make any kind of sense. The threat still seemed to continue, even though the event happened years before. Such people never feel safe with anyone, and with time, they withdraw into a shell. Soldiers who knew there was the possibility they would have to take someone's life are stuck. For some, it actually came down to either letting the enemy live and be killed, or killing them and staying alive. As the war went on, they lost something precious: their self-respect. Many men and women recoil inside when others call them a hero because, to them, doing these unmentionable things is anything but heroic.

God knows how the heart feels and the wounds it carries. In our world right now, God may permit what He hates, for the moment. Why? None of us knows why, and God does not always tell us why. As mentioned previously, when we ask why, in essence we challenge God to explain Himself to us. But God does not have to explain Himself to any of us. We cannot forget that when God created the world, all was perfect until sin changed us. We were given a free will to choose to love God or not to love Him, to obey Him or not to obey Him. We chose to live apart from God and do our own thing. Humankind chose not to obey God, and the world changed forever. Tame animals became wild. Earthquakes rattled the ground and destroyed people and their property. Fires broke out and claimed everything in their path. Floods washed away precious memories and uprooted treasured relationships.

This was not what God created. This was what we became through choices that free will allows. Adam and Eve chose sin by exercising their free will. Could God have stopped them? Yes, but He would have had to take away their free will. It is the same with us. If our life is threatened, in order for God to stop this terrible thing from happening, He would have to take away the free will of the person harming you. If God took away one person's free will, He would have to take it away from all of us, for He is just. With sin, everything changed, and to top it all off, Satan is the ruler of this world. Yet if we call on God, He will step into our great pain, cover it with His peace, and bring real freedom to our heart. God never wastes any pain.

At this point, our question should change from why to what, and depending how spiritually mature we are, this can be done. "Heavenly Father, what do You want me to do with this event in my life? What do You want me to see, or learn, and take away from it?"

I have read accounts of soldiers and others, and personally witnessed God restoring their shredded and tortured hearts. Even individuals who had to endure enormous suffering from the Holocaust now live life in complete peace. True freedom reigns in their hearts. Why? Because God is greater and more powerful than all evil combined. He is stronger than any person driven by the enemy to use their free will and inflict terror upon humankind.

The third worst pain a person can experience is being sexually abused or raped, especially if the event was endured for a long period of time. People who suffer through these kinds of events are changed forever. Only God is able to disconnect, heal, and restore what was taken, stolen, and destroyed.

Countless women and men have shared with me the terrible effects of being raped or sexually abused. In most of these stories, the violation took place in their own homes, by their parents or a relative, the very people who were supposed to protect them and keep them secure. After the first incident, others took advantage of them by repeating the same degrading acts. When I looked into their eyes, I saw horror and disgust. When the pain from the damage came to the surface, it was almost like the person was vomiting. Several individuals did grab a wastebasket and dry-heaved as the pain and memory of the event surfaced.

Their sexuality was changed forever, and in a sense, the natural cycle of the sexual development stages never had the opportunity to continue. In essence, their sexuality was awakened too early, before reaching the Sexually Mature Stage. Even after marriage, the sexual area will not function well. They are still stuck in the Infant or Toddler Stage of their sexual development. One husband shared with me that it felt like his wife is like a stiff board just lying there, enduring the process, not able to enjoy it or share the experience with him. The losses she experienced the day everything changed were many. If it were not for Jesus, who is willing and ready to give back what was stolen, she would have no idea how to get healing in the area of her sexuality.

The fourth deepest pain a person can experience is the pain of adultery. This is a deep betrayal, and the resulting pain and damage can be too deep to bear. Countless couples have confessed going astray and find themselves in a sexual relationship with someone outside of their marriage. The pain and destruction they cause themselves and their spouse can be clearly seen in their eyes. Their inner heart and soul were ripped apart. Can God step into this great pain? Yes, He can and He will, if we allow Him to make something beautiful out of this heap of ashes. One question may have surfaced in your mind as you read these last two points. I asked myself this question after wrestling with the principle God place before me: Does God require people who were sexually abused to reconcile with their abuser?

Let me first unpack the word *reconciliation*. According to the Cambridge Dictionary,[1] reconciliation is "unifying with a person and forming a friendly relationship with that person again." Reconciliation is an action word; so in essence, one would need to do something to make it happen. There is much misunderstanding between reconciliation and forgiveness. The victim needs to come to a place and eventually forgive the abuser to guard against the root of bitterness and hate and begin their own healing journey. Forgiveness will only change their heart, not the heart of the abuser. The abuser must experience a genuine transformation of heart and character before trust can be restored again or reconciliation is even possible.

This brings us to the following question. Should a sexually abused person reconcile with their abuser? From what I have observed is after the sexual abuse has taken place or has continued for some time, there is a brief moment where the abuser comes to his/her senses and pleads with the victim to reconcile with them. Often the abused wants to give them another chance and against all warning signs begins the process. However all too often the abuser's good intentions weaken and he/she returns to their former ways making reconciliation impossible.

Reconciliation is only possible when the victim can forgive from the heart and set new guidelines to establish trust again and when the abuser genuinely repents and has a transformed heart and new character that proves them to be trustworthy. God does not condone or approve any kind of abuse, but He does call on the sexually abused person to come to a place to forgive them.

I'm not sure about you, but in my case, none of my abusers have come to me and asked me to forgive them. No one has even said, "I'm sorry," and this is the case for most sexually abused individuals. Does God still ask us to forgive them, even if they don't admit to what they have done? Yes, He does. Forgiveness cannot wait until you feel like forgiving because you will never get there. It cannot wait till the other person comes to you because, as already mentioned, this may never happen. We need to forgive as soon as we can. Only then will Satan's power over us be broken, and bitterness and hate will not find its way into our hearts. I know this is easier said than done. Even after I became a believer in Christ Jesus, it still took me years to finally forgive all the individuals who sexually abused me. But we must try. You see, Jesus Himself showed us what to do; He did not wait for those who were crucifying Him to apologize and ask for forgiveness.

We all know trust can be broken in an instant. Rebuilding trust is like building a bridge. It requires someone to put down one brick at a time until the abused person is satisfied. This process can take a long time and requires genuine honesty between the two individuals who want to reconcile. Sometimes, at this stage, the best intentions go out the window. You see, victims need adequate time to have proof the offender is truly sincere. They will place a watchful eye on the offender, who will need to demonstrate to them that they are truly trustworthy.

For instance, take a married couple where one party commits the sin of adultery or has an emotional affair. Both partners need to seek God as to their future. Now that the deed is done, what can the offender give to make everything right again? Nothing. All there is left to do is for the adulterer to ask for forgiveness, and for the betrayed spouse, as soon as he or she can, to grant forgiveness for the pain and consequences her or his spouse caused them. Now if you are such a victim and God clearly directs your steps and asks you to stay in the marriage relationship, then the same formula has to be applied: Forgiveness + Trust = Reconciliation (perfect harmony). Without these elements, a good marriage is not possible.

In the marriage relationship, the spouse who was the adulterer needs to come to his or her spouse and ask specifically what he or she needs to do in order to rebuild trust. The wife may ask her husband to never be alone with a woman. It could be that a husband needs access to his wife's social media and e-mail accounts. If the offender is willing to reconcile, each of these needs or assignments will be a welcome task to be fulfilled to the letter. On the other hand, when adulterers bristle and complain of the freedom they will lose, they most likely had no interest in reconciling in the first place.

Deciding to reconcile or not is entirely God's call. If He does ask you to do this, He will equip you to feel His presence through the process. As you can imagine, I hated my sexual abusers, and I was not able to forgive them for years. When I finally granted complete forgiveness, I spent a lot of time in prayer, asking God what to do next. God met me and spoke to my heart, and I knew exactly what I had to do.

If sexual abuse or rape has taken place, the formula for reconciliation will be the same. God does not require me to be reconciled with my abusers if they haven't asked me to forgive them or are not trustworthy. It would be too dangerous to engage with such an individual again. It is too risky. God does ask of us to truly forgive them from our heart. If, after true forgiveness has taken place, and reconciliation is not possible, God may call on you to pray for their salvation because He died on the cross for them and wants to redeem them, as well.

Areas Where We Have Been Sexually Abused

I said above that the third greatest pain a person can feel is sexual abuse or rape. The heart becomes damaged as a result. When we think about what sexual abuse is, only two thoughts usually flash in our minds: being raped, or being forced by someone to perform sexual acts. These are only two forms of sexual abuse, but the list is much longer and includes much more. Some things mentioned in the following list are familiar to us; others may surprise us.

We have been sexually abused or victimized

- when someone lusted after us or after another. This can damage you and change your view about your own sexuality. For instance, if a man is into pornography, he begins to lust after women, who feel violated, even though they may not know what is really happening. It is the way the man looks at her. I've often asked my husband to trade places with me in a restaurant because I felt the eyes of a man undressing me, and I was extremely uncomfortable and quite embarrassed. A little girl can be damaged by a father who lusts after women.

- when a person has touched us in an inappropriate personal area. These areas should never be touched by anyone. I have heard older individuals recounting memories of being touched by someone while swimming or being lured into the barn. The shame and feelings of being exposed still felt as if the event had just happened yesterday.

- when we have been raped. Rape can also occur on a date if the girl says no, and the man presses ahead anyway, forcing himself on her. Rape is a violent form of sexual abuse and carries with it long-term scars and horrible damage.

- when someone has exposed us to pornographic material of any kind. This begins a process where thoughts about sexual activity turn negative. Porn changes sexuality. I have heard from men who were deeply involved in pornography; after a while, they hated women and loathed them in some way. On the one hand, they lusted after the women on the pages or in the videos, but on the other hand, it made no difference in their behavior. In their minds, the question is, *Why would these women do such a thing?*

- when parents exposed themselves to their children. Unknown to them, the child feels violated and shamed. Throughout history, we find parents who consider it normal to walk around the house in front of their children half-dressed or entirely naked. They never consider the young minds and tender hearts that are not equipped to handle this kind of exposure. Deep feelings of shame enter their young hearts. Also, if other adults expose themselves to children, the damage that occurs is felt for years to come.

- when other children (or teens) have made fun of our private parts. Each of us develops differently, physically, and this includes the development of our sexual parts. Teens are often required to shower with each other, as in gym class. Statements of comparison, or mocking, or making fun of a teen injures them. That teen's thought patterns about their personal sexuality change completely. This kind of teasing can begin while still in the elementary stage. Children can be cruel in falsely evaluating each other's progress through comparison. All too quickly, labels are given: wimpy, little, or whatever suits them to best make fun of private parts and other developmental sexual stages. The child will be devastated for years to come, often right into adulthood.

- when incest was committed against us. No person, close or a distant relative, has the right to take advantage of children in their charge. With incest, fear of telling is instilled in the victim. Relatives get away with sexual abuse for years by making the child keep the secret. When children do tell an adult, they are often not believed because, if it were true, one would have to face a husband, wife, sibling, or other relative who has indeed sexually abused the child. Children often choose not to tell their parents, other family members, or adults outside of the home, for fear of not being believed. They don't feel anyone can protect them.

- when someone has sexually harassed us. A lot has changed in the workforce, and we can be thankful for women who have had the courage to no longer put up with this kind of behavior from male coworkers. However, sexual harassment is not limited to females. Men have also been sexually harassed by women. This is not common and is definitely under-reported. People who are harassed feel violated, and deep shame settles in their heart and creates a lot of pain.

As already mentioned, this list is not extensive by any means. It is a beginning for us to consider the different areas where sexual abuse can occur. These events can have devastating consequences, often felt for a lifetime. The sufferer, in many cases, is ashamed and may have even made a vow to themselves to never, ever tell anyone of these humiliating experiences. That's what I did.

When a person is sexually abused, and it is their first sexual encounter, even if the event is not violent, the person's sexuality is awakened. I shared with you earlier, God has a timetable for waking up our sexuality, and if this takes place at a very young age, everything from that day on will in some way run backwards. It's like a motor running the opposite direction to its design. I have encountered many women who were sexually abused as girls by other women, as it was in my case. Because a woman woke up their sexuality and brought them to arousal, their sexual desire from that moment on was for women instead of men. Men have said that after a man sexually abused them while they were still little boys, their sexual desires shifted from that moment to men. The nature of a man's first arousal continues to be stirred in their bodies. In this case, it was a man who stimulated and woke up the sexuality of the boy. When we have been sexually violated, things change forever, like the life of this nine-year-old foster child.

While we were foster parents, our life occasionally intersected with other foster parents. In one of these meetings, a foster mom shared with me the saddest story of a nine-year-old girl who briefly lived in their home. As the woman recalled the story, I could see in her eyes how this foster child, and what had happened to her, deeply affected her heart.

This woman's family had been selected to foster this girl. Theirs was a close-knit family, and they had lots of love to give to the children who were placed in their home. Shortly after the girl arrived, a discovery was made. The very first evening, as the family settled in the living room with popcorn to enjoy a movie together, something out of the ordinary happened. Sitting on the couch were the foster mom, the foster father, their daughter, and the foster girl. The movie began, and this nine-year-old girl began to touch herself.

Nobody yelled; no one yanked her hands away. The foster mom just got up from the couch and gently took the young girl by the hand and asked her to please come with her. In the girl's room, this foster mom held her and loved her and told her in a soft voice why she should not touch herself in this way in public. They rejoined the family, and for the rest of the evening, this girl leaned her head on her foster mom's shoulder, perfectly content and happy.

A few days later, the school called, asking for the foster parents to come in as soon as possible. As they sat in the principal's office, the parents were informed that their foster child was engaged in touching herself in the classroom. The principal was almost tongue-tied. She informed the foster parents that the teacher had applied disciplinary action by having the child stand in the corner. The hearts of these foster parents ached for their precious foster daughter. When the couple returned home with the child, she told about the full impact of the teacher's actions. The girl had not only endured the isolation of standing in the corner, but had also endured the laughter of all the kids. The foster parents just held her, and together they cried.

A short time later, the social worker contacted the foster mom to arrange a home visit. During the visit, the social worker discussed the child's behavior in school and then provided new information about the sexual abuse she had endured while living in her birth parents' home. The case worker also informed them the decision had been made to transfer her to a group home where she would receive the proper help and supervision she needed. She would be placed on medication and receive cognitive counseling to change her behavior.

The foster parents were devastated. Both knew deep in their hearts that this behavior was not a willful act of defiance. They knew medication would not heal the deep wounds she carried in her heart from the sexual abuse she experienced at such a young age. The foster parents pleaded on behalf of this girl. Both knew full well this behavior that manifested itself was a response to soothe the deep wounds in her heart. Her pain was so severe, she had found a soothing method to settle the hurt in some way. No pleading would help. That very day the child was removed from the home.

When the woman came to this point in the story, she could no longer hold back the tears. She cried for this girl because she knew she had deep pain in her heart that had created this in her life.

This girl is one of thousands of individuals who at one time were sexually abused. They can no longer cry because all of their emotions are stuck inside. Not only do girls suffer the traumatic events of sexual abuse; countless boys have become victims, as well.

If a boy is sexually abused, he loses his identity and struggles for the rest of his life to accept who he is. I have seen the deep agony in the eyes of men who have sat before me. With their wives listening, stories of sexual abuse came to light. The shame is so deep, the events so horrific, the memories so debilitating, with no way out. It will take years for a sexually abused man to talk to anyone about what happened. Most men never tell a living soul about what took place in that barn, house, or room. They simply continue living life while silently carrying the wounds in their hearts. The degrading acts performed on their bodies are forever seared in their memory. Only Jesus is able to step into the heart, remove the pain, and heal the damaged heart. He is able to restore fully what was taken.

When I've sat with individuals who have been sexually abused, I've realized their precious gift from God, their sexuality, was shredded to pieces. Many years after the sexual abuse, their bodies are physically mature, but they still behave like little children and have never fully developed sexually or emotionally. In marriage, they never fully experience the beauty and wonder of becoming one sexually with their spouse because the memories haunt them all the time. Sexually abused people never really accept their body as good or beautiful. They never see themselves as pure. All this was taken from them and replaced by shame and self-hatred.

One woman recalled how she looked forward to her wedding night, when she would be one with her beloved for the first time. When the wedding night arrived, however, it was all but beautiful. The moment they came together, it was like something snapped inside of her, and all she could do was scream and flee from the bed. She ran into a corner and curled up in a fetal position, crying hysterically. Unable to help, her new husband sat on the bed and watched his bride crumple on the floor. He was stunned, as he had no idea what had just happened.

He went to his wife and gently lifted her into his arms, and after her sobs had somewhat subsided, he asked her if he had hurt her in some way. The woman could only shake her head, and for the next several years, what should have been a celebration of their love became hurried affairs, done quickly, just to get it over. One day in prayer, she can ask Jesus for the reason for her behavior, whether something had happened to her when she was little. In prayer, Jesus lets her know what took place a long time ago. When she was very young, a man had sexually abused her, and the abuse continued for years. She had completely disassociated from these memories and had lost all connection to these events. The sexual abuse was so horrific; the only way she could process what was happening at the time the abuse took place was to put it somewhere deep within her heart and mind. Then on her wedding night, she crashed.

In prayer, she can ask Jesus to restore her sexuality. Jesus will put the pieces of her broken heart back together. With Jesus by her side, the woman can fully remember all that had happened to her. The pain of the sexual abuse will be fully realized. That man had robbed and stolen so much from he; he destroyed her sexuality.

Praying with a Sexually Abused Person

All victims, especially sexual abuse victims, have to learn to fall in love with Jesus again. Their first love was destroyed by the perpetrator, who has now become the new face of God. It is extremely difficult to assist sexually abused people because, at some point, benchmarks were established. Benchmarks are specific events victims might decide on that they think will help them move ahead with their pain. If the benchmark is that the individual is caught and incarcerated, this will do nothing to repair the damage that was done or take away the pain the victim carries.

The next benchmark might be that the person receives the maximum punishment the law can give. What about the pain? Will it go away? Will the world be okay again? No, not really. So another new benchmark has to be set up. Sexually abused individuals feel very dirty and struggle to come to Jesus. I often encourage them to put all of their memories in a box, and we will take out one memory at a time and bring Jesus into their pain.

Over the years, many individuals have asked for my help in dealing with past sexual abuse issues. As I became acquainted with them, many made it very clear that if I were to ask them to forgive their sexual abusers, they had no intention to do so. Their abusers had taken so much from them already, there was nothing left. I would simply say, "Well, then, don't forgive them right now. Wait till you are ready. God will give you all the time you need to eventually grant them forgiveness."

Their eyes would get really big, and they would say, "You have no idea what this person did to me."

No, I did not. But I told them that if they wanted to share it with me,

I would listen. They would look straight into my eyes, lean forward, and with a low voice, as if someone was listening in, begin to unfold their story.

In many cases, it started when they were in grade school, and someone they knew gave them a ride home from school one day. The individual did not take them home right away but instead drove into a forest and took advantage of them there by forcing them to do certain things to them. The children were so afraid and scared that they did as they were told. After it was over, the individual made them swear to never tell a soul or they would be punished. In the years that followed, at unexpected moments, this person would show up, take them away, and sexually abuse them again. These girls and boys were barely able to leave their homes to go to school, afraid the abuser would come and snatch them away. They stayed in their bedrooms in order to be safe, away from the perpetrator, all the while keeping their promise. They never told a single person what was going on.

If the abuser died at some point in the future, were these precious ones then able to go on with life, without being afraid to leave their home? No, the fear continued. Peace never comes, no matter how hard they tried.

As these folks shared their memories with me, they would arrive at a point where a sinister look would come upon their face. They would ask me, "Do you know what I want to do with him [or her]? I want to buy an ax or something similar. Then I want to go to the cemetery and dig them up with my bare hands. When I have them in front of me, I want to chop them into a million pieces."

As I listened to them, holding their hands, I asked, "And then what?"

They would begin to repeat this little phrase over and over again, "And then what? And then what? And then what?"

Before I knew what was happening, they would put their head on my shoulder and sob. Their tears came like a flood. I just held them and let them cry. Through their tears they would say, "Help me to forgive him [or her]." After some time, they would quiet down, and I would ask if I could lead them to Jesus in prayer. They would nod their heads, and we would begin. I gave them the words and encouraged them to repeat these words to Jesus.

First, we asked Jesus where He was when the first sexual abuse occurred. Jesus let them know He was in their heart. He saw everything they endured, how they suffered, and how they were hurt.

Then we asked, "Why did I have to suffer?"

Jesus let them know these individuals used their free will and chose to hurt them. In order to stop them, God Himself would have had to take away their free will. Their heart understood they suffered because of the choice this individual made. At the same time, they saw the tears Jesus was crying for them.

A little while later, they asked, "Jesus, have I ever forgiven _____ from my heart for hurting me for all those years, for all they took away from me?" No, they had never forgiven them. "Do you want me to forgive them today? My heart hurts so much. Can you help me to forgive them?" They saw and understood that Jesus had helped them all along the way. He was close to them, and He was holding His little boy (or girl) in His arms.

It is very important to give victims the opportunity to forgive God for allowing the abuse to happen. We can pray something like this: "God, I trust You. I forgive You. I don't understand the bigger picture, but I know You love me. You love Your children. I want to hold on to You and not let any bitterness against You settle in my heart. I choose to hold on to the scripture, 'Trust in the LORD with all your heart and lean not on your own understanding' (Proverbs 3:5 NIV). 'Your own understanding' in this context means having the answer to the question 'Why?' This scripture clearly gives us insight to not seek the answers to why but rather to trust God and ask Him what, instead."

There was one more thing we needed Jesus to disconnect. We needed Jesus to take away the pain the person had caused them, and to replace all that was taken from them. Jesus did as they asked. He placed in their heart a new peace and innocence for the childhood they had lost, and so much more. Next, they wanted to know if their heart was pure and if everything was restored again. Could Jesus somehow let them know their heart was now pure? At times, Jesus gave them a picture of Himself standing in front of an altar, waiting for his bride, dressed in pure white. Or sometimes, it was a picture of Himself meeting them in a beautiful meadow filled with white flowers.

Often, when the prayer time was over, the tears flowed some more, but not because of the painful events they just had relived. These were tears of freedom and joy. In prayer, we also asked Jesus to give them back the gift of sexuality, as He had created it for them to enjoy this gift with their spouse.

Sexually abused victims have bitterness in their heart against their abuser. They carry guilt if they participated in the sexual activity or had a certain degree of enjoyment in what went on. In this case, forgiving themselves will bring freedom to their hearts. The journey to healing can be instantaneous, or it may be a process. This is up to God. I encourage people not to travel down their corridor of memories without taking Jesus with them. One day, the sun will shine again, and the painful event will be only a sad memory because they will truly be healed and free. Many years ago, I read a headline in a magazine that said, "Sexual violation was not your choice, but recovery is."

Pain So Severe One Mutilates the Body

If the sexual abuse continues for years, the shame becomes more and more intense. It can become so intense, people need to destroy their own body with the purpose of somehow stopping what is going on. Self-mutilation becomes the next step in fending off their abuser and ending the constant pain. The pain in the heart is far greater than the pain endured by the sexual abuse. The only way victims know to stop what is going on is to self-mutilate or make their body unattractive so the abuser leaves them alone. We may not be able to imagine deep pain like this. Cutters use a knife, scissors, razor, or other device to inflict pain on their body. The pain feels good while the heart hurts. They have no other way to stop the pain in their heart except to inflict pain on their body. They will release the tears they're no longer able to cry by seeing the blood flow from their body.

Likewise, individuals who have had to endure years of sexual abuse deliberately change their physical body by gaining excessive weight. Alternatively, some starve their body by withholding nutrients, with the intent of changing their physical appearance; all this, to make themselves unattractive in order to prevent future sexual abuse. A completely new image is created, one that fosters rejection.

Some individuals have confessed to torturing animals because the pain was just too great to hold in any longer. In some way, the animal became the object of the victim's rage. The mutilation would be inflicted on the animal instead of on him- or herself. Children can hurt so badly, the only way to bring relief to their hearts is to hurt someone else. In many cases, these are kids who cannot hurt the abuser. They cannot stop what is happening. The pain inflicted on the animal is the pain they cannot unleash on the abuser.

One final thought comes from a woman who wrote these words to me: "The shame and the need to destroy my body was like a movie playing out silently. Jesus showed me I no longer have to punish my body. I took Jesus's hand, and together, we traveled down the corridors of my secret life. He took all my shame and the ugliness of this body and sealed it with a triumphant, final thrust into the dark grave of death. It's done and over. It is finished. As I prepared to take Communion, I looked and saw the scars on my arms and legs, along with the scars hidden on my mutilated body. I finally realized it is over, I am free."

Her mutilated body is no longer a reminder of what she had to endure. She no longer copes by inflicting unimaginable pain on herself. She can now identify with Jesus, who is wearing the scars for her.

How to Reset Your Heart in Your Sexual Life

1. Begin by celebrating who God created you to be. Whether you are a girl or boy, man or woman, rejoice and accept your sexuality. God knows what is best for us.

2. Have the courage to list, on a sheet of paper, all of the immoral activities you've allowed to be a part of your life. You can also use the "Moral Failure Worksheet" in the *Biblical Counseling Workbook* This will be very difficult to do. Be encouraged; what the Holy Spirit uncovers, the blood of Jesus has already covered.

3. After you have identified your moral failure issues, begin by renouncing each activity and asking Jesus to give back the ground you gave to the enemy through that activity. Prayerfully stay in contact with Jesus; ask Him to bring someone into your life you can be accountable to.

4. Write your personal story and compare your sexual development with the sexual stages described in this chapter. If, at some point in your life, your sexuality was not able to grow and mature, bring this issue to the Lord and ask Him to resolve it and heal it for you.

5. If, at any time in your life, you were sexually abused or violated by others, go to Jesus. When you are ready, grant forgiveness to your sexual abusers. Release them to God. If you choose not to

work toward forgiveness, you will remain in unseen chains until you do so. I understand your heart, and I hear you. You want to be vindicated, cleared, and declared free from all allegations. Yet God's Word is clear; it is His prerogative to vindicate you. The Lord will take care of it. All you need to do is get out of His way.

6. If you live for revenge or choose not to forgive, God will get out of the picture and back away, leaving you to your own devices.

7. Take time to grieve what was lost. You have lost your innocence, your purity, your security, your healthy sexuality, your trust, and so much more. When we grieve, we begin to release the pain within us, and our heart is prepared to forgive. If we never grieve our losses, Satan uses this left-behind pain to enslave us again.

8. One concept overlooked by so many is, God does not ask us to trust our abusers. But He does ask us to forgive them and release them from our heart, forgive them for the pain and consequences they caused.

9. After all your moral failures have been confessed and put under the cross, one final request needs to be granted by Jesus. Your heart needs to know if you are sexually pure again. In prayer, ask Jesus to show you a picture of how He sees your pure heart. I wish you could see some of the pictures I have gracing my office walls, pictures of healed, pure hearts, transformed and made new by our Lord, Himself.

10. Establish your sexual safe place, by setting appropriate boundaries in order to stay sexually pure. More on this in chapter 6.

My Personal Sexual Healing and Restoration

During my school years and in college, I was very promiscuous. There was nothing to lose. Other than my career, which I really loved, my private life was on the brink of disaster. I had long ago left my church affiliation and my home. I thought I was just a bad girl, yet in reality, I was looking for love and attention. What I thought was love was a short physical moment spent with a man, and in the end, it cost me every time. My heart was lonely, frightened, and not functioning. I did not know at the time that my heart was locked away and could no longer feel anything. Looking back, I feel like I was stuck in the elementary stage of my sexual development. In many ways, I behaved like a six- to ten-year-old, seeking what I thought I needed. I had no idea what to do with my sexuality except to give it away and let others use it to their heart's content. It left me empty yet looking for more. My heart distrusted every man. Over time, I felt no guilt in using my sexuality to get the attention I desperately longed for. In those brief moments, I felt that I belonged to someone who cared for me.

Years later, I met a man, my future husband, Mike, who saw me in a different light. Mike was not like the other men, wanting sex. He just wanted to be with me. He called me every day, and we arranged to meet for lunch. Sitting on a blanket out in a meadow, we shared a meal together, all the while talking and enjoying each other's company. After several months, I actually felt something stirring in my heart. Eventually, I had to admit to myself that perhaps what I felt for him was real love. Not only did Mike shower me with his presence and with meals; he actually had a genuine interest in who I was.

After six months, he popped the question. Would I marry him? Wow, I did not see that coming. He actually wanted to marry me. He had no idea what he was getting into. But I immediately answered, "Yes," that I would love to be his wife. Six months later, we were married. A few months after our wedding, I left Germany and my sinful lifestyle behind. I was ready to begin a new chapter in my life. My heart was fearful because I had no idea how to be a wife or, if children were to be a part of our life together, how to be a mom.

The day I said, "I do," to Mike, I knew my heart stored many secrets: secrets of being sexually abused, secrets of my involvement with other women, and secret memories of many years of using my sexuality to gain acceptance and love from others. I never wanted anyone to know how desperate I was for love. To tell you the truth, I really had no idea how needy and starved for love I had become.

Years before I met my husband I consciously took these secrets and placed them deep inside my heart. To insure these secrets stayed in place, never to surface again, I sealed the deal by making a vow with myself. A vow is a promise not to be broken or violated. My vow was to never, ever tell anyone of my past sexual abuse or allude at any time to my wild life. I believed this vow would serve its purpose by eventually bringing me a person who could truly love me for who I was, not for what I was willing to give to them. Or if everything failed, this vow would at least provide me with men who were willing to give me a little, with no questions asked.

Now that I was married, I could certainly not risk losing my husband's love by telling him my deepest secrets. My vow also included my resolve to take these secrets with me to my grave. There were moments in my marriage where I felt a strong desire to tell my husband everything but, repeatedly, I pushed all thoughts of disclosure way down deep. The longer I held on to my secrets, the tighter the fear of discovery of who I really was gripped my heart. Of course, the strategy of the enemy was at play. He had me bound for years helping me believe I was really the instigator in every instance of my sexual abuse, not the victim. It was almost as if he whispered these words in my ears: "If your husband knows about your past, he will not love you anymore. And if others know about your past, they will not want you either."

As already stated, I simply could not risk losing the love of my husband or alienating him from me. So I pushed my secrets deep down in my heart, and I pushed God aside, as well. Not even He would have entrance into the secret chambers of my heart.

The years went by, and I fumbled along in the area of my sexuality, never really knowing what was expected and what I should expect. In many ways, I felt like a little kid each time we came together. Yet, as my heart came closer and closer to Jesus, this old vow would raise its head again and again. My heart became desperate. My sins refused to stay in my secret place. I could fully identify with David when he said:

> When I kept silent about my sin, my body wasted away Through my groaning all the day long. For day and night, Your hand [of displeasure] was heavy upon me; My energy (vitality, strength) was drained away as with the burning heat of summer. Selah. I acknowledged my sin to You, And I did not hide my wickedness; I said, "I will confess [all] my transgressions to the LORD"; And You forgave the guilt of my sin. Selah. (Psalm 32:3–5 AMP)

After twenty-five years of marriage, I could no longer stand it. I finally had the strength to face God. The moment I sat down with God, the tears flowed, and broken-up words came from deep in my heart. It almost felt like I was purging my heart, vomiting out all its ugliness. I cried what seemed like buckets while pouring out all of my sins to Jesus. All the while, in some miraculous way, I felt Jesus very close to my heart. He wept for me, His precious little girl who was robbed of the good gift He gave to me the day I was fashioned by Him inside my mother's womb. It had all become so distorted. The gift of pure sexuality was stolen from me and left my heart wounded, damaged, and in pain. My heart knew this was only the beginning of my journey with God because if I could not forgive my abusers and myself, my inner healing could not be complete. My heart was overwhelmed with grief for the losses I had experienced, for the choices I had made. In my grief, I clung to the Father, crying from deep within my soul. I allowed myself to just cry till my inner being felt relieved. Eventually, I was ready and pleaded with God to give me the strength to forgive my father and mother for not being there for me when I needed them. I forgave my abusers for all the things they did to me and all they took from me. I was able to truly let them go and release them to the Father. Without hesitation, I handed each one over to Him, symbolically extending my hands to God. After I released my abusers to God, I also asked Him to restore and help me to mature in the area of my sexuality and allow me to experience His gift to the fullest. In prayer, I asked God if He sees my heart pure and whole again. I felt such a peace and quietness in my heart; the message from God was unmistakable, and my heart was fully restored.

The most difficult part for me was telling Jesus about the things that I had done, but once again, He gave me all the time I needed and waited till I had the words to speak. I was able to forgive myself for all of my past choices and actions. My heart felt pounds lighter, refreshed, new in some way. I wanted to sing. I was free of the vow, the promise I made to myself, and the bondage I allowed the enemy to establish in my heart. I felt clean and pure.

Looking back, I still remember how God met me and revealed Himself to me on that day. The longer I prayed, the freer my heart became. I was able to take a deep breath. The vow was finally broken, and Satan could no longer hold me as his slave. At the end of my prayer time with my good, good Father, I asked Him if He wanted me to share my past with my husband. I made a deal with God: I would wait for Him to lead and specifically show me the right moment to open up my heart to him (and also give me the right words to say). I realized my husband had inherited all of my unknown secrets the day we were married. Yet secretly, I was hoping the day would never come when I had to share with him all of my past sins and sexual abuse.

The weeks came and went, and I had no indication from God to go ahead and share my past with Mike. Months went by, and I almost forgot my end of the bargain. So I thought, *We are good*. But God did not forget. He wanted to teach me to trust Him completely. Almost one year later, when I was on my knees asking God to choose the day, the moment, the time to open up my heart to my husband, God reminded me of my promise to Him. When the quiet voice of God spoke to my heart, it was clear what I had to do next.

On this particular day, I was in the kitchen, heating up our soup for lunch. The kids were in school, and Mike just leaned on the counter, watching me as I carried on. I instantly felt the prompting of the Lord on my heart and knew this was it. This was the moment; this was the appointed time. I could have easily dismissed the voice of the Holy Spirit or made excuses, but I knew it was time. I turned off the stove, walked over to Mike, and reached out to hold his hands.

Before I revealed my secrets, I reminded him of some peculiar questions I had been asking him for the past several months. I said I wanted to share with him the reason for these questions, why I was testing him and challenging his love for me. For instance, I once asked him if I had kept secrets from him and eventually told him the truth, would he still love me? Another time, I made a comment that there might be things he did not know about me and then asked, if I told him, would he still care about me the same way he did now, no matter what these things were? I also told him there was something he didn't know about me and asked if he would look at me differently if he knew?

Every question I asked was met with an understanding heart. Every time I asked him, he took me into his arms and just cared for me.

So now here we were, standing in the kitchen, holding each other's hands. I bravely lifted my face to look into his eyes and began by saying that what I wanted to share with him needed to be told all at once; I asked him to just listen and not interrupt while I spoke. He agreed, and I forged ahead. I opened up my heart and told him all about my sexual abuse and sexual involvement from the past. I watched him closely, afraid of how he would react. Tears flowed from my eyes, not because I still felt pain in my heart or shame for my sin, but because I had withheld the truth from my husband and had not trusted him with my past. I saw the pain in his eyes, and before too long, they were filled with tears. Now the tears were rolling down his face for me, his wife. He not only heard my words, but his heart heard and understood the pain from my childhood and adult life. What came next was so overwhelming and unexpected. My husband lifted me up and carried me to our living room couch. He gently sat me on his lap and just held me for a long time. We both continued to cry in each other's arms. Eventually, I heard his gentle voice, slow and filled with deep emotion. He prayed to our heavenly Father. The words I heard found their way into my heart. My husband was not praying for me. He was praying to God, asking Him to forgive him for not knowing of my deep pain. He asked God to show him how to care for my heart and how to care for all areas in my life. After what seemed like an eternity, he turned his head around and looked at me. He asked me to forgive him for not knowing.

I assured him I had made a vow and lived this vow to the letter, that if God had not chased me down and wanted me to deal with these unresolved issues in my life, I would have taken the things that happened to me to my grave. One more time, Mike closed his eyes, and I joined him, this time to give God praise for the healing He had brought to my heart. The love we felt at this moment for each other has endured for all these years and still remains to this day.

Was my journey complete? No. All of my secrets were now in the open. I had forgiven the people who had sexually abused and hurt me. I had forgiven myself. Looking back, I wish my journey of coming to freedom had happened sooner, but I realize it was shame that kept me from getting help from anybody, including God.

Now God had another assignment for me. About a year after my confession to my husband, I felt God speaking directly to my heart during my prayer time. It was a specific message. His words to my heart were,

"Ellen, I entrusted you with this pain because I know what you will do with it." It took me a long time to unravel this mysterious message, but it eventually made perfect sense. I realized that by calling me to this task, God prepared me to conform to His image and give Him His rightful place, trusting Him. Unmistakably, my heart understood my next assignment, the next step God wanted me to take to complete my healing journey. God asked me to pray for my sexual abusers to come to know Him as their Lord and Savior. In essence, God's assignment was for me to pray for their salvation because He died for them, and He wanted to redeem them, as well. This meant I would be with them in heaven, forever.

I was hesitant to pray for them. I did not want to be with them in heaven; I wanted them to suffer, and I wanted revenge. Once again, God and I went around and around, till I finally surrendered to Him: "Not my will, but Your will be done." At first, my prayers were not as sincere and heartfelt, but as the years went by, my prayers for the salvation of my sexual abusers became more urgent. Yes, I wanted them to come to know Jesus and be redeemed, to experience His love and forgiveness for their own healing. I made myself a new vow: to pray for these individuals till I no longer had breath in my lungs.

You may wonder what happened to my damaged heart, which was frightened and shivering in the dark attic. As I already shared with you, first, the inner heart of this girl was changed into a large, beautiful jeweled heart that Jesus held in His hands. Second, the glory of God Himself shone down on His little girl, bathing her with His love. Then Jesus met me in a dream, embracing me with all of Himself, and when I talked to Him about my sexual abuse, the final healing took place. Jesus took the girl out of that attic and placed her in the woods, my safe place with Him.

As of this writing, I am still very happily married. Each day seems to be a celebration because we are truly one in our hearts. I continue to grow and mature in the area of my sexuality, and I am finally able to look at this part in my life as a true gift from God. I feel beautiful, pure, and celebrated. Often during my prayer times, God reveals to me how precious I am to Him. No longer do I see myself as a victim or damaged goods. God has proven Himself to me by sticking to what I now know about Him. He never wastes any pain. Don't get me wrong; God does not need pain to fulfill His purpose in our lives, but He knows none of us can travel through this life without getting hurt in some way. Our enemy, Satan, uses our pain to destroy us. He almost succeeded with me. God, on the other hand, uses these past hurtful issues to step into our hearts and bring healing to it.

You might ask the question, what if memories of my past sexual abuse flood my thoughts again? Then what? Do I need to go back to God and start all over again? No. After my initial prayer time with God, I felt within my heart I should break off all contact with individuals who were similar to my abusers. Of course, by now I lived in America, so breaking off all contact with my abusers was not an issue. I would recommend it for the purpose of allowing yourself to be truly healed.

Just imagine you are rushed to the hospital with acute appendicitis. You have the operation, and now I, your best friend, come to the hospital for a visit. The first thing I do is throw a punch, with my fist, directly into your freshly operated wound. It bursts open, and once again, you need to be stitched up again. This is similar to being in the presence of your sexual abuser; you cannot heal because his or her constant presence will serve as a reminder of what happened. The heart needs time to heal; you need to give yourself all the time you need to heal.

Over time, I found I could actually be with individuals who were similar in build or had the same demeanor as my sexual abusers. I realized my heart was free. Today, I can travel down memory lane, and no shadows frighten me. No dark corners grab me by surprise. I can see all of my life as a reel in front of my eyes, without feeling any pain. Of course, I choose not to stop at some of my memories and let the full impact of what had happened overwhelm me again. No, I remind myself at these points that it is finished. At the same time, I have made it my practice to pronounce a blessing on all the people who have ever hurt me. When I bless them, my heart in some way feels blessed, as well.

My desire is for you to find this freedom for yourself. Go to Jesus and invite Him into all these areas in your life. Then ask Him to help you to continue with your sexual maturing process so you too can fully enjoy this good and perfect gift from our good, good Father.

As of this writing, I no longer counsel but am available to come to your church or gathering to talk about my personal journey and healing process. I am also blessed to train others in the heart counseling model and present a variety of topics to interested groups. Please refer to the back of this book for my contact information.

Or if you need help with this part of your journey, please refer to the back of this book to contact Caring for the Heart Ministries. A gentle, caring secretary will help you make contact with someone who can help you. They will have assisted countless others by leading them to Jesus.

CHAPTER 6

TO BE WHOLE: GOD'S ULTIMATE GOAL FOR US

LORD my God, I called to you for help, and you healed me. (Psalm 30:2 NIV)

You are my hiding place; you will protect me from trouble and surround me with songs of deliverance. (Psalm 32:7 NIV)

All of us were created with a physical body, and at the moment God breathed His breath into our nostrils, we became living souls complete with an emotional component and a free will. God also placed within us an eternal part, the spiritual; we were created in the image of God. We were also created as sexual beings, either as a boy or as a girl. If one of these four areas is damaged or out of alignment, we cannot function the way God intended. The process of growing and maturing in our physical, emotional, spiritual, and sexual life is necessary to live in harmony with God and ourselves. If, at any time, our life is intersected by events that damage or destroy our heart, we have the ability, with God's help, to reset our life and begin living in harmony with God again. Resetting our hearts requires us to fully examine the four topics presented in the main chapters of this book.

How do we keep our collapsing world propped up? Why do we do this? Because we can function when we pretend all is well, and as such, we don't have to deal with our issues. We never consider the concept of being whole, well, and healthy. We can hardly imagine what our personal world would look like if we were whole rather than broken. To be whole in our physical, emotional, spiritual, and sexual life seems like a far-fetched fairy tale. Is this even possible, or is it some kind of wishful thinking? As we look around, we see broken people, lonely individuals, and bitter hearts: men, women, and children who have been wounded deeply. Society is seemingly uninterested in what is happening with them. Our voices cry out, yet nobody listens, and our deepest needs go unfulfilled. In some unexplained way, we are stuck, unable to help even ourselves. Over and over again, we silence our inner hunger for someone to love us, respect us, take note of us, pay attention to us, and make us feel important and valued. We press all of these deep needs way down in our hearts to keep ourselves from going crazy or from appearing to others as being high maintenance.

We also live in a world where we seldom deny ourselves anything that brings us pleasure. We are saturated with electronics that appear smarter every day, and as a result, we disconnect from people and connect to the superficial instead. Machines engage our interest much more than human beings, who appear complicated, overwhelming, and often out of sorts. It is just easier to invest our efforts elsewhere. If we asked the average person, "Do you believe these electronic relationships are real emotional connections?" the answer would be, "Yes." In reality, we are lonelier than ever before. Inside of our being, we have an unmet need; we cannot even put a name to what it is we need. At times, we venture out to identify what our true need really is. We believe perhaps it is spending time with a person. Before too long, we realize just spending time with a person does not fill the void we have in our hearts. Could it be we need more money to replace the emptiness? Not really. Countless wealthy individuals enjoy many external benefits, and their hearts still crave and long for some unseen deeper relationship.

External things do not last, they do not satisfy, and they never fill the heart. Humankind has learned that what the world has to offer always leaves us in want. Even Solomon wrote in the book of Ecclesiastes that all earthly treasures are meaningless. I believe this is true. Aside from God, all is meaningless. We convince ourselves it is different for us, that these things will be sufficient to meet our deepest needs. However, the Creator of our hearts knows what we require, and He instills in us a deep hunger for one fundamental thing: Our deepest need is to be loved and to love others. It was God's idea to place this capacity to love in our hearts because we would otherwise not have the idea to love anyone, including Him.

> We love because He first loved us. (1 John 4:19 NIV)

Only after all of our unresolved issues have been unlocked and dealt with can we freely give love and receive love from others. When true freedom reigns in our heart, we will be able to take our eyes off ourselves and focus on the needs of others, thus fulfilling their deepest needs.

When I counseled people, I always asked what they really needed. I often said, "If you could give me three words or statements to describe what would make you the happiest girl [or guy] on the face of this earth, what would they be?" They could not answer because, first of all, no one had ever asked them this before. Secondly, they could not identify what they needed. I finally started recording a list of words and short statements that I call healing words. (You can find a list of the healing words in the appendix.) I collected these words and statements, along the way, from individuals who were complete and whole. This list of healing words became the best tool for me as I assisted others. It helped give them a voice, as they could finally identify what they needed. It never failed. Women have checked short statements on their sheet such as "included," "paid attention to," "valued," "listened to," "important," "together," and "protected," just to name a few. Men, on the other hand, have marked words like "admired," "complimented," and "respected"; they want to hear someone say, "I'm proud of you" or "You are awesome."

Whole and Complete in Our Physical Life

In the second chapter, we looked in detail at how the physical body needs to grow and mature in order to be fully available to God, and to be able to manage the ups and downs we face as we journey through this life. The physical body may have been perfect at birth, but along the way, things can change. Accidents and sickness can cause loss of limbs. Unforeseen events can result in disfigurement. Prolonged use of medication or misuse of drugs can create negative effects on our physical bodies and how they now function. None of us should ever take our physical body for granted. God has given us this one body; we need to be good stewards and keep our body in the best shape we can.

In order for us to be completely whole in our physical life, we need to reach the mature stage. In other words, we need to be fully developed in our physical person and totally accept our physical stature, no matter the shape of our body. Only then will we have the capacity to accept the physical changes we may face during our lifetime. If we have reached this maximum level of maturity in our physical life, we will be able to completely accept it. For instance, our body at some point becomes dependent on others having to care for it, even to the extent of round-the-clock physical care by a family member, caregiver, or institution. We will not only be able to accept this season in our life, but we will be able to adapt to a new normal while enjoying the next day.

If we are in this stage of our life, physical pain can be a constant companion, and this can determine whether we have a positive or negative outlook on life. During these times, we need to cling to God even more. One option is to look ahead to the blessed hope. Believers can find comfort in the fact that one day, physical suffering will cease, as we are ushered into the everlasting arms of Jesus. At this point, all of our earthly, physical suffering will come to an end.

> He will wipe every tear from their eyes. There will be no more death or mourning or crying or pain, for the old order of things has passed away. (Revelation 21:4 NIV)

> We know that the whole creation has been groaning as in the pains of childbirth right up to the present time. Not only so, but we ourselves, who have the first fruits of the Spirit, groan inwardly as we wait eagerly for our adoption to sonship, the redemption of our bodies. (Romans 8:22–23 NIV)

A member of my family was born with a genetic defect, and the prognosis revealed that as she continued to grow physically, her life would be very different from others. As I watched her inner struggle and warlike attitude, it became a challenge for me to stay positive and encouraging.

One day, a thought flashed through my mind, and I said to her, "You don't have to love what is happening, but you could try to make friends with your physical body."

If we can make friends with the setbacks we experience in our physical bodies, then in essence, we accept what is happening. Then we will find the path to establishing our normal more easily and quickly.

No matter what is going on in our physical bodies, God will use it, if we offer it up to Him. Ministry does not depend on what we look like or what we can do physically. The opposite is true. For instance, take Paul, who was called by God to go to the Gentile world and preach the gospel. At some point, Paul prayed to God for healing of a physical issue he had.

> Therefore, in order to keep me from becoming conceited, I was given a thorn in my flesh, a messenger of Satan, to torment me. Three times I pleaded with the Lord to take it away from me. But He said to me, "My grace is sufficient for you, for my power is made perfect in weakness." (2 Corinthians 12:7b–9 NIV)

As I celebrate my birthday each year, I am aware of how rapidly things are changing in my physical body. I realize I am no longer twenty years old. It is difficult to acknowledge and accept that at some point, we need to slow down. On the other hand, I find a certain quietness has enveloped my physical body at this time in my life. One of my priorities is to be in the best physical shape possible at any age, and in order to accomplish this, I give my body what I believe is optimal fuel. Over the years, I have allowed myself more rest without feeling guilt or remorse. At first, this was very difficult, but I listened to my husband's advice and scaled down my physical activities. God gave a command to Moses concerning the tribe of Levi; He said:

> "In regarding to the Levites: From 25 years old or more, a man enters the service in the work at the tent of meeting. But at 50 years old he is to retire from his service in the

work and no longer serve. He may assist his brothers to fulfill responsibilities at the tent of meeting, but he must not do the work. This is how you are to deal with the Levites regarding their duties." (Numbers 8:24–26 HCSB)

One last thought on the subject of the physical. Woman and men are different, and we must take into account that men bond or connect through the physical. What does this mean? First, they connect by being fulfilled sexually. It is their release. Second, they connect when they hear respectful statements as we use our physical voice. When Mike takes care of an outside work project, I take a lawn chair and situate myself within his sight and voice range. Every once in a while, I say something like, "I really appreciate you doing this" or "You are really strong." Statements like these fill the heart of a man and let him know you respect him. Respecting a man will go a long way. I must caution you, the statements must be sincere and genuine.

Words and conversation are needed to reach the heart of a woman, as well. Women use many words and give detailed accounts as they express themselves, for the purpose of fulfilling their need for love. If a husband takes the time to listen intently to his wife, her heart will be filled. The husband who wants to bond with his spouse needs to be genuinely interested in all she wants to say. Only then will the magic of connection occur within her heart. In both cases, whether man or woman, physical voices are needed to establish a heart connection with the other.

Whole and Complete in Our Emotional Life

In the third chapter, I wrote about our inner emotional being. As we unpacked this area, we discovered that most individuals never consider that their deep-seated emotional pain was perhaps caused by others in their past. People live with these emotional wounds, and their damaged heart does not have the capacity to grow and mature. This results in a life like an emotional roller coaster. If the inner pain is too great, we can actually lose the ability to differentiate between the truth and a lie because all we feel is pain. No matter how old we are physically, we still hear the damaging words uttered by a parent or caregiver, words that damaged us. Like fiery arrows, they continue to find their way deep inside of our hearts. Most of us have no idea how wounded we have become or how to deal with our damaged heart.

If our emotional life does not have the opportunity to fully develop, we will not be equipped to handle life's difficult blows. If our heart, our inner emotional being, has been wounded or damaged, we will have this invisible disability that nobody can understand. We try to explain to others the best we can how we feel, but they cannot put the pieces together. If we actually try to put this puzzle together ourselves, we are also at a loss. Deep down we know something is not right, but we cannot put our finger on what it is. We need to allow Jesus to shine His light on our emotional heart because He has seen and heard everything we have experienced in life. We seldom, if ever, come to Jesus for our emotional health, and for this reason, we suffer in silence, coping in some way. Even our closest friends and family members do not understand what is happening.

In chapter 3, I explained how we can actually have a very young emotional heart inside of us. In other words, our emotional heart can get stuck at a certain age level. Physically, you may be sixty years old, but emotionally, you can be six years old. If we have to function and live with a very young heart, it will become very difficult to shoulder daily responsibilities or find any kind of fulfillment. Imagine: Would we expect a six-year-old to care for an entire household, to parent children, to be a helpmate to a spouse, and on top of all that, to work every day? Could he or she do it? I believe not. In the same way, if the emotional heart of a person is very young, they will struggle to manage their life. All of our decisions will be influenced by this immature, young emotional heart. Just like a physical disability changes everything, emotional pain interferes in our daily life; our choices and activities.

As already mentioned in one of the previous chapters, more and more individuals reach out to mental health providers to find ease and relief from their emotional struggles. They seek a diagnosis and find themselves relieved at having a name for their condition. It almost seems people accessorize with a title of some sort. It is now hip to be declared bipolar or be stamped for life as having a personality disorder. I fully realize these conditions are real in many cases, yet we often see individuals being overdiagnosed and placed on medication right away. A question arises in my soul: Is this God's plan and design for His creation? Where is God in all of this? Do we still need Him or is He being replaced by a pill? Please do not get me wrong. There is a place and time for professional intervention and short-term use of medication. But is medication the real answer for emotional issues? Or are we simply knocking out our emotions so we are able to be a part of society? When our emotions have been numbed, we comply. We walk around as in a haze and no longer fully participate in life. A person becomes a shell, trying to fit in, but in essence simply exists.

Can God step into our emotional pain and bring freedom? Absolutely. In so many cases, this is exactly what has happened. When we give Jesus full access to our heart, it's like having a personal encounter with Him. He steps into our pain and transforms us from the inside out. Healing of the heart is only effective if it occurs from the inside out. No outward protocol can heal a wounded heart and restore our emotions. The heart can once again accept love from God, as it flows from His heart to the tormented soul. We can always go back to medication if need be and at the same time give God His rightful place to bring healing to our inner pain.

We need to give Jesus the opportunity to step inside all of our pain, remove it, and replace it with all the good things we never received. Only then are we completely whole and emotionally healthy. To stay free, there is no option to hide ourselves on an island, to guard our heart so it will never get emotionally hurt again by anyone. No, the solution is to find a person we can completely trust and emotionally connect with. This trusted person should be your spouse, if you are married, or a close friend. This individual needs to care for your heart in such a way that your emotional needs are met, so that your emotional heart will never go back to the age it was when it was wounded in the first place.

To establish this complete trust, we begin by sharing with them our past history so they never repeat our core pain issues again. If you don't already have such an individual in your life, pray and ask God to send you the right person. I recommend keeping it gender friendly. A woman needs to give full access to her heart to another woman. The same applies to a man.

After my husband fully understood the condition of my heart and how old I actually was emotionally, he looked into my eyes, held my hands, and said, "My love, would you forgive me for never caring for your heart the way you needed me to? I had no idea. I was so focused on my own needs that I never considered there was something you really needed. Now I understand you were never loved, by anyone. Can I care for your heart for the rest of our days together?"

My heart melted, and I was ready for anything.

As already shared with you in chapter 3, my husband wasted no time, got right to it, and fulfilled my deepest need to experience a true father figure. At the same time, I felt nurtured and cared for by him. He not only became my surrogate father figure but also the mom I never had and still longed for. To this day, I still marvel how my heart grew up to my physical age within a two-week period. I know it worked, and it will work for you as well.

Each of us needs to be ready and willing to begin our own personal journey in order to be whole. If you follow the steps in "How to Reset Your Emotional Heart," you will be well on your way. To continue living in what I call "ongoing freedom," the emotional heart needs to be explored from time to time, with the purpose of checking to see if we still experience total peace in our hearts. If you choose to leave a stone unturned, the results may not be as I experienced them.

The emotional side of things is very important if you are a woman. You see, a woman bonds and connects through the emotional. Nothing spells connection more for a woman than when her heart is spoken to. For this reason, it is dangerous if men in the workplace or community reach the heart of a woman by making heart statements. Heart statements go something like this: "You are the most beautiful thing I have ever seen" or "The color of your dress is perfect for you." Compliments and flattering statements go directly to a woman's heart, and if she does not hear them at home from her husband, other men, without knowing, can fill her empty heart. Have you ever heard the saying, "Sex starts in the kitchen"? Yes, this is exactly true in the case of a woman. A man, on the other hand, doesn't respond to emotional statements in the same way; he will always be more connected in the physical world.

Whole and Complete in Our Spiritual Life

We looked at the spiritual side of things in chapter 4. We realized growth and maturity are required to live the Christian life to the fullest, the way God had intended. God's desire is for us to move into a deeper relationship with Him. In the first chapter, I covered the concept of a spiritually mature person who is able to move from asking God, "Why?" to seeking a new direction from God by asking Him, "What do You want me to do with this?" or "What is Your plan in this circumstance?" This is the case especially when we come to a crossroads in our life. I often find it invaluable to diligently search through God's Word for what it has to say about an issue I am facing. If the Word is not against my direction and the peace of God reigns in my heart, I go ahead with my plans. If my heart is not at peace and my direction does not align itself with God's Word, I choose not to follow through with my plans. If we take these extra steps to discern God's will, we can accept the peace of God with confidence and proceed in the direction He points out for us, without fear.

Many individuals have been spiritually abused by pastors and leaders who are supposed to be shepherding the church, binding up wounds, and going after lost sheep, but these overseers were out to feed themselves. God spoke on this subject:

> As surely as I live, declares the Sovereign LORD, because my flock lacks a shepherd and so has been plundered and has become food for all the wild animals, and because my shepherds did not search for my flock but cared for themselves rather than for my flock, therefore, you shepherds, hear the word of the LORD: This is what the Sovereign LORD says: I am against the shepherds and will hold them accountable for my flock. (Ezekiel 34:8–10a NIV)

Spiritual leaders often use scripture to help others in their time of need, yet sometimes, people feel beat up, judged, or overwhelmed. If scripture is laid on top of a heart filled with pain, the heart cannot fully receive the scripture, as powerful as it is. First, the pain must be removed. Then scripture can find its way into the heart. For this reason, counseling based entirely on using scripture alone will not yield the desired result of freeing the heart.

As I prepared to meet clients, they often ask, "Should I bring my Bible for our sessions?" I reply, "You are more than welcome to bring your Bible;

however, we will give Jesus full access to your heart first, in order for you to experience freedom. Then we certainly can open up God's Word and together read what He has to say on any subject."

As already mentioned in chapter 4, a woman at my first church offered me a rare opportunity just as I was starting out in my spiritual life. Her mission was clear: She wanted to disciple me. I affectionately call her my "spiritual mother" because she took the time to teach me how to live this Christian life and also prepared me to minister to others.

My discipleship lessons started with finding my way around in the Bible and eventually looking up Bible verses for myself. As I gathered up courage, I eventually ventured out to attend Bible studies. To my surprise, I discovered I was not alone in my spiritual journey. I knew I was an infant in Christ, new to the faith, new to everything. My heart was so eager to learn, and I often became frustrated because I felt I was way behind. Yet, I was determined to follow my spiritual advisor and forge ahead into unknown territory.

Chapter 4 also covered my actual service in the church, which had its beginning when I volunteered in the nursery holding babies, talking to mothers, and playing with the other kids. I also helped in the preschool class. Wow, the kids in this age group already knew who Noah was and about a man named Jonah, who was swallowed by a fish. Where had I been all of my life? I had some catching up to do.

Not too long after this season in my life, I was asked to consider teaching a Sunday school class for young kids. Was I ready? What if the kids asked me a question, and I didn't know the answer? I panicked, but my heart trusted in God, and I had to try. I had so much joy serving these kids, and we all learned the lessons together. The kids had no idea I was just a half-step ahead of them. Quietly, without me even knowing it, I slipped from the Spiritual Infant Stage to the Spiritual Small Child Stage. My heart was energized, and as my lessons with my spiritual advisor continued, my hunger to know more and teach more became very obvious.

After about a year, I was promoted to teach children's church. Now I was with the bigger kids, and I had to be on my toes to be ahead of the game. At this time, my knowledge of spiritual things had expanded quite a lot, but I also realized that the more I studied the Bible, the less I actually knew. As always, God was my guide, and the motto I had established earlier served me well: "Where God guides, He will provide."

My spiritual journey did not end with teaching these kids. Eventually, I graduated to teaching the adults, and the meat of the scriptures became my reason for teaching Bible studies. Digging into God's Word always satisfied me, and giving out the scriptures fulfilled me. The cycle of receiving from God and then sharing with others reminds me again, as previously stated, of the Jordan River and the Dead Sea. Unlike the Dead Sea, with no outflow, thus the reason for its name, the Jordan River has an inflow and an outflow and is therefore healthy. In much the same way, I wanted to be a Jordan River: healthy, vibrant, flowing, giving and receiving, not only from God, but also from others He was sending into my life.

Have I arrived at the Spiritual Mature Stage, or am I still spinning around somewhere in the spiritual cycle? To tell you the truth, there are days (and even weeks) where I find myself living exactly at the mature stage, when all of a sudden, without warning, I regress. I have discovered one thing, however. I don't like to stay there very long because my heart longs for more closeness with my heavenly Father. I also realize, as long as I live on this side of heaven, my efforts to always be completely spiritually mature will depend on my close relationship with God. If I do slip back, I don't beat myself up. I find a way to get back on track. Most likely, it will be like this until the end of my earthly days.

You too will find yourself cycling in and out of certain stages, but you should never go as far back as the Infant Stage or be satisfied to remain there. Others depend on you, and God needs each and every one of us to minister to His creation. Make it a priority to pray and seek out a spiritual advisor, a mentor who is willing to disciple you, so you too can move from one spiritual stage to the next more easily and realize when you are too far away from the good, good Father. Spiritual food is needed in the same way that physical food is needed: for life, so you will not die. You can die spiritually and not even know it. When a trial comes your way, it will be a sure test of how you respond and how well you endure the difficult circumstances. Trials are always a spiritual opportunity for us to grow and mature in Christ.

If we consider male and female, or husband and wife, the spiritual area is a very important heart connection point. Growing and maturing spiritually creates a special bond within any relationship. The connection is felt deeply in the heart because it is focused on the Lord and not on self. We are all attracted to individuals who live a mature spiritual life and demonstrate to the world that God is still on the throne and that He cares affectionately for all of humankind.

Whole and Complete in Our Sexual Life

In chapter 5, we discovered how even in our sexual life, God needs for us to grow and mature. This topic is often neglected, but it must be reckoned with in order for us to be completely whole, especially if sexual abuse was a part of our past. The memory of the event will be forever etched in the mind of the victim and, in most cases, become the new future of the person. These results are tragic, since sexual things will take on a new meaning. No longer can sex be enjoyed and celebrated as God intended. However, a bad beginning does not have to lead to a bad end, and our past does not have to define our future.

If the person has enough courage to disclose to a trusted friend or spouse the sexual abuse they had to endure, the next step will be to bring the individual to Jesus, and together, they will deal with the event, in prayer. After the sexual abuse has been dealt with, it will be time to allow Jesus to fill the heart with all the good things that were stolen by the abuser.

One woman asked Jesus if He could restore her heart by giving her a picture of how He sees her purity. Jesus showed her a box decorated with lots of jewels. She said the box glittered so brightly, she understood its message. With this picture, Jesus gave her a new start; her life is now on a new path. She will always have this memory, but now, every time she is tempted to visit these events again, she can go to her healing picture and put it on top of the bad memory.

It is vital we take complete inventory of our past in the area of our sexual life. Only when we enjoy the gift of sexuality to its fullest are we complete and whole in the area of our sexuality. As already mentioned, this is God's gift for a husband and wife to enjoy together. In order to experience sexual fulfillment, healing and restoration has to occur. However, we cannot build our marriage relationship entirely on our sexual experiences. You see, we may lose the ability to engage in sexual activity one day, and if the marital relationship was built on sexual satisfaction alone, there will be nothing left to hold the couple together. God's desire is for us to be connected emotionally, on a heart level, with each other, and also with Him. Only then will we be completely satisfied.

I would like to add the following: If a sexually abused person has come into a marriage without dealing with the sexual abuse from the past, they need to realize the healing will be gradual. It is very important the spouse knows the details of the sexual abuse and gives you all the time you need to heal in this area. God will heal and restore what was lost.

A couple comes to my mind who came and asked for help. Before too long, a discovery was made. When she was a teenager, a group of guys raped her. She had never before disclosed any details of what happened, not to her husband or any other living soul. But for some reason, she wanted to do it, right then and there. She not only talked about some of the details of the event, she added that her husband was doing some of the same things even to this day. When he did them, she felt violated all over again. One specific action was him running his hands up her legs. This activity should not have created pain, but in her case, she had been violated in this area. It had become a constant reminder of what she endured while being abused.

As he listened, his heart was touched by her story. He started to cry because his heart was in tune with her heart. Finally, after the woman had poured out her heart, he looked into her eyes with tear-stained cheeks and said, "From this day on, I want you to tell me right away when I do something that hurts you or reminds you of your past."

A few months later, she called me. She shared with me that the night before, she actually wanted her husband to run his hands up her legs. At first, he did not want to do it. He was hesitant, but she encouraged him to go ahead. The moment he laid his hands on her legs, she felt a warm sensation, no pain, no memory of the sexual abuse, only pleasure. She cried on the phone and said over and over again, "Jesus healed me. He healed me."

Where am I in my sexual life? Not where I once was. I'm totally transformed, healed, restored, and able to celebrate this awesome gift from God. Never in my wildest dreams did I ever consider that my sexuality would be restored. God did it, and the years I have left will prove He is the victor, and I am the benefactor of this victory.

In isolated moments, if I choose to dwell on my past, feelings of shame and guilt can still spin me into a dark alley. Occasionally, there are days I regret waiting so long to bring all of my pain from the sexual abuse and from my promiscuous lifestyle to Jesus. Not in my wildest dreams could I have imagined the tender heart of Jesus and the complete forgiveness He granted me by fully restoring me. Today, should my past want to overtake me, I take the pictures I received from Jesus and quickly lay them on top of the memories, and very soon, my sexuality is whole again. My former experiences will always be a part of me, and if I want to, I can access them readily. Satan, my enemy, would love nothing more.

My husband gave me all the time I needed to share my personal experiences with him and not shy away from the details. He was very sensitive about my past, and he never seemed repulsed by me in any way. His total acceptance of where I had been, what I had done, and what was done to me only created sadness in his heart. He once told me he would like to "knock out" the people who had hurt me, but I assured him there was no need for that. What I needed from him was to love me just the way I am. My sweet husband is so caring and gentle. My past never entered the area of our sexuality again.

If I did not have Jesus helping me forgive my sexual abusers, my heart and my sexuality would be in a total different place. No matter what kind of a husband I'd have had, these unresolved issues would have always crowded out our intimate times. Today, I can honestly say I'm free to love, I'm free to give myself sexually to my husband, and I feel completely whole.

In the sexual arena, a bond or heart connection can only be established between a man and a woman if they give themselves freely to each other. All past physical, emotional, spiritual, and sexual issues need to be resolved. Then the sexual area will be a true celebration, the icing on the cake to enjoy, without having to worry about calories. I believe the sexual area is our gift from God, the culmination of our love for each other.

Physical Safe Place

You may wonder, "What in the world is a physical safe place? Why would you need a physical place of refuge? What is the purpose of having a place like this?" I asked myself these same questions, and after I established my first physical safe place and used it, the benefits became clear. Seeking a physical safe place has nothing to do with going to a sheltered area because your life is in danger or because your current location is no longer safe. No, the physical safe place I'd like to introduce you to is actually what I call a "detox" place. At times, the physical demands of life can become too much for us. The constant onslaught of hurtful comments from others can stab us deep in the heart, and when we feel we are on the brink of blowing our lid, we can go to our physical safe place and verbally detox with God.

For me, it began when both my husband and I found ourselves storing up feelings of frustration, anger, and disappointment, and other unhealthy thoughts. At one point, for example, my physical appearance did not please others, and all I wanted to do was run and hide. This happened when we first entered into full-time ministry. I had no idea what to expect, and in my fantasy, I established this wonderful world of being needed, appreciated, and wanted. To my shock and surprise, there were times of pain, frustration, and loneliness. People attacked me for my physical appearance. Some found my appearance unacceptable. Whenever I left my house, it felt like I was under constant scrutiny. I was evaluated based on someone's perception of who I was supposed to be. For some, my hair was too long; for others, too short. Sometimes, my skirt was too drab. Other times, it was too colorful. The criticism spun me right back to my childhood years. Once again, my mother's voice echoed in my heart, finding fault with me.

It was then that my husband and I established our first physical safe place. I knew I needed a literal physical place I could escape to and vent my frustrations to God, where I could feel totally acceptable to Him, physically. If I didn't have this place, I would have vented with my beloved or spewed my inner pain toward my kids. I didn't want to engage in this kind of behavior. So we decided to find our safe place, sooner rather than later.

The day we decided to intentionally look for this safe place was kind of special. We were willing to travel a few miles from our home, though later on, some of our physical safe places were within walking distance. They were always outdoors, in nature. Looking at the sky or at your surroundings often creates a sense of calm and comfort. Out in the open, surrounded by nature, provided the perfect setting for our purposes. As we started out, our intent was to find a spot that was not easily seen from the road. We travelled down a dirt lane to see what was around the next bend. Suddenly, right there in front of us was a small turnout. So we parked the car and took a few steps up the gentle rise. We found ourselves standing in a small grove, sprinkled here and there with boulders, small plants, and wildflowers. From this spot, we could not see the road. This little grove was private and exactly what we were looking for.

We took each other by the hands and dedicated this place to God. We shared with Him that the days we would come to this place would be difficult ones. Most likely, our hearts would be wounded; our frame of mind would not be the best, and even if we were very upset or even angry, would He just be there for us? We asked God if He would listen to us and minister to us while we poured out our pain and hurt. As we ended our prayer, we promised God we would wait for Him to center our hearts and soothe us with His love and presence, before we went home. As husband and wife, we made up a simple phrase to let each other know when we needed to visit our physical safe place. This way, we would not worry when the other disappeared.

Standing in this peaceful place, we felt physically safe and close to God. We used our physical safe place whenever we felt we needed to detox with God and avoid the danger of detoxing with our loved ones. If we didn't have this special place, we most certainly would have let out our frustrations on each other or on anyone who might have crossed our path. By going to the physical safe place, we gave God the opportunity to reset our hearts so our physical person would once again display that we functioned in harmony with God, others, and ourselves. Our physical safe place served the purpose of bringing us back to peace and harmony; it also made us feel totally accepted by God in our physical body and appearance. Our world was good again.

Emotional Safe Place

It sounds kind of strange to have an emotional safe place. What purpose would such a place have? How does such an idea even work? Why would anyone need to seek out an emotional safe place? Ever since Jesus gave me my emotional safe place, my heart has been able to fend off damaging arrows that could have easily wounded my heart all over again.

Each of us can greatly benefit from having an emotional safe place, a place where we can go in our minds when others repeat the hurts we experienced in the past. We live in a world filled with people who, out of their own pain, continue to hurt others. In most cases, it is not their intent to hurt us; however, if they never dealt with their own unresolved issues, they will function out of their pain.

For instance, in my personal life, I was first rejected by my parents. So every time others reject me or create feelings of rejection, my heart feels the same pain I experienced when I was little and still living at home with my parents. Should a person, right now, reject me again, it is actually a repeat of what my parents started. My parents were the first people in my life to introduce the pain of rejection. From that day forward, individuals have just repeated it again and again.

Rejection is not my only core issue, I have discovered. I have several core issues, and it seemed there was always someone who kept stepping on one or more of them. I was unable to stop them and had no idea what to do with the constant pain. Eventually, I felt the need to separate myself from these individuals, till my heart healed, and I could handle their personalities without feeling rejected by them.

Everything changed when Jesus gave me my emotional safe place. He reset my heart the moment I gave Him permission to step into my pain. And at this point, Jesus placed a picture within my mind and heart. This beautiful gift from Jesus became my emotional safe place. How can you get your own emotional safe place? In chapter 3, I described in detail how I applied this in my own life. The following is a brief summary:

Remember that you will be piecing together a puzzle, beginning with your earliest memories. Always keep a permanent record, your personal story, on a piece of paper, as best as you can recall it. Then begin to put the puzzle pieces together: who was the first person who created the pain? Next, find the answers to several questions: How did my heart feel when this happened? Where did the event take place? How old was I when the first damage occurred? You may be surprised you are unable to remember events from your childhood; the memories may be sketchy. It may seem like your childhood has been wiped away. Don't worry. Jesus was there every step of the way while you were growing up. He will reveal your past and unfold it for you.

It is not uncommon for people to subconsciously or unknowingly lose memory of certain events in their life. If the pain is too great, we can detach and separate from it all; we can also disassociate. Disassociation is to put dramatic events completely aside in our minds in order to function in life. God gave us the ability to disassociate from horrific circumstances. When children are abused, the only option available to them is to disassociate at the time the abuse is happening. God's intent is not to leave these unresolved issues sitting there. He will allow time to pass. When a child has reached adulthood, or whenever God believes the moment is right to access these episodes again, God Himself will begin to give reminders of some unresolved issues that are still lingering in the heart. These reminders from God can come through experiencing flashbacks, dreams, unrest, or anxiety. People need to carefully examine their past, or have others assist them, to discover the root cause of unresolved issues. God has a way of bringing these things to the forefront, and He waits for the person to deal with them. He wants the opportunity to bring healing to our hearts.

Again, please refer back to chapter 3 and read the points in "How to Reset Your Emotional Heart." Familiarize yourself with the steps you need to apply to come to freedom in your emotional life. Before you end your prayer time, ask Jesus to give you your emotional safe place. Ask something like this: "Jesus, there will be moments and days when others repeat that which brought pain to my heart in the first place. What do you want me to do when others reject me? Can you give me a picture, a song, a verse, or a Bible story, and place this in my mind? When others reject me, can I go to this emotional safe place You give me today whenever I need too?"

The moment I asked Jesus these questions, I immediately saw a picture of myself at the edge of a forest. I was sitting, leaning with my back against a large tree trunk. My legs were drawn up. My eyes were resting on a green meadow just within reach, and the rays of the sun were streaming in from all sides. Right next to me sat Jesus. I did not see Him or touch Him, but I knew He was there, my protector and Savior. I felt completely safe, accepted, loved, cherished, and so much more. As I continued to pray through my emotional pain issues, more pictures and verses came to me. I can readily access any one of these should someone step on my core pain issues. If I place the picture of my safe place on top of the rejection pain, my heart will immediately feel at peace, and the presence of God becomes very real.

Spiritual Safe Place

Individuals who have been spiritually abused by a pastor, leader or another person, need to have a spiritual safe place. Since my spiritual upbringing was far away from anything God intended, I treasure my personal spiritual safe place, where I can be with Jesus, right away, no matter where I am or what is going on at the time. So what exactly is a spiritual safe place, and how do you get one?

It took me awhile to figure out how to pursue a spiritual safe place. Many times, I needed to know Jesus was with me in a much more concentrated way. I sought to somehow involve God's Word in the process and allow it to saturate my whole being and, at the same time, feel spiritually safe. My quest yielded an answer, and today, I'd like to introduce you to the most effective way I've discovered to establish a spiritual safe place. My answer came through my friend, who shared with me the following principles. At first, they sounded rather strange and unfamiliar, out of the ordinary. However, the longer I mulled them over in my mind, the more attractive they sounded. They revolutionized my walk with Jesus. My friend threw me a lifeline when she introduced me to what she calls meditation talk.[1]

Many of you are familiar with memorizing scripture. I am fascinated when individuals can recite entire portions of scripture from memory. In my case, memorizing anything always had its challenges, and I never felt up to the task. It could be because some of my pain issues were created by a teacher who had us memorize all the names and dates of various wars and recite entire poems from memory. It was not the activity of memorizing. It was the humiliation of being asked to stand in front of the entire class and endure the snickers and mocking faces of my classmates. Since one of my core pain issues is rejection, I felt utterly rejected by all of my peers and by my teacher. The longing, however, to hide God's Word in my heart has always been there.

Let me share with you how you can have a spiritual safe place that no one can ever take away from you. My friend affectionately used the acronym of "M&M" for the meditation talk. Sounds yummy; I love M&Ms, and I'm guessing many of you do, as well. Such a sweet treat. God's Word is not only sweet but also powerful. It is precious and yummier than any candy here on earth. The concept of engaging in this M&M method with God is profound, refreshing, and stimulating.

The following steps will connect you intimately with God and open up His Word to you in a new light. Once you begin, it will challenge you. As you practice the M&M method, you will discover you have walked with Jesus. The first "M" stands for "memorize." Well, look at this, there is that word: *memorize*. We will be considering a different way you can memorize. The second "M" in M&M stands for "meditate."

I'd like to begin by unpacking the word *memorize*. We are all familiar with the conventional process of memorizing scripture. First, we choose a portion of scripture and put to memory the name of the book, the chapter number, and the verse reference. Then, to be successful, we read, recite, and repeat the process till the scripture is firm in our mind. This activity takes discipline and certain effort. It is wonderful to load up the heart with such rich treasures we can access at any time. The Holy Spirit will bring back the Word of God when we need it most, if it was truly put to memory at one time.

I found this to be the case when I cared for Alzheimer's patients years ago; then, years later, when Mike and I had the opportunity to hold services at a nursing home, the patients afflicted with Alzheimer's freely recited God's Word, word for word. We witnessed firsthand the recollection of God's Word by individuals who could no longer remember their own name or anything else. Yet they fondly completed scripture verses my husband read to them. We felt honored and touched when the Word of God flowed out of their mouths and hearts, as if it was just put to memory yesterday.

Some of us are endowed with a wonderful ability to memorize easily. One of my roommates in college had a photographic memory; I was jealous of how easily she could memorize entire chapters. I had to labor for my grades. I challenge you to keep at it and try to put key verses to memory for the purpose of sharing the gospel with others. Nothing can compare with actually possessing the Word of God in your heart.

Then there is the process of meditation. This is our second "M." Memorizing scripture alone is not beneficial because we would miss the real intent of the exercise. Only if a scripture is imprinted on our heart and mind will we realize its full impact and know what the verses say to us. Many of us fall short in this department; it takes extra effort to allow the Holy Spirit to teach us what God wants to say to us through a particular verse. So when memorizing, most of us focus on quantity rather than on quality. The quality of the memorizing is meditation. With the M&M method, you actually accomplish both quality and quantity in a slightly different way, yet the meditation will be more effective.

Following are the steps for your M&M session. First, select a small portion of scripture. I recommend the text you choose is not too large; keep it to a single page. After you have settled on what you want to read, make yourself comfortable by sitting in your favorite spot. Read your text over several times. You want to familiarize yourself with the content of the text so well that you would be able to share what you have just read with another person. Before you go to the next step, you should have the story firmly in your mind; you know what is happening or understand what the parable or story is talking about. (in this case memorizing looks different as what we are used too). Of course, if you are away from home or at your workplace, you want to go back to a passage of scripture you have already put to the M&M experience and enjoy it again.

Now comes the fantastic part. The next step of meditation is to shift your focus to the actual content of the text you just read. Ask Jesus to teach you what He wants you to know about the verse you selected. Seek some privacy where you can enjoy quiet and stillness in your soul. Begin the process of meditation by simply concentrating all of your attention on each specific verse. At the same time, you will focus on God, putting your full attention on Him in order to truly enjoy His presence and your fellowship together. You can close your eyes if that is helpful. Walk with Him through the passage of scripture. At some point, isolate specific words or a sentence, and think about what this means to you personally, or what God wants to say specifically to you.

The following is a small example. If my selection is Psalm 23, I will read it over several times. When I'm ready to meditate on this wonderful chapter, with my eyes closed, I imagine myself walking with the Shepherd. I might ask myself, "Is there anything I want in addition to what I have right now, here, being with Him?" I may not come up with anything because, as we are walking together, I'm completely content. After a little while, I continue through the passage of scripture with my Lord. We lie down next to the quiet waters, and there I pour out my heart to Him. I let Jesus restore my soul. I allow the scripture to remind me that moments may come throughout my life where I find myself in a dark valley, the valley of the shadow of death. I will reaffirm my commitment to Jesus not to be afraid because I know He is always close by. His rod and staff protect and comfort me always.

As I continue to meditate on this portion of scripture, I am so engaged with Jesus, it almost feels like I'm there with Him. The scripture comes alive. I experience the truth I am reading; at any time, I can go to this selection again and continue the meditating process or go over the same images again. I have found the longer I practice M&M, the more I want to do it. Entire chapters have come alive for me and will forever be etched in my mind and heart. This is my spiritual safe place. These are the places I go whenever I feel judged or criticized by a fellow believer, or when I'm about to teach a group or lead a Bible study, or when I have been invited by a church to speak to hurting hearts.

In these times, I want to draw extra strength from God as my mind and heart rest on my M&M sessions. The pictures I see in my mind will serve as my forever spiritual safe places. No one can take these away from me or alter them in any way. I can access specific verses, not by giving you the chapter or by reciting a scripture passage word for word. I can retell the content of the story, or parable, or a certain event that took place in scripture, by being so familiar with the text that it resides in my heart. To summarize our spiritual safe place: it is found in God's Word because only there do we find truth.

Sexual Safe Place

You may not have heard of establishing a sexual safe place, but this is exactly what I had to do. A sexual safe place is a must, no matter where you are in your physical life, no matter how old you are in your emotional heart, or what stage you find yourself in your spiritual life. It is essential and necessary.

What exactly is a sexual safe place? Setting up a safe place involves establishing boundaries and drawing a line in the sand, so to speak. If you know your parameters and others know your limits concerning your sexual life, you will always feel safe and protected. These boundaries you erect are your sexual safe place. To begin setting up these boundaries, you will have to answer this question: What guidelines do I want to follow and am

I willing to keep? It is foolish to set up lofty goals you have no intention of keeping. This is similar to people declaring New Year's resolutions. If you do not give them some thought and consider all the obstacles that will surely come your way, the first stumbling block in the road will lead to failure and giving up. If you set a boundary not to kiss a man (or woman) until you stand with them at the altar, you have to set up guidelines early on in order to keep that goal. Society, friends, and family members may not share your vision. You will be on your own. The strength and willpower you need has to be fueled by your close relationship with God, and for this reason, you must move sexually from the Infant Stage to the Mature Stage.

As a woman, your emotional needs must be met without giving in to sexual activity. For a man, it is vital to train yourself to be self-controlled and not to give in to your strong sexual desires. God knows your sexuality will awaken one day, and for this reason, young men and women are to seek a marriage partner and enjoy this gift of sexuality God has given. Healthy sexual boundaries will not only keep you from immorality. They will help you to maintain a healthy physical, emotional, and spiritual life.

Setting up boundaries starts early in life; the sooner, the better. You make the choices because you are the one who must decide what the boundaries are and put them in place. There is a whole world out there that is sexually involved at a very young age; the sexual tsunami is not easy to escape. In order for you to make a commitment to them, your plans must be firm, unwavering, and reasonable.

Let's go back to the sexual development stages I wrote about in chapter 5, beginning at the infant, toddler, and kindergarten stages. Infants cannot set any kind of boundaries. Actually, the opposite is true. The adults in their life need to set boundaries for them. In this stage, we have our first exposure to anyone setting a limit as to what is acceptable in our life. We find out, as we get older, there is always someone who sets standards for us. Toddlers and smaller children can be introduced to boundaries. They need to be taught that sexual touch is that which includes any part of the body that is covered when wearing a bathing suit, and it's not permitted by anyone who is not involved in their personal hygiene care. When children are a bit older than a toddler, between two and four years old, they should be able to answer these questions: "Who is allowed to touch you?" and "Where can they touch you?" If they do not know the answers to these questions, how can they know there are boundaries concerning their sexuality? Small children would not know they are being sexually molested if they never learn where others can and cannot touch them. Toddlers are able to say, "No." They can run away or tell an adult what is happening, thereby keeping themselves safe from perpetrators.

When we explore the Six- to Ten-Year-Old Stage, sexual boundaries are essential. Children are in the world and exposed to all kinds of different people who may not have set sexual boundaries in their own life and could potentially harm them. By this time, it should be clear not only to the adults, but also to the child, who is allowed to touch the sexual areas. The elementary age child may not be able to clearly define boundaries for themselves, but they understand that their sexuality is totally private.

At the Puberty Stage, the game changes, and by this time, the hormones are going crazy, and the sexual appetite is felt. Before children reach this critical age, the trusted adults in their life must explain what boundaries are.

As shared with you earlier, we prepared our children by teaching them healthy sexuality. When they reached their sixteenth birthday, we did something special to help them commemorate the day and cement in their own hearts to choose purity till marriage. We proposed to our children to consider having their first date with Mom or Dad. Dad would be our daughter's first date, and I would be our son's first date. We were comfortable with our children engaging in group dating, where they could exercise their decision-making muscles as they encountered various situations. You see, we can teach good things and read about healthy sexual living, but if we never get the opportunity to put it all into practice, how will we become aware of how difficult or easy this is? For this reason, we gave our kids the freedom to go on dates with the opposite sex when they reached their sixteenth birthday. We made it clear it would be best to start out with double-dating or going out with a mixed group. This was so they could familiarize themselves with the behaviors and actions of the opposite sex outside of Mom, Dad, or a familiar relative.

The invitation to be my son's first date was accepted. I asked him to choose the place he wanted to dine, the clothes he wanted me to wear, and whatever else he could think of, to make our date special. When the day arrived, it was magical in many ways. I saw my son in a totally new light:

as a young man, no longer a child. My heart was so proud. Of course, our daughter and her dad planned their own special date. As we were seated in the restaurant and enjoying our meal together, even my son could sense the importance of this occasion. We chatted easily with each other. After we finished eating, we just lingered, enjoying each other's company. This was the moment I had been waiting for.

I sat back, looked at my almost-grown boy, and said, "I not only wanted to be your first date. I bought a special present for you as well. Before you accept this gift, I want you to promise me to give it some thought before you accept it."

My son was curious, cautious, and unsure of how to respond, so I continued. I opened my purse and took out a small box. Ladies, you know that when a small gift box is produced, our hearts get excited because we hope it holds a ring. You guessed right. The little box I placed in front of my son did hold a ring. It was not a sentimental ring or a Claddagh ring (which stands for love, loyalty, and friendship). No, this ring had a totally different meaning. It would serve as a reminder for him of having made a promise to himself to remain pure till marriage.

I opened the box to reveal its contents and said, "Son, this ring is unique. If you choose to accept this ring and proudly wear it, you would be choosing to keep yourself sexually pure till your future wife removes it from your finger and replaces it with your wedding ring. Not only that, but you would be committing yourself to set up boundaries so you can keep your promise. What I'm asking you today is a lot. Please give this some deep thought and do not take it lightly. I will keep this purity ring until you give me an answer. Very soon, you will go out into the world; your dad and I can no longer shield you or make decisions for you. These will eventually rest on you. In the area of your sexuality, you will have to decide what you want to do with it because it will be your constant companion for the rest of your life."

Before I knew what was happening, my son took the ring from the box and slid it on his finger.

My heart did a little flip. He truly wanted to do this, and I was so proud of him. A small certificate also came with the ring. I handed the piece of paper to him and asked him to sign the certificate. This would be the act of driving the stake in the ground for him.

I added, "Son, this ring will be a visible reminder of the promise you made today. The promise you are making is not for me. It is for you, and as your mom, I have the privilege of being a witness to your choice. I want to add, however, if you decide to open the white box, the gift of sexual oneness you should only enjoy with your future wife, or engage in any kind of sexual activity with others, I will always love you, and God will always love you too."

Preparing our children for sex was as natural as eating dinner at our house. So we knew we could wait to present the idea of the purity ring until they reached the age we had set for them to begin dating. If parents wait till their children reach the age of sixteen before having a conversation about sex, it may be too late. It cannot wait. It is our privilege, as parents, to guide our kids in all areas, to give them the best possible start in life, and help them be successful in all areas. We know that giving away our sexuality too early will only lead to giving it away again, and again, and again. Our physical body will feel used and taken advantage of. Our heart will emotionally struggle and begin to feel neglected, and our spiritual life will suffer because God seems far away.

As their caretakers, we can spare our kids a lot of pain. Young people need to be familiar with the concept of boundaries and know how to set boundaries; then it's up to them to keep them. If adults set up boundaries, the teen may end up not having the motivation or desire to abide by them. They may believe these rules were good enough for the parents when they were young, but things are different now. If they set the boundaries themselves, the responsibility for their actions will rest on their shoulders, and they will have created their own sexual safe place.

If you are a single person, you know full well how hard it is to keep yourself sexually pure. This is why you need to establish specific boundaries for yourself and for others. You might want to consider who to keep company with, decide what kind of TV programs or movies to watch, determine where you feel sexually safe when outside of your home, decide whether you will ever be alone in a room with a person of the opposite sex, and so on.

Another question has to be answered: What boundaries must I set for my own personal life that enable me to live sexually pure before God? These areas need to be explored, considered, and dealt with, so the boundaries are solid, and life can continue in a smooth way. Drawing close to God will help you remain pure in your sexual life.

In the dating world, the temptations are at their highest. Without good ground rules and boundaries, you may find yourself in a situation you cannot handle. Dating can be fun without opening the Pandora's box of sexuality. However, as we hold each other and care for each other, we need to consider the physical contact points. The more physical we are, the stronger our sexual response will be. I've always loved to dance; however, this innocent activity includes close physical contact. For this reason, a dating couple needs to decide what kind of dancing they engage in. We need to exercise self-control if we want to remain sexually pure.

While dating, we want to know the other person and discover all we can about them. Of course, we are sexual beings, and our attraction is not only about looks and personality. We are sexually attracted to each other, as well. Countless couples have shared with me that when they decided to move to the next level and became sexually involved with each other, at that point, all talking and communication stopped. The physical was always chosen, or even demanded (generally, not by the female, who often gives in to the pressure from the man because she cannot stand the thought of losing him). If we step over the line and engage in premarital sex, we usually continue for the very reasons I already mentioned.

Premarital sex is a sin. If we step over the line, we can confess we have sinned (1 John 1:9), repent of our sin, and agree to sin no more, even as Jesus told the woman who was caught in adultery, "Woman, where are they? Did no one condemn you?" She answered, "No one, Lord!" And Jesus said, "I do not condemn you either. Go. From now on sin no more."] (John10b–11 AMP).

Married couples need to establish sexual boundaries, their sexual safe place, in order to remain pure and faithful to each other. We make these commitments to ourselves and to our spouse in order to honor them. The last thing we want to do is betray them and break the promise we made to each other, "to forsake all others." If you are not willing or able to forsake all others, it is best you do not get married. Getting married announces to the world that there is no other for you but your spouse. She is your one and only; your husband is the only guy you will ever be with, sexually. The enemy does not believe in these kinds of commitments, and his goal is to derail you. As you know, married couples will have roadblocks. All too soon, the honeymoon ends, reality sets in, and the marriage bed is not the blissful fantasy we envisioned. This is the time the enemy will step in. You see, Satan is an opportunist and a master timer. He will wait for the right moment to do what he does best, that is, to deceive you.

Healthy sexual boundaries for married couples should include commitments to never be alone with someone from the opposite sex. This is similar for single people. Making a covenant with your eyes, as Job stated in the Old Testament, is vital: "I made a covenant with my eyes not to look lustfully at a young woman" (Job 31:1 NIV).

In a marriage relationship, there is no keeping of secrets (except for presents you want to surprise your loved one with). What I mean is, no passwords should be private, and all on-line accounts should be accessible to the spouse. Our lives should be like open books so two hearts can relax with each other. Once these areas have been violated, trust is broken. Rebuilding trust takes a long time and a lot of effort. Married couples need to guard themselves against the kind of activities they enjoy with other married couples, and how often. The relationships will be sexually healthy if all parties involved have healthy relationships with their own spouses. When the marriage of another couple is in trouble, the risk of getting emotionally involved is much greater, and emotional attachments can lead to physical things.

Widows and widowers once enjoyed sexual intimacy with their beloved. One day, this ended, with the death of their spouse. New boundaries need to be established in order to remain pure. Widows and widowers need to consider getting their emotional needs met from different sources: enjoying mixed-gender group activities or a hobby that can be shared by staying on task, without sexually intimate interaction. Both need to safeguard their sexual life and find others who can provide what is needed emotionally, in a healthy way.

Helpful Tools to Remain Whole

Daily life and all its demands are not only challenging but exhausting, as well. How do you stay whole and healthy, with so little time to spare? If we are fully mature in our physical, emotional, spiritual, and sexual lives, then we have gained much ground. If we have set up our safe places, our journey through life will be easier. Now all that is left is to continue to be intentional, to be proactive, and to keep all four areas in freedom.

What does being proactive and intentional look like? What can we do to keep ourselves on track and not lose sight of our goal to stay whole? The following are some ideas I have applied in my own life and recommend to others. You see, we need to put reminders in our life, so we never forget. As you read through the list of recommendations, you can decide how you'd like to commemorate what God has done in your life. Instead of staying on a vicious cycle, going one step forward and two steps backward, you will have tools on hand to help center yourself on Christ.

One suggestion is to keep a journal. Contrary to common belief, this is not only an activity for woman or young girls in puppy love. It does not entail writing down gushy, mushy stuff. The kind of journaling I want you to get hooked on is unlike anything you may have considered before. It is profitable for men and women, young and old. These records will be open and available for all to see. No, this is not a private affair where you write down what is happening in your life from day to day. Nor is it a recording of some kind of secret dream or wishful thinking. This kind of journaling is for you to record the progress of your healing journey and of staying in freedom. If you choose this option, record as often as you can because these words, on the paper, will be your lifelines for years to come. Following are some options for different types of journals, along with some other ideas to help you remain whole.

Victory Journal: Ebenezer

The first tool I would like to offer for your consideration is a Victory Journal. Keeping a Victory Journal is not limited to literally writing on a piece of paper with a pen; it can also take the form of an "Ebenezer." The primary function of a Victory Journal is to provide a record of what God has accomplished in your life, so you will never forget. You will be able to look back in an instant and recall what God has done for you in the past. A Victory Journal, or Ebenezer, is a record kept so others can see when God has shown up in a miraculous way. I personally call these miracles "God moments." Before I flesh out these principles a bit more, please allow me to give you a brief background on the Ebenezer, describe what it is exactly, and explain where this concept actually originated.

An Ebenezer is not the character in the familiar Yuletide play, *A Christmas Carol*; this name and its meaning is taken directly from the Bible. It is related to times when God supernaturally intervened on behalf of the Israelites, as described in the Old Testament accounts. The leaders of the nation of Israel knew exactly what God wanted them to do, and when they fulfilled His command to the letter, He rewarded them with a great victory. This victory that was given by God was commemorated by erecting an Ebenezer. An Ebenezer consisted of stones piled on top of each other, or arranged in an order prescribed by God. Its purpose was as a permanent reminder for the people to be able to look back to an occasion when God had met them and gave them victory. It was Samuel, the priest, who first named the piling up of these stones "Ebenezer," meaning "the Lord has helped us." In essence, an Ebenezer is a "stone of help."

> Then Samuel took a stone and set it between Mizpah and
> Shen, and he named it Ebenezer (stone of help), saying,
> "Thus far the LORD has helped us." (1 Samuel 7:12 AMP)

From this day forward, the Israelites would continue the practice of erecting these stone markers, as demonstrated by Samuel, to serve as a permanent reminder of God's intervention in a difficult circumstance. At times, God Himself instructed the Israelites to establish an Ebenezer. The pile of stones marked the very spot where God defeated the enemy or turned a trial into a blessing.

No one, not even Satan, or your family members, or anyone else, can take away the victories God gives exclusively to you. These victories, or Ebenezers, are not only for you to keep and hold dear, but also for others, to point them to God when they face their own trials. Each one of us needs to intentionally look at our life and identify our victories, possible places to erect an Ebenezer in order to never, ever forget the times God fought for us, and we were victorious because of it. As it was for the Israelites, we need to record our victories as a chronological, historical account of God working in our lives.

Other entries you can include in your Victory Journal are what I call "Blessings in Disguise." What do I mean by this? You see, when I look back at my sexual abuse, I now know I would not have prayed for these individuals if God had not called on me to do so. It is my prayer that each and every one of them will come to know Jesus Christ as their personal Savior. The privilege I now have to pray for their salvation is indeed a miracle, and I want to mark this prompting of the Lord and my obedience as a victory in my life.

Your Victory Journal may not have many entries, but what you record in its pages will be powerful and will never lose its impact on your life. Likewise, your Ebenezers will be few, but at the same time, they will be extremely important reminders of God's interventions in your life.

I am able to go back to whatever entry I want to read, and the presence of God will still overwhelm me. The tears will flow again, and my heart will be touched by how God intervened in a seemingly impossible circumstance. These are my victories, miracles God performed in my life. He will do the same in your life. Your Victory Journal will be filled with powerful memories you would have lost if you had depended on your memory alone.

One woman shared with me some of the entries from her personal Victory Journal, and I almost felt like taking my shoes off. It seemed we were on holy ground. Her account of how God met her in a specific and terrifying moment was miraculous, and it could only have been accomplished by God Himself. This permanent record of God's intervention in her life is there for her when she finds herself in the midst of other trials. She can go to her Victory Journal and draw new strength. She can't know if God will once again intervene on her behalf, but she has the record that He can. It is up to God if He wills.

Another woman told me she went out to her physical safe place, taking a special collection of different-sized stones with her. Each stone bore a powerful message of how God reached into her life when there was no way out. On one of the stones, she had recorded with a permanent marker how God had revealed Himself, that He was present every time she was sexually abused by one of her family members. Also written on one of the stones were these words: "God cried for me, understood me, felt my pain, and I was never ever alone." Every time she visits her Ebenezers, her stones, she feels immediately close to God. She once placed some of these stones under her Christmas tree. This signified to her that no earthly present could compare to what God had done for her.

This is powerful. My personal Victory Journal has become an unexpected tool. When Mike and I were raising funds for our move to Africa, we found ourselves in many different churches. On several occasions, as we arrived at a church, the pastor or an elder greeted us, and they would ask if I would speak to the ladies.

I would reply, "Yes," and then ask if they could give me a moment, that I would be right back.

You know what I would do next? I would find the bathroom, lock myself into a stall, and pray. I would ask God to lead me to a portion in my Victory Journal I had started in the back of my Bible a long time ago; I asked Him to point out what He wanted me to share with the ladies. You know what? It never failed. I would know exactly what to share with the ladies, and all of us were blessed together as we experienced a little bit of heaven on earth.

Gratitude Journal

The second tool is also a journal where you can record what God has done in your life. I call this a "Gratitude Journal." Here, you can commemorate all the special blessings you've received throughout the day, the week, or the month. You will be able to hold on to your personal blessings because this journal is filled with them.

As I record my blessings in my Gratitude Journal, I often wonder if there were blessings God could not give me because I had insisted on going my own way. One day, after spending some time in prayer, I reflected on this thought and began to imagine the beautiful pearly gates, the entrance to heaven. Because I had heard so many stories and tales of Peter being the first person to greet us there, he was there in my imaginary story. I know our arrival in heaven will be nothing any of us can imagine, but for what I was seeking, it was the perfect picture.

In my imagination, Peter greeted me and offered me a private tour of heaven. Right after we walked through the magnificent pearly gates, one enormous building loomed directly in front of us. The structure was so large, I could not see the end of its length or its height, yet Peter took me past the door without entering.

"Wait a minute, Peter," I said. "Aren't we starting our tour of heaven by seeing what's inside this building?"

"No," he answered. "We will not enter this building."

Of course, my curiosity was stirred, and I started pestering Peter to allow me to peek inside this very large warehouse. I was convinced it held a great mystery. I wanted to see, with my own eyes, what is stored in heaven that requires such a large building.

So Peter gave in, and we entered the large complex. I saw rows and rows of shelves, all looking the same and reaching into infinity. All of the shelves were the same size and held white boxes, all neatly arranged next to each other. *What could be stored in these white boxes?* I wondered.

I had barely completed the thought when Peter chimed in, "Each of these boxes belongs to someone, received the moment they were born."

So I have a white box in heaven with my name written on it? I thought to myself. *This sounds exciting.*

I boldly asked, "Can I see my box?"

Before I knew what was happening, we stood before a box bearing my name. I was not sure I really wanted to know what this box held, but we had come this far; I might as well remove the lid and take a peek.

Just before I lifted the lid, I heard Peter's voice: "Each box stores blessings God could not give to people because they chose their own way over His." At this point, my heart became sad. In my imagination, I realized, if there were such a thing as a white box stored in heaven bearing my name, it would contain many blessings God withheld from me. There were many times I determined to do my own thing. My heart felt a deep loss.

This is just an imaginary story, but I hope you get the point. I want all the blessings God has for me, and I want to receive all the good things God planned for me to have. This is the reason I started my Gratitude Journal: to never forget each precious blessing from God. Most of the blessings He has given me have come in the form of people He placed in my life at just the right moment, when I needed them most. If I had missed these saints, I would have made different decisions, and my life would have taken a different path.

Writing Letters to God

Another way to remain whole and healthy is to write a letter to God. Letters to God can be filled with thanksgiving, or you can vent to Him and express what is in your heart. You can record the journey of your life for others to read. You may want to begin your letter to God in this way: "Dear Abba, Father," or "Dear God, remember when You … when I …" Keep writing till you run out of words and have spent your soul on this piece of paper. Gently fold your letter and place it in an envelope. Over time, as you stack each letter on top of the other, take a colored ribbon and bind them together. You could use different colored ribbons for different kinds of letters. For instance, choose a red ribbon for happy letters you wrote to God, or green when something really exciting happened, or blue for special moments when God seemed even closer than before. You decide what to do and how to keep these letters.

If you have written letters filled with painful memories, and some later time God spoke peace to your heart and you were able to forgive a person, you might want to destroy these letters, thereby closing the door. Or you could take a big fat red marker and write these words on top: "Finished, paid in full." Next, you could go to your Gratitude Journal and record how God took a mess and transformed it into a message, or turned a trial into a triumph. Or you can write in your Victory Journal that you were finally able to forgive.

Letters can also be written to people who at one time influenced your life. We never want to forget these interventions. I call these people God has sent my way "my angels on the sidelines." These angels on the sidelines come to us seemingly out of nowhere and disappear in almost the same fashion. How awesome is it to leave behind letters of that nature. Your children and family members will be immediately ushered into God's realm, where angels live and function as special messengers of God. The people who will read the contents of these letters will know, without a shadow of a doubt, God is still on the throne.

If you choose to write letters, or you would rather keep a Victory Journal or a Gratitude Journal, or set up Ebenezers, these precious recordings can become your legacy. You may want to pass them on to your children. There is no greater treasure to pass on to the next generation than to share with them what God did in your life.

Returning a Blessing

The last idea I would like to pass on to you came to me via a request from God. It proved itself powerful in my life and changed everything. Before I share with you what God revealed to me, let me point you back to the four main chapters, where I fleshed out how God wants us to grow and mature physically, emotionally, spiritually, and sexually. In each of these chapters, you read about my personal story, my journey, how my heart was damaged and filled with pain. You followed the steps I applied to come to freedom. In this last chapter, my emphasis is on how to stay in this newfound freedom. If you choose not to take steps to keep this freedom, before you know what is happening, you will find yourself with a heart filled with pain again. This last step will safeguard you, in a way, to prevent this from happening.

You wonder, what could be so powerful that it would keep one's heart free? Your question deserves an answer. After I made peace with God about the past issues and the current condition of my physical body (chapter 2), my focus shifted to my emotional issues (chapter 3). As I invited Jesus into all of my pain, He took it away and replaced it with all the good things I needed. I then turned my attention to unresolved spiritual problems (chapter 4), and it took me almost two years to finally clean up all my sin issues and establish a great relationship with God. I had no idea my heart held so much bitterness or how prideful I had become. I was confronted with my rebellious ways and had to acknowledge and repent of my sinful, immoral lifestyle. Finally, it was time to face my sexual issues (chapter 5), where Jesus helped me forgive my abusers and brought healing. After all of these areas were addressed and true freedom reigned in my heart, God gave me my final assignment to return a blessing when a person has hurt me in some way. This proved to be the key to not allow others to fill my heart with pain again.

As previously mentioned, there was a moment in my healing journey where I understood, with my heart, what God really wanted to say to me. He had allowed these events in my life, and He knew what I would eventually do with it all. What do I mean? I understood God had entrusted me with all the things that happened to me, not to punish me, or to teach me a lesson, or to make my life miserable. No, on the contrary, God wanted me to come to a place where I would be able to completely trust Him, no matter what was happening in my life, and see the bigger picture.

> Trust in *and* rely confidently on the LORD with all your heart_And do not rely on your own insight *or* understanding. In all your ways know *and* acknowledge *and* recognize Him, And He will make your paths straight *and* smooth [removing obstacles that block your way]. (Proverbs 3:5–6 AMP)

I know what is going through your mind right now. I thought the same thing: How can we tell people who have endured horrible torture to trust God? How can we witness the untimely funeral of a child and tell family members to trust God as they visit the gravesite? I don't understand it all, but I do know God permits what He hates, and He allows evil to exist and influence our lives. For this reason, you and I need to live in the light of our real home, eternity. I had to give God His rightful place in all areas of my life, whether I agreed with Him about what was happening or not. He knows best, and all He wants me to do is to trust Him completely. This is why I want to encourage you to move from spiritual infancy to spiritual maturity. Walk with God, and don't get stuck if circumstances get difficult.

Once again, I used my imagination to hold fast to what God wanted me to know. Ever since I found this powerful image, I've been able to use it to focus my mind back on God. The image is of a very large box. This large box has my name written on it, and God Himself gave it to me the day I was born. I call this box my life box. This box is filled with packages. God's purpose in giving me this life box is for me to reach inside, at certain appointed times, and take out the next package. All the packages are different sizes. They are labeled with a description of their contents; however, I can only read the label after the package is in my hands. Sometimes, when I have lifted a package out of my life box, my heart has leaped for joy. Written on these labels have been things like "nursing career," "marriage," "adopt three children," and so on. There have been other packages I did not want to accept, because when I read the labels and fully realized their contents, my heart felt fear: "rejected because of gender," "sexual abuse," "never having children on my own," and so on. With each box I receive, I remind myself that a loving, wise, heavenly Father placed it there for me, and all He wants to know is do I trust Him completely with this trial and His plan for my life. I give Him the praise for all the good things He blesses me with.

You see, every time I saw a person who reminded me of the people who had hurt me, my heart constricted, and I felt the old pain again. In the past, I would just put another bandage over my bleeding heart. Today, I choose to bring the pain to Jesus and return a blessing. My heart came to understand that, in order to catch the fiery arrows from others and not let them penetrate and hurt me, I must fire my own arrows of blessing back to them. How do I do that? It is actually quite simple, yet tough at the same time. The moment I realize what is happening, I pronounce a blessing on the person. Returning a blessing instead of evil is very powerful and brings my heart right back to peace. It also leaves the person in God's hands.

Let me give you an example. From time to time, I find myself in the company of a person who reminds me of my mom. Her voice might be similar, or her character might be the same. Such a person can easily wound my heart again, especially if she is in my presence often, like a coworker or boss. When the arrows fly, instead of letting them hurt me again, I choose to return a blessing. This blessing will be in the form of a silent prayer like, "Lord Jesus, I don't know if my boss had a demanding morning, but you do. I ask you to just wrap your arms around her and let her know how special she is, and that you love her very much." Or I could say in my heart, "Heavenly Father, give favor and blessing to my boss today as she deals with all of the responsibilities she faces." Saying or praying a blessing on others is like asking God to protect them.

Your blessings will be short prayers on behalf of the person you choose to bless, and you will find your heart and mind will dwell on the blessing instead of on the arrows thrown your way. These arrows will not find their mark and will not inflict new pain. After my heart clearly had a handle on how to go about it, I put it to the test. I have not stopped giving out blessings since that first time. Start small, when you are ready. You see, there will come a time when you need to give account to Jesus, and He will reveal the motives of your heart. So if your motives are not pure, it is best not to pretend and give yourself a pat on the back for doing so well. No, these blessings you will pronounce need to be genuine and heartfelt. God wants us to see people as He sees them. He desires to give them what He freely gave us. First, He gave us the gift of free salvation, and we have the opportunity to introduce these folks to Jesus. Second, we can help them begin their own journey of coming to freedom in their physical, emotional, spiritual, and sexual life.

A Mature Person

Mature Christians are not afraid to go through the pruning process that God will, at times, choose for us. We need to see life from God's perspective because we are indwelled by the Holy Spirit, who is God. Each of us is a presenter of the living God to the world. Do we truly reflect God to this world? We do not represent God well if we act out in anger. Trials are our test of how we are doing, how we speak of God, and whether we can truly say, "It is well with my soul." An immature person will ask, "Why did God allow this to happen?" What does it mean when we say God is good? Is God only good when He gives blessings? At times, God is silent, and we long for an answer and it does not come. There is a reason why God is silent.

Take teachers, for instance. They speak, and instruct, and tell their students what they need to know, but when it comes to the testing time, teachers are silent. They want to know if you have learned what you have been taught. In the same way, God teaches us, and at times, He gives us a test to see if we are ready to go to the next level of the assignment He has for us. During these testing times, God may be silent. Like a teacher, He wants to promote us to the next grade level, and in order to do that, He needs to know if we have learned what He was teaching us.

It is during these testing times our weaknesses will surface. We can run to God, acknowledge this weakness, and allow Him to strengthen us. There is always a lesson for us in the storm. A fully mature believer will not be afraid of these tests. We can ready ourselves and be prepared, just like a student must study in order to be prepared for the test. We will only fail the test if we are unprepared, if we have never fully grown in our physical, emotional, spiritual, and sexual life. Maybe it is time to reset your heart.

There was a time I wrestled with the thought of God having to punish sin, till I came to the conclusion that it is actually God disciplining us when we have sinned. It is a good thing because it keeps us from sinning. In like manner, we discipline our children so they will not repeat an offense. God's laws are a protective barrier around us. We are free in Christ but need to come to terms that He is in charge.

Why do we need to reach maturity in the four areas I covered? Because there will be times we are faced with trials, and it will require tremendous faith and trust on our part to include God in these circumstances. We need to stop acting as if this world is our home and, in some bizarre way, trying to seek heaven here on earth.

As we get close to the author of love, God, we begin to learn to love as He loves. God will channel His love through us, and we will channel it to the world. Getting to know the heart of God should be our primary goal in the pursuit of growing and maturing physically, emotionally, spiritually, and sexually. With the assistance of the Holy Spirit, we can refashion ourselves in all four of these areas. God will re-parent us by being the parent we never had and perhaps still long for. He will re-father the fatherless and come alongside the grown-up person who never had a dad or mom to mirror the heart of God. In some way, God Himself will recreate us by healing our hearts. Only then can we look beyond ourselves to others who are still hurting.

If you are familiar with Mother Teresa, you may know she dedicated her life to the extremely poor in India. I believe Mother Teresa saw the face of God in the faces of the outcasts of Calcutta because each individual she ministered to was precious in her sight. She became the hands and feet of Jesus. How could she do that? I believe she found the answer to the question, What do I need to do in order to be completely whole and fully available to God? Each of us must seek our God-given assignments. He left us here on earth to represent Him, after all. If our hearts carry unresolved issues and pain, we will, in a limited way, be able to be the hands and feet of Jesus. Jesus wants you to write a new story, like He did with my life. Every day I choose to enter God's world, and He enters mine, I am reminded that God is in charge of Satan and the world.

Once Broken, Now Made Whole

In the previous chapters, you followed along as I shared my personal story with you. You walked with me as I shared my heart. Some of you felt my pain, and perhaps your own pain surfaced, as well. Some of you are ready to run to Jesus and allow Him to bring healing to your wounded heart. Like me, you long for the day when you can rejoice in what God has done. My heavenly Father performed a miracle in my heart by bringing me back to the way He created me. He loved me so much, He did not let me flounder through life as the person I had become.

Jesus healed me in my physical life, and together, we rejoice for me being a girl. He restored my spiritual heart because I now know who God really is. I had lost my way and lost my true identity, and it was Jesus who reached into my heart and healed me emotionally. For years, I longed for purity, second virginity, to be once again declared a clean and moral woman. Not till I gave Jesus full access to my past did I receive healing in my sexual life. And God not only restored me; He made me whole and complete, and He declared me pure. For years, I tried to fix myself, but all the methods I pursued left me empty. I even had the bright idea I could cure myself from the outside; all I needed was my strong willpower. I was so wrong. Only God can bring healing, and He does it from the inside out. All that is left is for me to tell you what my life looks like today.

When I entered into this broken world with my physical body, I was all intact and had all of my fingers and toes. But right from the start, I was rejected because I was a girl. Emotionally, I was broken and wounded. My heart felt the rejection. I knew I was not wanted and was not loved. Spiritually, I was separated from God, as we all are. Because we all have inherited Adam's sin nature, we all have sinned and come short of the glory of God:

> Therefore, just as sin came into the world through one man, and death through sin, so death spread to all people [no one being able to stop it or escape its power], because they all sinned. (Romans 5:12 AMP)

> For all have sinned and fall short of the glory of God (Romans 3:23 NIV).

In addition to the sinful nature I inherited from Adam, I was led astray by my spiritual advisors to follow a religion that, after my earthly time ended, would not lead me into the everlasting arms of Jesus, but instead, into eternity separated from Him forever.

I was sexually abused several times, and the gift of sexuality, as God had intended it to be, was taken away from me. It became a distorted thing, leaving me in a very confused and shameful state. I was deeply hurt, and it took me years to finally deal with the deep wounds in my heart.

My healing journey could not have happened if I had not included God. To my surprise, I had to start at my beginning, and with my own heart, understand how the hearts of my parents had been wounded before I was even in the picture. I was parented out of their pain. Once I realized how their hearts must have felt, my own heart grieved for my mom and dad for what they had lost and never found. My heart was ready to forgive, knowing we had all lost so much. The more I contemplated our losses, the more a sweet love for my parents washed over my heart. Both of my parents had already been dead for many years, yet my heart longed to have been given the opportunity to tell them personally that I forgave them. I would have also asked them to forgive me for never seeing their pain, for being focused on my own needs.

Along the road of my healing journey, I also discovered I had lugged around a suitcase full of facades and masks to hide behind, pretending to the world that all is well. I'm forever grateful to Jesus for taking away all of my made-up charades that kept others out of my heart. My own heart could not find its way out of my self-made prison. Today, I no longer want to hide or pretend. All is well. Yes, I still guard my heart a little bit. What does this mean? You see, I will always encounter individuals in my life I'll never be safe with, either physically, emotionally, spiritually, or sexually. So I choose to keep them at a distance. Then there is a special group of people who have earned the right to be selected, or have been chosen by me, to have complete access to my heart. It is my choice, and it is your choice, to be with those we believe are healthy to be around, in order for us to thrive again.

I also realize there was a time when I felt strongly that my husband needed to provide for all of my needs in the four areas of my life. I was so wrong. Of course, my husband needs to be there in all areas of my life, but if I demand him to be perfect and know exactly what I need at all times, this is unrealistic. Only God can be perfect, as He knows my true needs. The closer I draw to Him, the more evident this becomes.

In the same way, if we expect one person to meet all of our needs, should they be physical, emotional, spiritual, or sexual in nature, this is unrealistic. This is often the very reason individuals go from one person to another to seek fulfillment. It will never happen because the other person is often, themselves, on a mission to find someone who meets all of their needs.

Your person of trust, or your spouse, has unmet needs, and there comes a point in the relationship where we need to reciprocate what is needed. It is during our prayer times that we can discover what our trusted friend or spouse really needs. First, we can ask Jesus to show us a picture of their heart, how He sees it, and if it is wounded in some way. Next, we can ask Jesus to give us the keys to our loved one's heart. You may wonder what in the world these keys are. Well, as you know, keys open doors, and we all have our own keys we use to gain entrance to our cars and houses. In the same way, if we have the right keys to gain entrance into a person's heart, an emotional connection can be established more quickly. Keys are simply areas in which, at one time, a person had a connection with something, someone, or someplace. These were properly established way ahead of the current relationship and can go as far back as childhood.

The following are keys" I have found while sitting with countless individuals and listening to their stories. One man told his wife he loves to hunt. He reminisced about going hunting with his father and how this activity cemented their hearts into one. Now his father had passed away, but every time he goes hunting, it's like they are together again, connected emotionally.

One woman recalled running down to the creek behind her house, and as she would sit next to this bubbling creek, she told the moving water everything that was in her heart. Only the creek knew she was spanked till welts covered her body, or how afraid she was of being home when her parents were fighting with each other. As she spoke to the gently flowing water, she would fashion a boat out of some paper she had brought with her. After she poured out all of her heart, she would release the boat and watch it bobbing down the stream. In some way, the creek took all of her pain away.

In the instance of the man who loved to hunt, the key to his heart was doing this activity with his father. In the case of the woman, the creek became her only trusted friend and was now a key to her heart. Someone wanting to connect with them needs to explore these keys in a diplomatic way. What this means is to gently ask why this was important to them, how this activity affected their heart, and what they were feeling while engaged in the activity. The more information you can gather about these keys and how well they worked, the more specifically you can reach the heart of the person, and the better the keys will work. Now all there is left to do is to duplicate what the hunting adventure or the creek experience gave. You see, the connection was already there, and it worked.

My former clients were always stunned when I discovered the keys to their heart, and they often asked, "How do you know this about me?"

I would reply, "By simply listening to you, and watching your face and eyes. You gave me the keys to your heart, and when I tried them, I was able to open up your heart."

If I can use these keys and open up the heart of a complete stranger, then the person you want to connect with, the one you trust, can too.

I know all of my husband's keys, and I use them a lot to fill his heart and have a continuous heart connection with him. In turn, I have given him all the keys to my heart because I can trust he will never misuse them; he will use them only to connect his heart to mine. Keys cannot be given to a person who is not trustworthy, in the same way you wouldn't give your house keys to a person you just met.

At the time of this writing, I have reached the ripe old age in my physical life that puts me in the group referred to as over the hill. Some would even consider me ancient. My praise goes out to God because I still enjoy good physical health, in spite of some ups and downs. Knowing things can change in an instant keeps me close to Jesus. I have had the privilege of watching others deal with their physical challenges, and this spurs me on to keep my close relationship with God. I have witnessed the undying devotion to God of many who endured a lot of suffering. They have become my heroes. Testimony after testimony of these precious folks spur me on to reach for the same in my life.

My emotional life could not be better. I feel content, whole, healed, and totally restored. Not in my wildest dreams could I ever have imagined my relationship with God could be on such a level. I'm no longer struggling with anger or spending my energy seeking revenge. True peace is my daily portion, and I want more and more each day. Many times, I feel like a fountain of joy, able to dispense love, understanding, and acceptance to others. Before my own healing journey was even complete, God pressed upon my heart to sit with other hurting hearts and lead them to Him. Now my path has changed again. It is time to follow a new direction from God, to share with others what He has done for me, and to seek out individuals, couples, churches, and groups who would love to learn the heart counseling model.

When I examine my spiritual life, it is vibrant and exciting. My desire is no longer to just read the Bible but to allow God, through His Word, to read me. There is no fear of God looking into my heart and meeting me there. I want my relationship with Him to be open and honest and never, even for one minute, fall back to the spiritual void I had before. Each day, I long for His appearing, wanting to be with my Savior forever. My goal is to get to know God up close and personal. New songs fill my heart and lead me to the altar, and eternity is in front of me.

In the area of my sexual life, the healing I received was remarkable. I'm able to celebrate God by being unashamed of my sexuality. I have fully embraced my feminine side, loving each minute. Now when I look at myself in the mirror, I see what God sees. The images and experiences from my past no longer interfere with my sexual life. At times, I can still find myself wandering back in my mind to what was, but I do not linger there. Freedom to enjoy the gift of sexuality is my reward from God. I have forgiven my abusers, pray for their salvation, and declare blessings on their lives. Today, I have no enemies because true freedom reigns in my heart.

Even in the case of the people from Germany who sexually abused me, my heart is free. I spoke with God a lot, asking Him to show me if He wanted me to reconcile with them. Since I was far away from home, I had no idea where these individuals were in their spiritual life. Over a span of thirty-nine years of marriage and living in the United States, my contact was very limited. What little contact I had was with only my sister. My other acquaintances would most likely not feel a connection to me anyways. "Out of sight, out of mind" was our philosophy. I have made a total of three visits to Germany, and on each occasion, the condition of these individuals was very much the same as when I left. There was never the opportunity for me to let them know I had granted them forgiveness, and there certainly was never the time to establish trust. My visits were very short due to finances and time availability. I would need time to work all this through with them. So I continue to pray for their salvation, asking God to bring them to Himself, and I pronounce blessing on their lives, to keep my heart free.

Would I consider myself a whole person in my physical, emotional, spiritual, and sexual life? In many ways, yes. Are there times in my life when I seem to falter? Of course, but I know how to get back on track. I not only have the tools to stay in freedom; I have my Lord and Savior, Jesus Christ, to watch over my heart, standing by whenever I need Him. My heart is full with praise and thanksgiving, and nothing would bless me more than if your heart was as free as mine. God truly reset my heart, and the harmony we have together is priceless.

I now understand my story was given to me. I received grace from God and healing in all areas in my life. God used the bad things in my life to train me for His purposes. When God allows pain in our life, it is always for a purpose. It is for our good, to teach us and train us for the work He has for us to do. Today, I want my voice to join the voice of David as he prayed the words of this song to God: "God rewrote the text of my life when I opened the book of my heart to His eyes" (2 Samuel 22:25 MSG).

In closing, I want to share with you a few lines of the following poem, often recited by Corrie ten Boom because it summed up her story. Corrie found freedom in Christ in spite of all of her horrible experiences living through the Holocaust. She allowed Jesus to make her whole again, to reset her heart:

> My life is but a weaving
> between my Lord and me;
> I cannot choose the colors.
> He worketh steadily.

(*Just a Weaver*[2] by Benjamin Malacia Franklin)

Although my father and my mother have abandoned me,
Yet the LORD will take me up [adopt me as His child].
(Psalm 27:10 AMP)

CONCLUSION

Since I started writing this book, some trials have come and gone. As always, God was included in how I approached and handled these unexpected trials. Over and over again, I remind myself to stay true to the teaching of this book in my own life. Was it always easy to stay totally focused on God? No. I Often had to go back to the basics and start again, fresh.

So it will be with you. At times, you will feel you are going two steps forward and one step back, but in the end, you find yourself running to God, seeking His help to live this new free life again. It will not be easy. Countless opportunities will arise to derail you to spin you back to your old ways, but people who have tasted freedom in their heart will never settle for anything less.

Finally, living a life free in your physical, emotional, spiritual, and sexual life will put you miles ahead of many others, who still try to solve their issues with worldly advice and counsel. In the end, they will discover the results were not what they hoped for. Almost daily, I meet people carrying unseen burdens, reaching for anything to calm the storms inside. Women, men, and children alike, scratching and clawing for affection, to be noticed, to be wanted, and to finally receive the love their heart has never felt from anybody in their life.

It is my desire that in this book, you will discover your true heart, seek after true freedom, and settle for nothing less. We cannot always count on individuals to care for our hearts and meet all of our needs, be they physical, emotional, spiritual, or sexual. Only God is able to provide the right guidance for us in each of these areas of our lives. As the Psalmist wrote, "Your word is a lamp for my feet, a light on my path." I hope I have not only stimulated your appetite for what can be but also provided you with everything you need to start your personal journey to total freedom.

No longer do you have to live in bondage to your hurtful past or live with a wounded heart.

I would like to sincerely thank you for allowing me to be a part of your life and to offer you the gift of freedom in your physical, emotional, spiritual, and sexual life. It is possible only through Jesus Christ, our Lord. He has set me free in all areas of my life, and He wants to give you the same opportunity.

Please press on; never quit. Freedom is only a prayer away. If you need help, go to www.caringfortheheart@msn.com to find a list of caring counselors who would love to help you through this process. You have the potential to start a new way of life, or a new wave of excitement within the church, your home, and your community. I'm here to cheer you on, and I would love to hear about your personal journey. (no counseling will be provided via e-mail) You can contact me at eReachheart2@yahoo.com

As part of your new life, I would love to extend an invitation to you. Both my husband and I are available to come to your town, church, or group and teach the principles presented in this book along with the heart counseling model that set my heart free. For more information and a complete list of all the classes we offer at this time, please visit www.reachingtheheart.org

Love,
Ellen

NOTES

Chapter 1. Why Another Book?

1. Neil Anderson, *Victory Over the Darkness* (Regal Books, 1990, 2000 – A Division of Gospel Light), 11.
2. J. R. Tolkien, *The Lord of the Rings* (Allen & Unwin, 1949). 15.

Chapter 2. *God Wants Us To Grow and Mature Physically*

1. John Bunyan, *The Pilgrim's Progress* (John Bunyan 1678), 19.
2. Rick Warren, *The Purpose Driven Life* (Zondervan Publishing House 2002), 32.
3. George Merriam and Charles Merriam, *Merriam-Webster Dictionary* (Founded in 1831; original Noah Webster – Merriam publisher; United States), 33.
4. John Foxe, *Foxe's Book of Martyrs* (John Day 1563), 35.
5. J. Irvin Overholtzer, *Good News Club* (Child Evangelism Fellowship 1920), 35.
6. Kendrick Brothers Productions, *War Room* (Alex Kendrick and Stephen Kendrick 2015), 38.
7. William Cameron Townsend, *JAARS (Jungle Aviation and Radio Service* (Wycliffe Bible Translators 1934), 39.
8. Philip Yancey, *Where Is God When It Hurts?* (Zondervan Publishing House 1990), 42.
9. John Regeir, *Biblical Concepts Counseling Workbook* (John Regier 1999), 45.

Chapter 3. *God Wants Us To Grow and Mature Emotionally*

1. C.S Lewis, *The Problem of Pain* (CS Lewis © copyright CS Lewis Pte Ltd 1940; 91.), 75.
2. William Cameron Townsend, *Wycliffe Bible Translators* (William Cameron Townsend 1942), 83.

Chapter 4. *God Wants Us To Grow and Mature Spiritually*

1. Bruce Wilkinson, *The Dream Giver* (David and Heather Kopp, Multnomah Publishers INC. in 2003), 100.
2. Lance Latham and Art Rorheim, *Awana* (1950), 104.
3. Laureate Selma Lagerloef, *Jerusalem* (film 1896), 115.
4. *BibleGateway.com* (Zondervan), 121.

Chapter 5. *God Wants Us To Grow and Mature Sexually*

1. Cambridge University Press, *Cambridge Dictionary* (1584), 154.

Chapter 6. *To be Whole – God's Ultimate Goal for Us*

1. Merry Hamrick, *Meditation Talk* (Merry Hamrick 2011), 195.
2. Benjamin Malachi Franklin, *Just A Weaver* (first published in the late 1940's.), 221.

ABOUT THE AUTHOR

Ellen Stotts is a trained *Caring for the Heart* counselor as well as a teacher and trainer of this Biblical *Heart Counseling Model*. For the past twelve years she has had the privilege of sitting with hurting people and assisting them in coming to freedom in their personal and marital lives. In addition she has trained interested individuals in this *Caring for the Heart* counseling method so they could likewise help others come to freedom.

She and her husband were missionaries with Wycliffe Bible Translators. She then served alongside her husband as a pastor's wife, and transitioned into the role of a counselor. At present Ellen is a well-liked speaker, teacher, and trainer.

Ellen and her husband, Mike, founded *Reaching The Heart Ministries* in 2008, a non-profit 501© 3 ministry that has provided counseling using this unique counseling method to lead individuals to freedom in their heart. Now the emphasis is to train others. She has traveled statewide and abroad, speaking, training, and teaching others this approach of caring for hurting hearts and bringing Jesus into the unresolved issues of a painful past.

Ellen and Mike are the parents of three adult, adopted children and have one grandson. They reside in Arizona where the sun seems to shine all the time.

RECOMENDED READING LIST

CHAPTER 1 – WHY ANOTHER BOOK

The Upper Room John McArthur

In a borrowed or rented banqueting room atop some shop or large family dwelling in Jerusalem, the drama unfolded. The events and teaching recorded in John 13-16, commonly known as the Upper Room Discourse, reveal some of the most poignant and powerful promises for believers in all of Scripture.

Aha Kyle Idleman

The God moment that changes everything. We've all had an "aha moment" in our lives, an insight that changes everything. With everyday examples and trademark testimonies the text draws on Scripture to reveal how three key elements—awakening, honesty, action—can produce the same kind of "aha!" in our spiritual lives.

God Loves You Dr. David Jeremiah

God's love is perhaps one of the most misunderstood aspects of our heavenly Father's nature. Understanding that God is not just a loving God but *is* love itself, baffles believers and non-believers alike. Love is the very nature of God—making it impossible for God to be anything other than love.

CHAPTER 2 – GOD WANTS US TO GROW PHYSICALLY

The Purpose Driven Life Rick Warren

The Purpose Driven Life will help you understand why you are alive and reveal God's amazing plan for you both here and now, and for eternity.

You will be guided through a personal forty-day spiritual journey that will transform your answer to life's most important question: What on earth am I here for?

Where Is God When It Hurts Philip Yancey

"If there is a loving God, then why ... ?" No matter how the question is completed, at its root lies the issue of pain. Does God order suffering? Or did he simply wind up the world's mainspring and now is watching from a distance? You will discover God is neither capricious nor unconcerned.

Foxe's Book of Martyrs John Foxe

Historian John Foxe, recounts the lives, sufferings, and triumphant deaths of dozens of Christian martyrs. Some were people of rank and influence. Some were ordinary folk. Some were even his friends. Four centuries later, these deeply moving accounts of faith and courage mark a path for modern Christians to measure the depth of their commitment.

CHAPTER 3 – GOD WANTS US TO GROW EMOTIONALLY

Choosing Forgiveness Nancy Leigh DeMoss

There are no magic words or secret formulas for forgiveness. But there are biblical principles that can help you break free from bitterness and pain. In *Choosing Forgiveness,* discover specific strategies for putting God's grace and mercy into practice -- forgiving others as God has forgiven you.

Forgive & Forget Lewis B. Smedes

In Lewis Smedes's classic book on forgiveness, he shows us that it is possible to heal our pain and let go of the resentment that poisons us. *Forgive & Forget* will provide the energy needed to forgive our wrongdoers and release the feelings of hurt and anger that occupy our minds and souls.

Losing Cooper J.J. Jasper

This true account is the moving story of the Jasper family after the tragic death of their five-year-old son Cooper. The book chronicles their journey through darkness, but offers real hope to anyone experiencing trouble, trials, or tragedy. It shows how a strong Christian family deals with shock, loss, and grief from a Biblical perspective.

A Practical Guide to the Caring for the Heart Model of Prayer Marilyn Damron

This booklet explains and teaches people how they can lead others in prayer to be free from their past emotional pain.

CHAPTER 4 – GOD WANTS US TO GROW SPITUALLY

The Pursuit of Holiness Jerry Bridges

"Be holy, for I am holy" commands God to His people. However, holiness is something that is often missed in the Christian's daily life. That's because we're not exactly sure what our part in holiness is.

The Pilgrim's Progress John Bunyan

This famous story of man's progress through life in search of salvation remains one of the most entertaining allegories of faith ever written. Set against realistic backdrops of town and country, the powerful drama of the pilgrim's trials and temptations follows him in his harrowing journey to the Celestial City.

The Dream Giver Bruce Wilkinson

The Author shows us how to identify and overcome the obstacles that keep millions from living the life they were created for. He begins with a compelling modern-day parable about Ordinary, who dares to leave the Land of Familiar to pursue his Big Dream. With the help of the Dream Giver, Ordinary begins the hardest and most rewarding journey of his life.

CHAPTER 5 – GOD WANTS US TO GROW SEXUALLY

Every Woman's Battle Shannon Ethridge

Your sexual needs are far different from your man's. And they may be more dangerous. When does an affair begin? Not with the first forbidden touch…but with the first forbidden thought. Unexpectedly, you find yourself enjoying a powerful emotional bond with another man. You feel like you matter to someone again. And the door you thought was locked so firmly–the door to sexual infidelity–is suddenly ajar.

Every Man's Battle Stephen Arterburn and Fred Stoeker

From movies and television, to print media and the Internet, men are constantly faced with the assault of sensual images. It is impossible to avoid such temptations... but, thankfully, not impossible to confront them and gain victory over them!

Sex and the Single Life Hafeez Badku

Most singles, whether Christian or not, might describe their experiences with sex and love in one word: dissatisfied. Whether because of broken relationships, random hook-ups, romance novels, pornography, or casual sex, many have experienced nights of pleasure only to wake up to days of emptiness and regrets. In *Sex, God, and the Single Life*, the Author shares of his own journey from sexual regrets and frustration to sexual joy and satisfaction. Through an exploration of scripture and an honest discussion of God's purpose and design for real intimacy, this dynamic book will reveal the path to satisfaction that singles everywhere have been yearning for.

The Bare Naked Truth Bekah Martin

Purity. Sex. Boys. Waiting. There's something about those words that makes everything complex in a heartbeat, and raises more questions than answers. Is there something wrong with me if I don't kiss a boy after a date? Or am I doomed if I DID? What if waiting is just a one-way trip to life as a crazy cat woman? And what if I tend to, um, think about a certain boy in a certain way?

CHAPTER 6 – TO BE WHOLE – GOD'S ULTIMATE GOAL FOR US

Eternity Joseph M. Stowell

"Using heaven as our point of reference lends new balance to life on earth and provides fresh alternatives for a world filled with hollow pursuits", says this nationally known teacher and author. We belong to the world to come. In fact, since that world has already been planted in our hearts, we are already citizens of heaven.

Biblical Concepts Counseling Workbook John Regier

This course is designed to help individuals identify their spiritual problems they have experienced in life or marriage with the goal of resolving them by applying the principles given in the Word of God. Ten key spiritual problems that destroy a believer's joy, peace and fulfillment are identified.

Caring For The Emotionally Damaged Heart Workbook John Regier

Jesus focused on the heart of the individual to resolve the problems people encountered. Freedom can only come as change takes place in the heart. This course is designed to help a person to identify the emotional pain issues they have experienced in the past which have damaged the heart, and lead them to resolve these issues through prayer.

God Is Gracious Joann Nisly

You will find this devotional book goes straight to the heart. The reader will travel with Joann through her personal journey of healing.

APPENDIX

Chapter 3. *God Wants Us To Grow and Mature Emotionally*
    1. John Regeir, *Emotional Pain Words* (©John Regeir 1999; used with permission.

Abandoned	Can't do	Cut off	Driven
Abused	anything right	Damaged	Dropped
Accused	Can't Focus	Deceived	Dumb
Afraid	Can't	Defeated	Embarrassed
Agitated	measure up	Deserted	Empty
All my fault	Can't trust	Desires rejected	Excluded
Alone	anyone	Despair	Exhausted
Always wrong	Can't trust God	Desperate	Exposed
Angry	Cheap	Despicable	Failure
Annihilated	Cheated	Destroyed	Fear
Anxious	Coerced	Detested	Foggy
Apathetic	Condemned	Devalued	Foolish
Ashamed	Confused	Dictated to	Forced
Assertive	Conspired	Didn't belong	Forgotten
Avoided	against	Dirty	Forlorn
Awkward	Controlled	Discarded	Forsaken
Bad	Cornered	Discounted	Friendless
Belittled	Corrected	Disgraced	Frightened
Betrayed	Couldn't	Disgusting	Frustrated
Bewildered	respond	Dishonored	God can't
Blamed	Couldn't trust	Disowned	love me
Bombarded	anyone	Disregarded	God doesn't
Bossy	Criticized	Disrespected	hear my prayers
	Crushed	Dominated	

God is angry
  with me
God is never
  there for me
God is too harsh
Hate myself
Hated
Have influence
  over
Helpless
Hollow
Hopeless
Hunted
Hurt
Ignored
Inadequate
Incompetent
Inferior
Insensitive
Insensitive to
  my needs
Insignificant
Insulted
Invalidated
Isolated
Judged
Keep under ones
  thumb
Kicked
Knocked down
Left out
Lied to
Like a Zero
Lonely
Lost
Made fun of
Manipulated
Miserable

Mistreated
Mocked
Molested
Neglected
No good
No way out
Not cared for
Not cherished
Not good
  enough
Not listened to
Not paid
  attention to
Not safe
Not valued
Not wanted
Publicly shamed
Put down
Rejected
Repulsed
Resentful
Ridiculed
Ruined
Rule the roost
Ruled
Sad
Scared
Scorned
Second Best
Separated
Shamed
Shunned
Shut down
Silenced
Stepped on
Stressed
Stupid
Suffocated

Suicidal
Suppressed
Tired
Torn Apart
Trapped
Trashed
Tuned out
Ugly
Unable to speak
Unaccepted
Uncared for
Undesirable
Unfairly treated
Unhappy
Unheard
Unimportant
Unlovable
Unnoticed
Unqualified
Unresponsive
Used
Violated

Ellen Stotts, *Emotional Healing Words* (©Ellen Stotts 2014)

Accept me the way I'm

Always protect me

Ask me what I need

At times brag on me

Attend to my needs

Be loyal to me

Be my best friend

Be my protector

Be proud of me

Be save so I can open up

Be sensitive to my needs

Be there to lift my spirit

Be my fresh air

Encourage me often

Please focus on me

Give me hope

Trust me completely

Use a soft voice

Care for my needs

Celebrate my achievements

Accept my energetic nature

Celebrate my successes

Do not push me away

Come along side of me

Consider me important

Do not judge me

Do not ridicule me

Do you want to be with me?

Don't always blame me

Fill me up to overflowing

Find a remedy

Give me time to rest

Help me to be free

Help me to be restored

Help me to calm down

Help me to find direction

Help me to find self-respect

Help me to find self-worth

Help me to gain control

Help me to gain self esteem

Help me to love myself

Help me to relax

Hold me in high esteem

I need affirmation words

I need to be accepted by you

I need to be acknowledge

I need to be chosen

Hold me in your arms

Consider my dreams

I need to be claimed by you

I need to be found

I need to be honor by you

I need to be praised by you

I need to be valued

I need to be wanted

I need to feel competent

I need to feel free to be myself

I need to feel secure

I need to feel significant

I need to have value

I need to hear compliments

I need to know I belong

I need you to be attentive

I need you to be honest

I need you to be with me

I need you to caress me

I need you to cheer me up

I need you to fill me up

I need you to fill my cup

I need you to give me space

I need you to guard me

I need you to know I'm smart

I need you to
listen to me
I need you to
love me
I need you to
rely on me
I need you
with me
I want to be
connected
I want to be
happy
I want us to be
together
I want you to
love me
I want you to
notice me
Include me in
your life
Joined together
Keep me
Know I'm
intelligent
Let me know
when I please
you, do things
right
Listen to my
opinion
Look at me I'm
your treasure
Make me feel
found
Meet my
emotional
needs

Tell me when
you need me
Need you to
pick me up
Never
degrade me
Never force me
Never laugh
at me
Never look
down on me
Never make fun
of me
Never pound me
Pay attention
to me
Please accept me
Please care for
my heart
Cleanse me
Do not
offend me
Please hear
me out
Please honor me
Please listen
to me
Do not let me
down
Please pray for
me, daily
Do not
deceive me
Please treat me
fair
Please wait till
I'm healed

Promise not to
leave me
Protect my
name
Provide a safe
environment
Recognize me
for who I'm
Remember me
in the day
See me as clean
/ pure
See me as
having worth
I need to be
your one and
only
See me for my
potential
Share with me
when you
think about me
Show me respect
Take time to
listened to me
Tell me It's OK
Tell me to slow
down
Tell me to take
it easy
Tell me to take
my time
Tell me what
would you like
Tell me you like
what you see
Trust me

Try to meet my
needs
Understand how
I feel
Wash me with
God's Word
Welcome me
into your life
Be willing to
protect me
Would you
admire me?
Would you
celebrate me?
Would you like I
share my heart
with you?
Would you
nurture me?

Printed in the United States
By Bookmasters